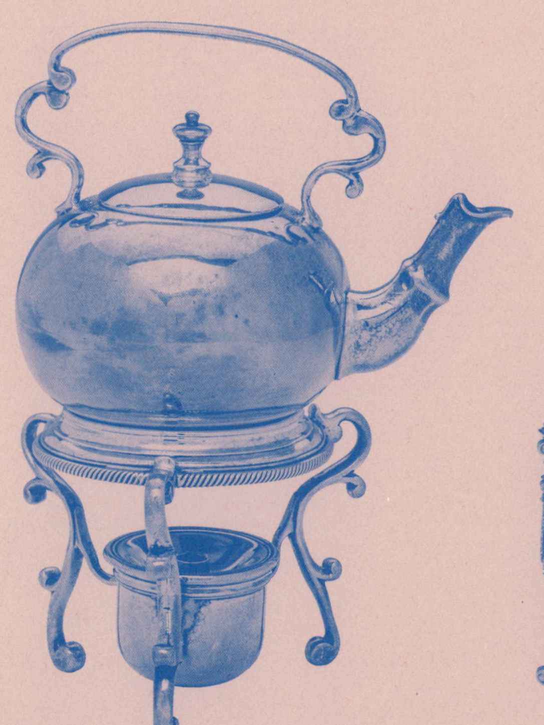

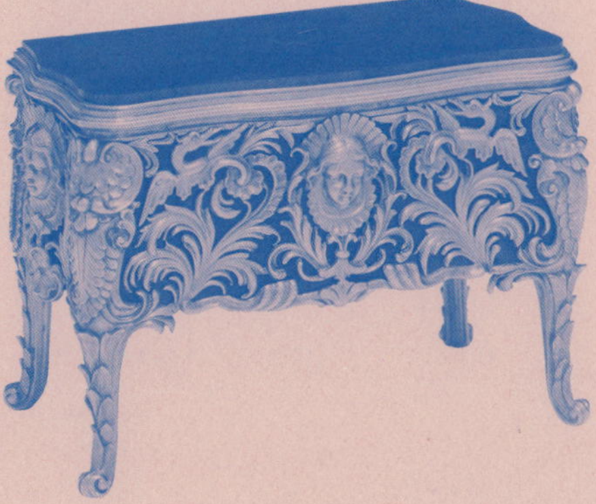

Tiny
Treasures

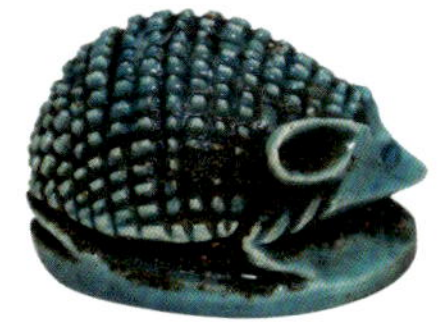

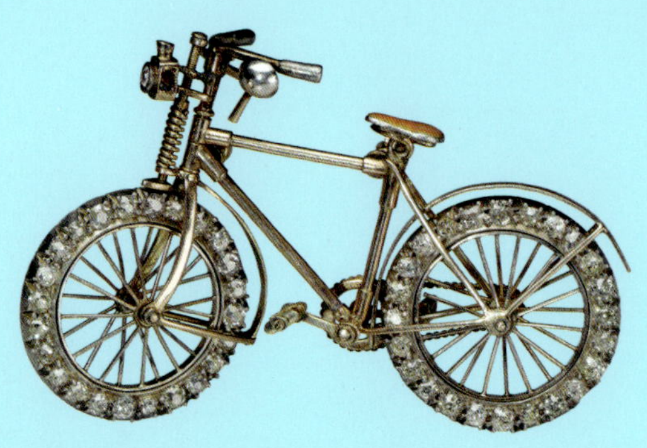

TREA

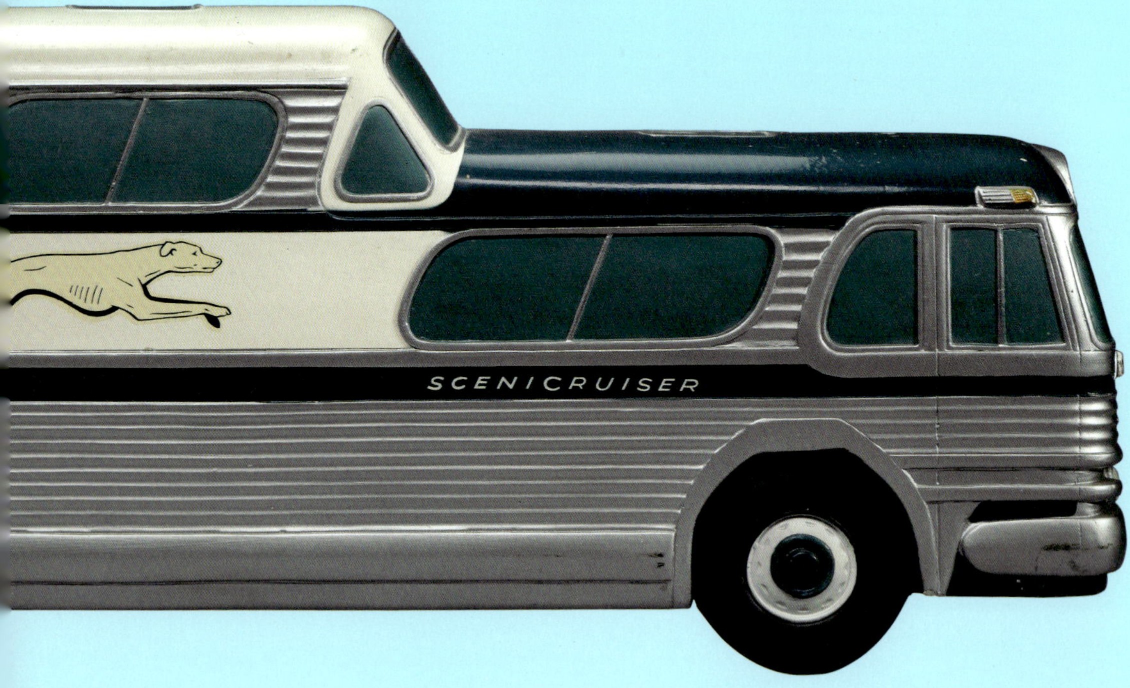

TINY SURES

THE MAGIC OF MINIATURES

Courtney Leigh Harris

MFA Publications
Museum of Fine Arts, Boston

CONTENTS

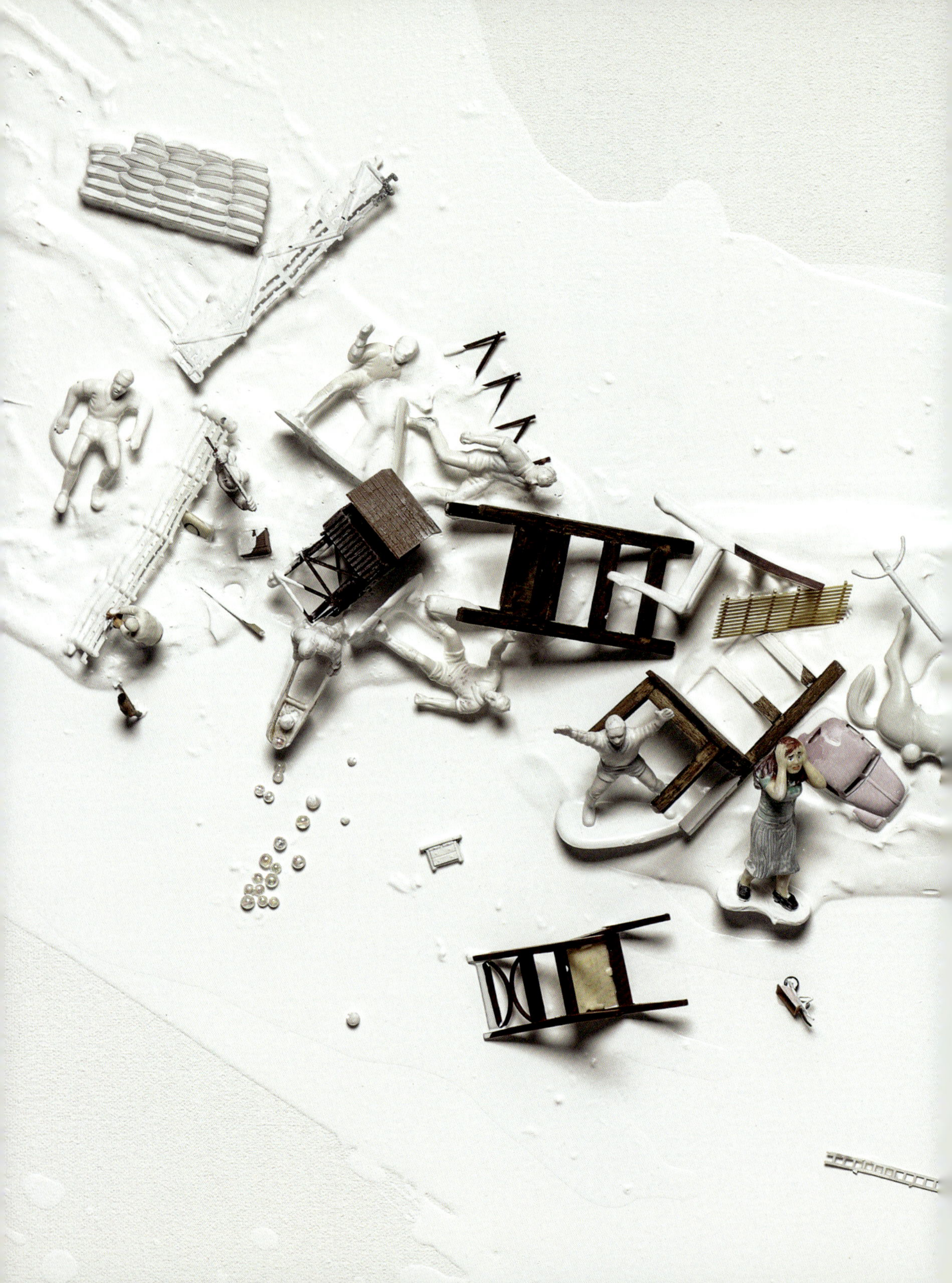

Director's Foreword

Tiny Treasures: The Magic of Miniatures asks why and how artists and artisans across time, place, and cultures have created compelling and powerful miniature objects. Drawing on the MFA's extraordinary collections, this publication and the exhibition it accompanies explore how tiny objects from ancient Egypt to the present day invoke divine protection or memorialize loss, assert their owner's status or their maker's skill, or simply surprise and delight. From tiny Egyptian amulets, to delicate Japanese *netsuke*, to minuscule French watercolors and Dutch dollhouse furnishings, these works' small scale and exquisite craftsmanship reward close looking by revealing worlds of meaning and beauty.

Many of these works have not been on view before at the MFA, or have been exhibited separately across the museum's galleries. Looking at them together enhances understanding of their materials and techniques, as well as their original purposes and enduring appeal. Contemporary works, including several by current Boston-based artists, show that miniatures continue to inspire artists today.

Generous support for this publication was provided by the Andrew W. Mellon Publications Fund.

We invite readers of this book, as well as visitors to the exhibition, to experience the breadth and depth of the MFA's collections and to make new connections between artworks that are small in scale but large in impact.

Matthew Teitelbaum
Ann and Graham Gund Director
Museum of Fine Arts, Boston

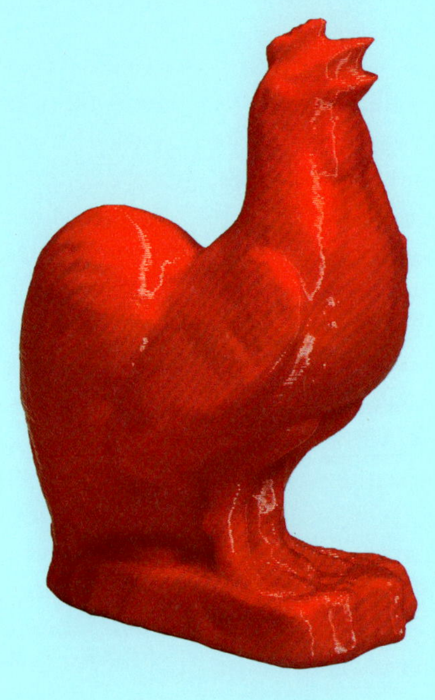

What Makes a Miniature?

Tiny is trendy. We are surrounded today by movements that encourage us to slow down and downsize. For many, the goal is to live simpler lives, in smaller spaces, with fewer belongings—think tiny houses, smaller footprints, decluttering, mindfulness, minimalism. Omnipresent smartphones (themselves miniature computers) bring popular culture and global phenomena into users' hands in a matter of seconds, giving them effective control of a universe of information, all reduced for a small screen. Still, in an ever-expanding world that prioritizes globalism, grandeur, spectacle, and immersive experiences, miniature objects can catch us off guard, stop us in our tracks, and force a different frame of mind.

It's all relative: scale does not exist in a vacuum. As humans, it is natural that we see scale in relation to ourselves and our bodies. A doll might seem large to a toddler, whereas it looks small to an adult. The inside of a transatlantic airliner is a large space—until one has to spend ten uninterrupted hours in it. All of this to say, scale is fluid and changeable.

We cannot talk about miniatures without considering scale. What is a miniature? While the word "miniature" might bring to mind various images, there is a standard definition that applies across the board. A miniature is, simply, anything that is smaller than its parent object. This explanation is important because it necessitates the existence of that parent object: miniatures cannot exist without them. They also are constructed objects and therefore imply the existence of a human creator. To make a miniature version of something, one has to understand and acknowledge the full-size object and then actively create the smaller version in its image. Importantly, however, miniatures need not be small. Throughout this volume, attempts have been made to indicate the size of the works of art illustrated. The aim is to demonstrate that although many miniatures are small, that is not universally true. They need only be smaller than the full-size version of themselves. A miniature whale could be more than 4 feet long, a miniature temple structure could still tower above a tall man.

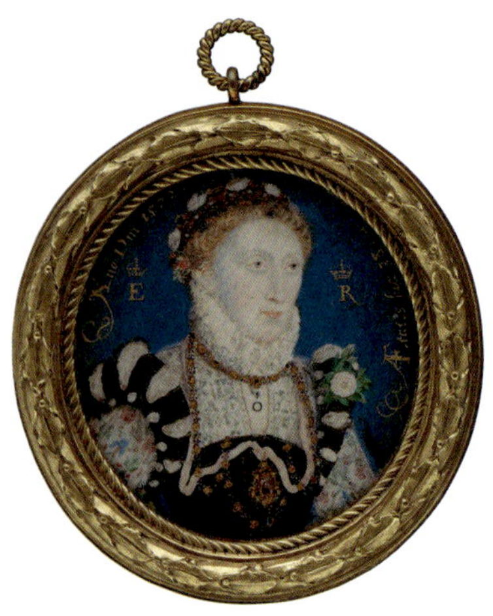

1. Nicholas Hilliard (English, 1547–1619). *Queen Elizabeth I*, 1572. Watercolor on vellum, 5.1 × 4.8 cm (2 × 1⅞ in.)

The flip side is that there are no miniatures in nature, as anything in the natural world is simply the size that it is, absent human interference or influence.[1] A fruit fly is not a miniature fly, a hummingbird not a miniature bird. They simply exist as they are. Yet artists working in miniature modes are particularly drawn to the natural world and tend to gravitate toward depicting natural phenomena and creatures, such as animals, birds, and trees.

The word "miniature" may conjure in the minds of readers certain types of objects. Many art lovers will be familiar with portrait miniatures and Indian painted miniatures, for example. Both traditions arose from the illustration of manuscripts and books. Within a European context, "miniature" has its origins in a Latin word referring to color, rather than size. Prior to the invention of the printing press, books were handwritten by scribes, usually monks. Although they commonly used black pigments, they also often used red—especially for titles and the initial capital letter at the start of a text. The Latin word for red is *minium*, and "to color with red" is *miniare*, terms that became strongly associated with the detailed illustration, or illumination, of manuscripts in the early modern period.[2]

In the sixteenth century, miniatures jumped off the manuscript page and became works of art in their own right. Most common were portrait miniatures, usually painted with watercolors or gouache on metal, card, or paper. Perhaps the best known of the miniaturists was an Elizabethan artist, Nicholas Hilliard, who created exquisitely detailed likenesses of members of the nobility and the royal court in the Tudor age (fig. 1).[3] Producing such precise paintings on a small scale (most are under 2 inches high) required remarkable technique. The tradition of painted miniature portraits continued well into the seventeenth and eighteenth centuries,

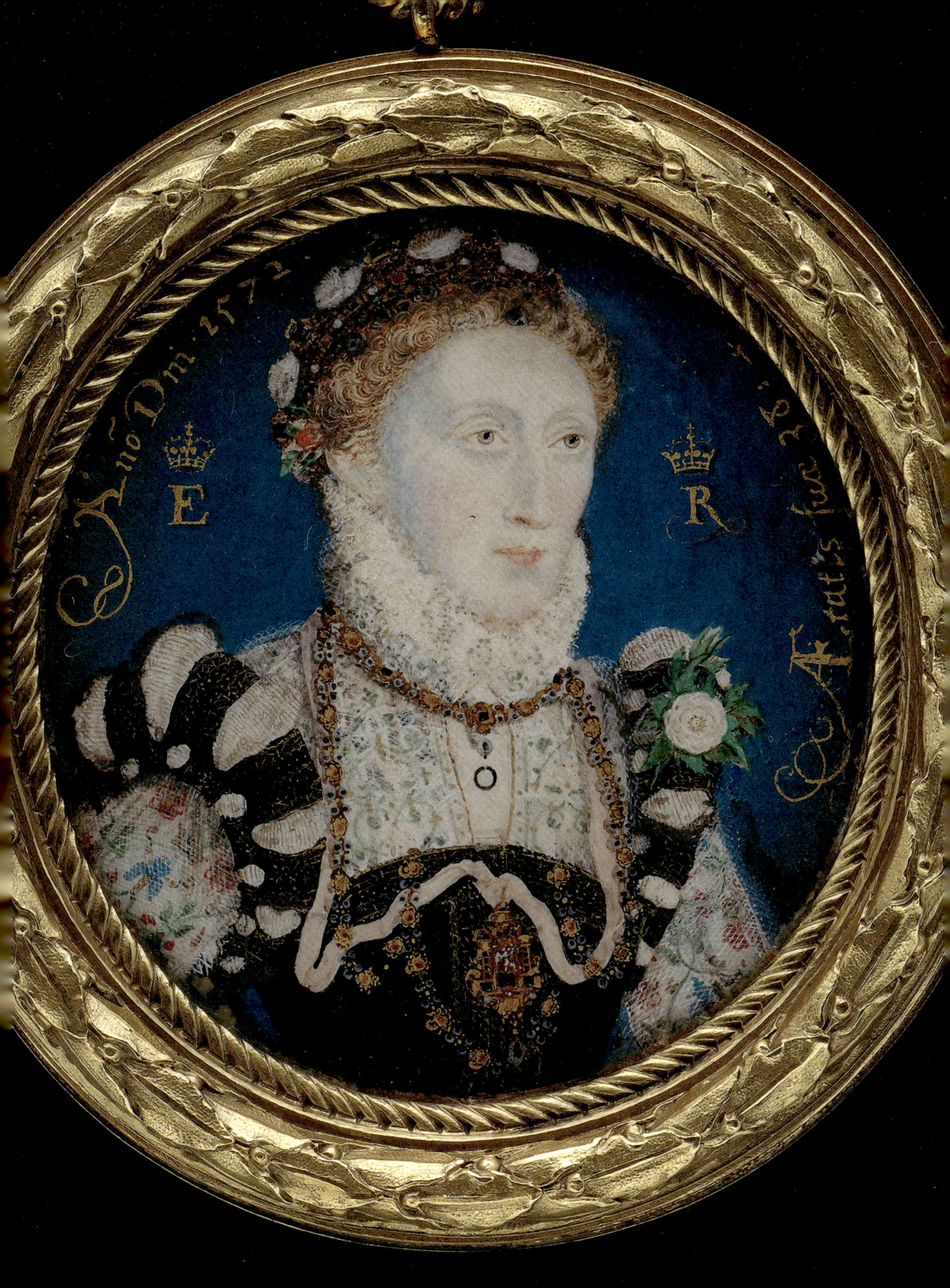

Ano Dm 1572
E
R
Ætatis suæ 38

when they gained popularity in early colonial America. Often associated with remembrance or grief, portrait miniatures were still common in the Victorian era and the late nineteenth century.

Indian, or Mughal, miniature paintings from the sixteenth century are an important field of artworks that are technically called miniatures, although they fall outside the scope of this discussion. These paintings are relatively small, painted in bright colors and with great detail. They served as illustrations for manuscripts and books. In their appearance, the Indian painted miniatures combine traditional Indian and Mughal imagery with influences from European print sources, which first became available in India around that time.[4]

While this survey seeks to examine miniatures made in a range of places, by many cultures, and through time, it is, of course, not possible to look to every artistic tradition. This study of miniatures is grounded in works from the Anglo-European/Western tradition, broadly from the early medieval period through to the modern era. The project later widened its focus to include a broader consideration of the pervasive interest in miniatures throughout human history, including selected works from ancient Egypt and Nubia, seventeenth- and eighteenth-century Japan, and contemporary artists around the world.

There are a few moments in Western history when artists particularly turned to miniaturization. Three such periods can be associated with major societal shifts. The first was the age of exploration in the fifteenth and sixteenth centuries. As travelers journeyed far from home in search of new continents and unmet civilizations, the world as it was known both expanded and became smaller. Maps reflected new lands, and explorers and traders brought back fascinating objects from their travels. Rulers of European nations, in particular, and wealthy collectors acquired items from across the distant seas and arranged them in elaborate collectors' cabinets, or *Kunstkammern*.[5] These display rooms and cases became microcosms of the entire world, as seen in both natural and manmade objects. This sort of allegorical miniaturization was

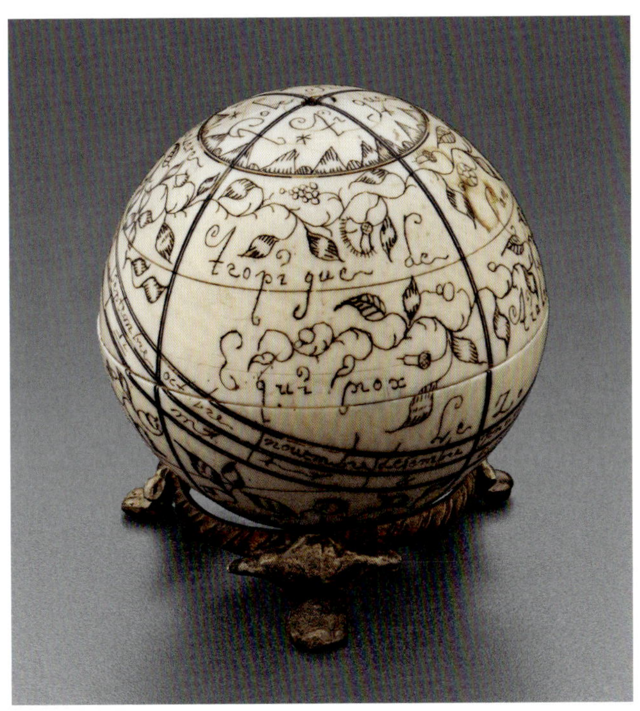

2. Terrestrial globe compass, France (Dieppe),
around 1675–85. Ivory with ink decoration, brass compass,
diameter: 5.7 cm (2¼ in.)

mirrored in the creation of new objects by European artists inspired
by the expanding world. Works like the Dieppe ivory globe compass,
from the late 1600s, speak to this impulse (fig. 2). In its day, the
globe was both an exquisite work of art, with its smooth, turned-
ivory surface and delicate inked decoration, and a practical item—
the globe unscrews at the equator to reveal a compass. Possessors
of this intriguing object and others like it would have been able to
show them off to their learned friends and thereby highlight their
own knowledge of the world. The owner of the Dieppe globe could
literally hold the whole world in the palm of his hand. With the additional detail of the compass, he also would have held the means by
which to navigate and order that changing world. The age of

exploration prompted a reordering of the world by
scholars and artists alike. It must have been disorient-
ing to know that the world was expanding, while
not knowing much about the "new" lands. Certainly,
objects that spoke to this reorientation in thinking
proliferated during the period.

The second major shift that spurred the making
of miniatures occurred in the late seventeenth century
and into the eighteenth, when science flourished
during the Enlightenment. The scientific instrument
that relates most directly to the history of miniatures is,
of course, the microscope. While microscopes, and
other contraptions with lenses, had existed from the
end of the sixteenth century, it was not until the 1660s
that they began to be used for true scientific inquiry.
The breakthrough moment for microscopes and the
general public's knowledge of what they could offer
came in 1665, with the publication of Robert Hooke's
book *Micrographia*. Hooke made modifications to
the existing microscope technology by mounting the
lenses and finding a way to illuminate his specimens.[6]
With the improved visibility, he was able to create
exquisite illustrations of what he observed. Perhaps the
most famous image from his volume is that of a flea,
depicted in microscopic detail in a large fold-out
engraving nearly 17 inches long (fig. 3).

This image must have been a revelation when it was
published in London. To see an insect so small that it is
barely visible to the naked eye, clearly laid bare with all
of its parts on display—how could one not have been
dazzled by this scientific development? In the same way
that the age of exploration prompted a rethinking of
our place within it, the enlargement of something so
minuscule must have made viewers sense a similar
shift in their role in the world.

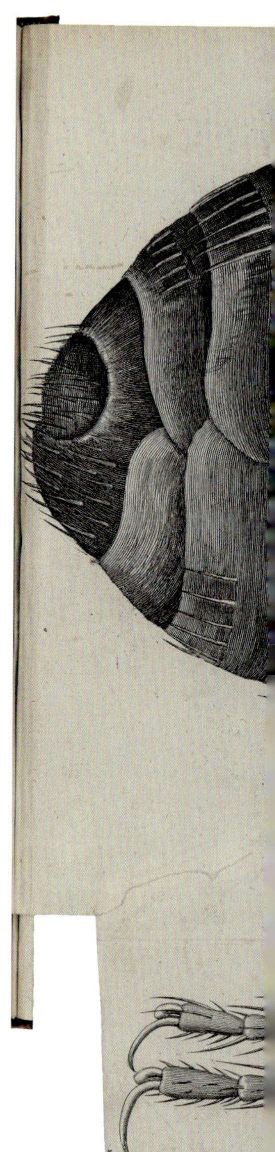

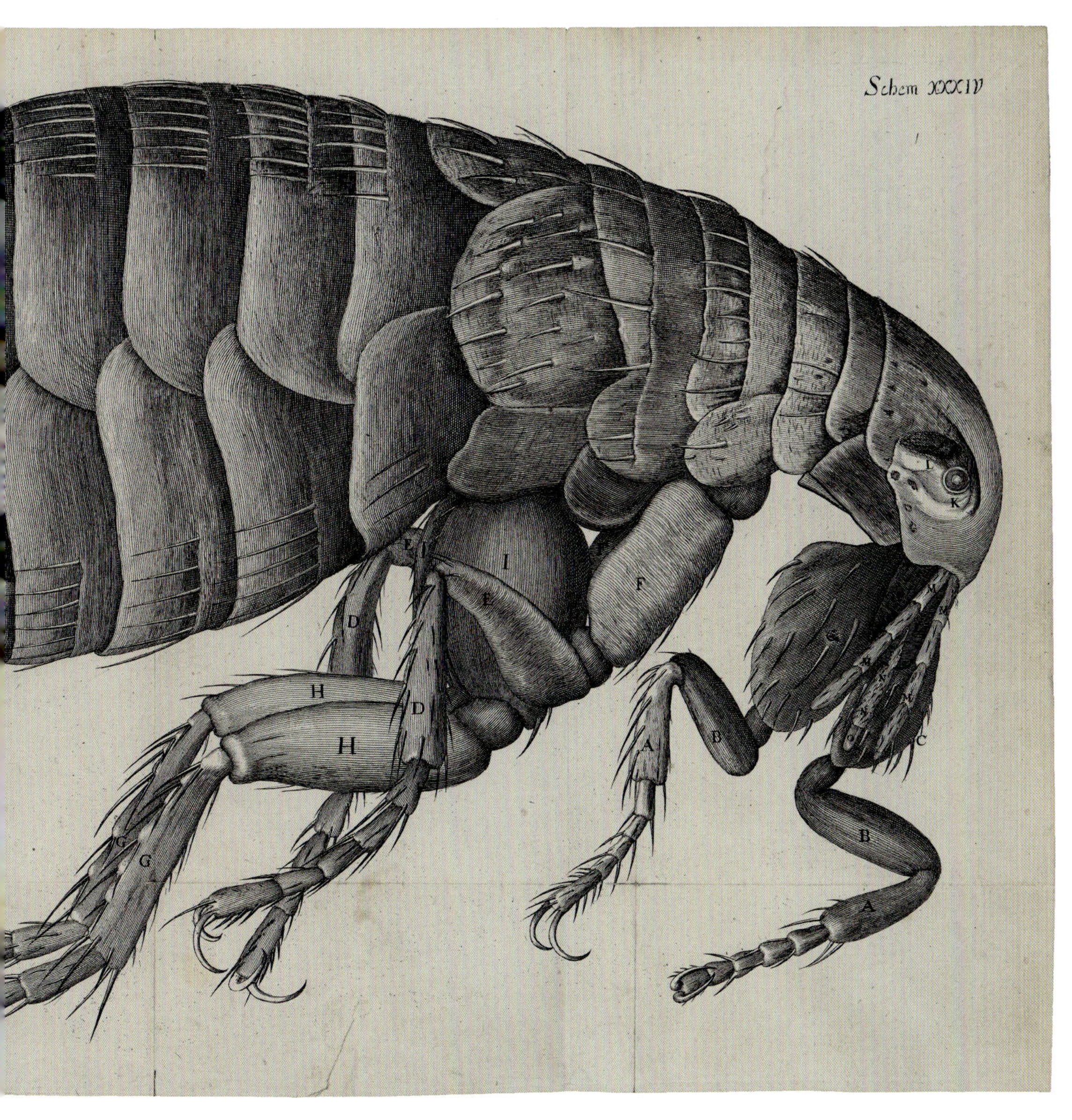

3. Robert Hooke (English, 1635–1703). Engraving of a flea, from *Micrographia* (1665), 33 × 43 cm (13 × 16⅞ in.)

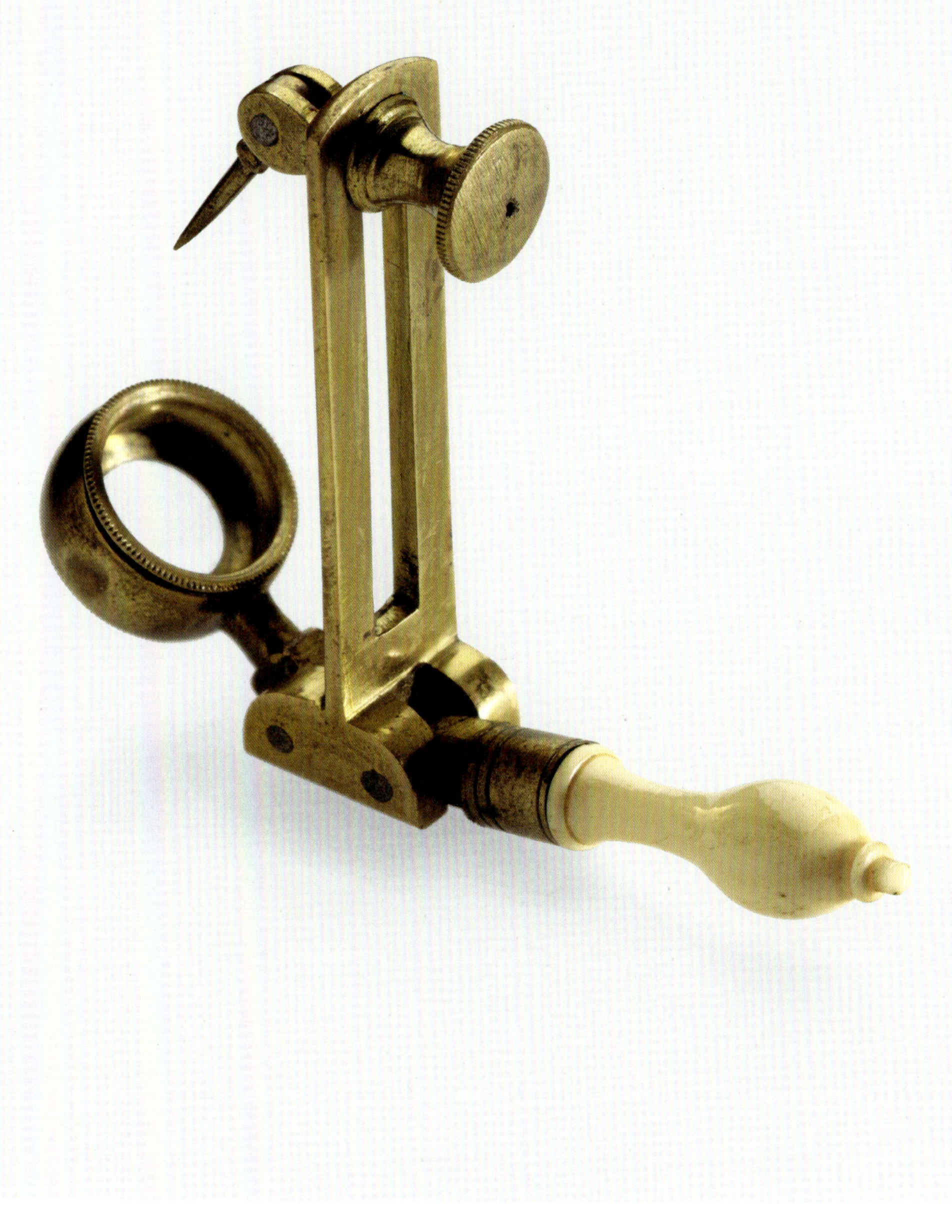

4. Miniature magnifying glass, possibly English, 18th century.
Brass and glass lens with ivory handle, length: 5.2 cm (2 in.)

An object that speaks to the craze for microscopes and scientific discovery, even among dilettantes, is a miniature portable microscope or magnifying glass (fig. 4). Too small to actually serve any scientific purpose, it was likely more of an accessory or fashion statement for a wealthy owner. It would have been possible to wear it on one's wrist and so keep it easily accessible. (The desire to look at something in detail could strike anywhere.) This charming object features a small lens and a pin for holding in place whatever unfortunate creature the amateur scientist wished to examine.

It is no surprise that the introduction of the microscope and microscopic images into the general consciousness prompted responses in areas beyond the scientific. Perhaps this is most notable in the field of literature, where one of the best-known books of the first half of the eighteenth century takes miniaturization as a theme. This is, of course, Jonathan Swift's *Gulliver's Travels*, published in 1726. Although Swift's traveler, Gulliver, actually visits many lands on his journeys—including one where everything is gigantic (Brobdingnag), it is his first stop in Lilliput, where everything is miniature, that remains firmly ensconced in Western popular culture and literary history.[7] The Victorian era's obsession with microscopes is also tied up with a popular interest in tiny or invisible beings, such as fairies. Once scientific instruments had revealed a world teeming with small creatures like fleas, writers and artists with active imaginations envisioned entire magical worlds that people could not see. If a drop of water was full of microscopic bacteria, could not the forest air near Cottingley, England, be filled with fairies and sprites?[8]

The third moment of miniaturization can hardly be called historical, as it is ongoing. The past four decades have seen the explosion of the Internet and its migration into our pockets with the advent of smartphones. Now that we have the ability to access all of the world's knowledge with the swipe of a finger, does the world become smaller or larger? Since the advent of the World Wide Web in the late 1980s, many artists have turned to working on a gigantic scale to try to grapple with the phenomenon of the shrinking world. The gigantic, necessarily the opposite of the miniature, entails the remaking of an object on a massive, often grotesque scale, as in the work of such artists as Richard Serra, who uses huge pieces of steel to create landscape sculpture, and Robert Smithson, who literally shaped the fabric of the earth into the best-known example of land art, *Spiral Jetty* (1970). The gigantic can also be immersive. We need look no further than museum exhibitions of the 2010s, such as Yayoi Kusama's *Infinity Mirror Rooms*, to see the popularity of this approach.

Other artists demonstrate a wish to get back to something basic, something fundamental—to escape the gigantic expansion of the real world and the art world alongside it. Pursuing pure technical achievement on a small scale is one option that some have explored. The Japanese artist Yagi Akira, for example, creates perfectly formed porcelain boxes, each one smaller than the next, that fit within each other—recalling Russian nesting dolls—down to the smallest item, a single die (fig. 5). Akira began making his nesting objects in the 1980s, combining in his own work the precision of his grandfather, a master porcelain maker, and the innovation of his father, an avant-garde ceramicist.

Alongside the immersive and the gigantic, we find a steady trend among artists to go small—choosing, perhaps, to work in the genres of model making, miniature painting, or photography. And through their decision to eschew the monumental, their work often takes on a quiet dignity. A Boston artist, Chris Templeman, harnessed modern technology in the form of 3-D printing to create miniature versions of a Chinese ceramic rooster in the MFA's collection—produced at roughly one quarter of the original size. Over the course of 2017, the Chinese calendar's Year of the Rooster, a 3-D-printing "vending machine" dispensed 2,017 miniature

5. Yagi Akira (Japanese, born in 1955). Nesting covered boxes, 1994.
Porcelain with pale blue glaze; largest box, height: 17.1 cm (6¾ in.)

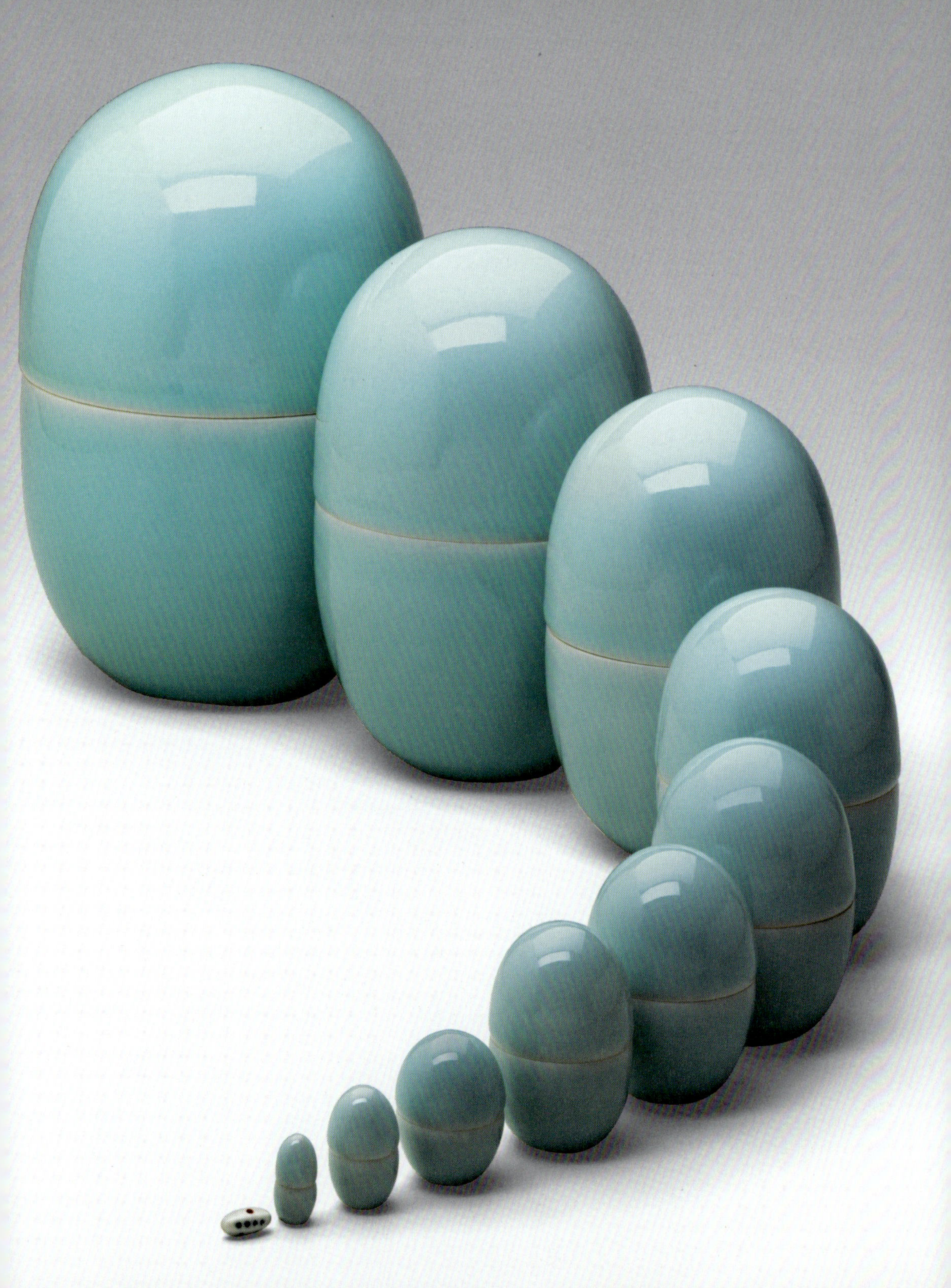

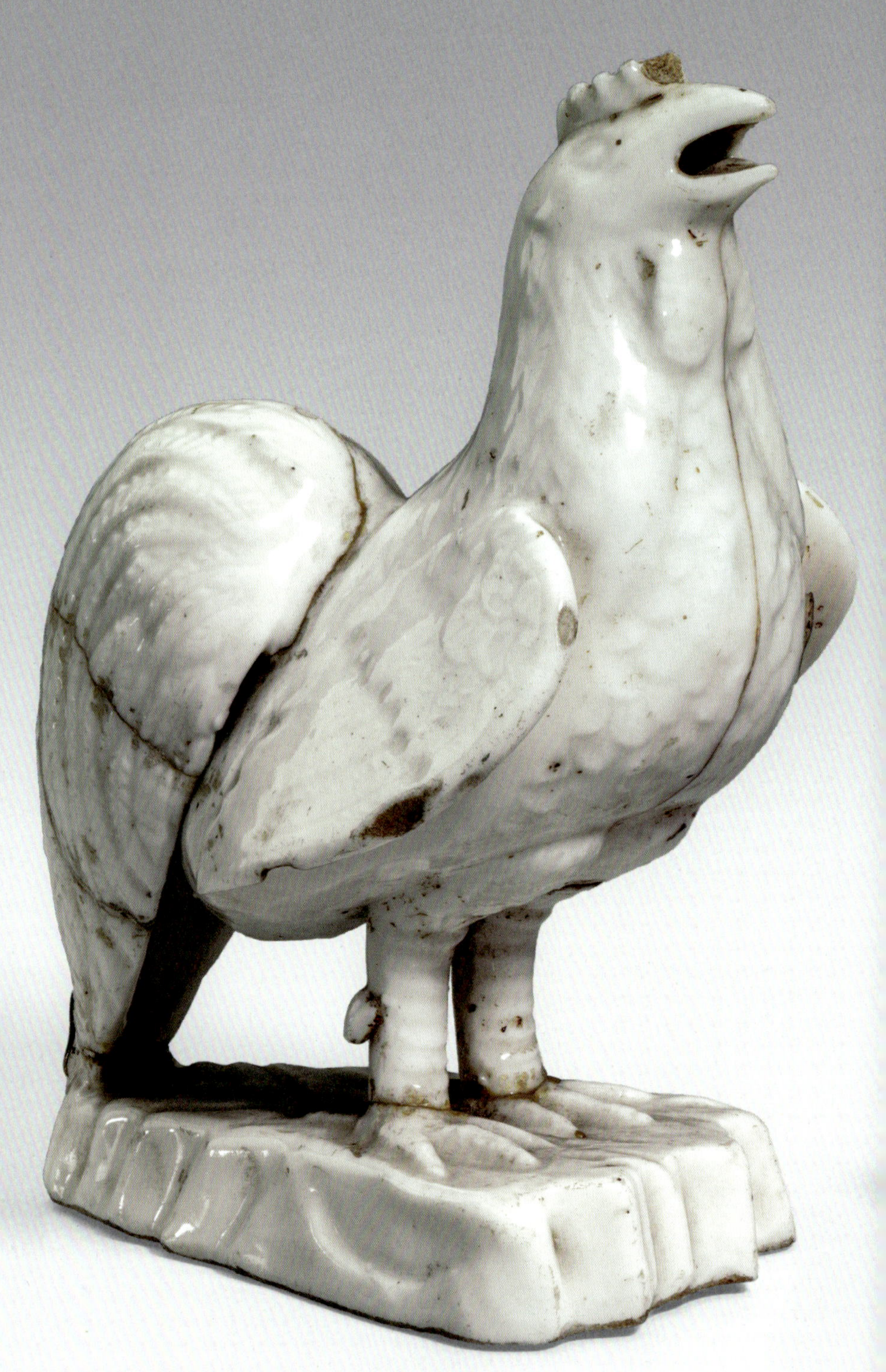

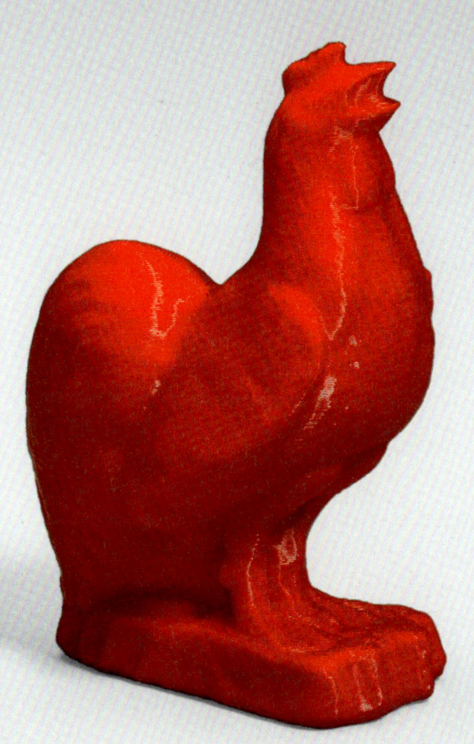

6. *Left*: Rooster, Chinese (for export), mid-18th century. Hard-paste porcelain, height: 15.9 cm (6¼ in.)

Right: Chris Templeman (American, born in 1979). *"Make and Take" Rooster*, 2017. 3-D-printed polyactide (PLA) plastic, height: 8 cm (3⅛ in.)

roosters, thus simultaneously commodifying and democratizing the original figure (fig. 6).

More recently, the world has faced another profound period of change and destabilization. Beginning in 2020 the global coronavirus pandemic meant that for most of us the world shrank down to the size of our living spaces. Artists responded in different ways to the closure of galleries, the pause in the art market, and the merging of work and home. The artist Eben Haines found himself forced to stay at home, unable to access his usual studio space. Furloughed from his job as a graphic designer at the MFA, he created a new kind of space for artists where they could create and show their works on a miniature scale, the *Shelter in Place Gallery* (fig. 7). Haines put out a call for artists to submit small works of art, which he displayed in a physical miniature gallery and photographed so that they appeared to be in a full-scale exhibit; then he posted the photographs on Instagram.[9] The *Shelter in Place* project garnered lots of participation from artists in the Boston area and beyond; it even hosted an exhibition curated by Michelle Millar Fisher of the MFA and was acquired for the Museum's permanent collection in late 2020. Many of the artists who took part played on the miniaturization theme by also making scaled-down packing crates, pallet racks, and machinery for the "gallery work" performed by Haines and his cofounder, Delaney Dameron. Our inherent connection to small things from our childhood makes us open to engaging with miniature objects as adults. The appeal of *Shelter in Place Gallery* lies not just in its democratization of gallery display space during the pandemic, but also in our enjoyment of the "trick" played on our minds and our eyes by the illusion of the miniature gallery.

In the midst of the months of quarantine and isolation, 2020 also brought great unrest, as it became a year reckoning, both in the United States and globally, with persistent racial inequity, the legacies of colonialism, and police brutality. Artistic reactions to these issues have been broad; it is not yet possible to point with specificity to a generalized response, whether miniature, gigantic, or normally sized.

The twenty-first century has seen a rising interest in gender equity as well as racial equity. Within the museum field, this has led to a desire to rectify the long-standing bias toward works by male artists. Many museums are making efforts to acquire works by female-identifying artists, to fill gaps in our historical knowledge as well as to broaden the histories shared with the public. The artist Katarina Burin highlighted this need in the field of early twentieth-century architecture by creating the persona of a Czechoslovakian female architect, Petra Andrejova-Molnár, or P.A., to whom she ascribed an uncompleted commission from 1932–34 for a fictional Hotel Nord-Sud. Burin made all of the elements that might have constituted P.A.'s body of work for the project, including design drawings, stationery for the hotel, a prototype nightstand, and a scale model of the building (fig. 8). Architectural models, though largely beyond the scope of this book, are also part of the story of miniatures. Here, Burin's imagined model of P.A.'s commission seeks to place female architects in history, acting as an important corrective to our accepted understanding. She uses the miniature form by necessity and achieves something that would not have been possible at full scale in the real world.

When people think of miniatures, they often think of dollhouses and their furnishings. These are the kinds of miniature objects that many of us have lived with and enjoyed, either as childhood toys or adult hobbies. Like the world of animals and plants, the miniaturization of the household and domestic sphere is a natural subject for artists. There is something straightforward and compelling about shrinking down a desk or a cup to the size for a doll or a tiny house. As such, this is a useful way to start to think about miniature objects as art, given their links to childhood memories and our familiarity with their full-size versions.

However, it is easy to fall into the trap of associating miniatures exclusively with children. Although Susan Stewart, one of the most important scholars in the field, makes a strong connection between miniatures and nostalgia for lost childhood, that interpretation risks oversimplifying them.[10] Nevertheless, there is some

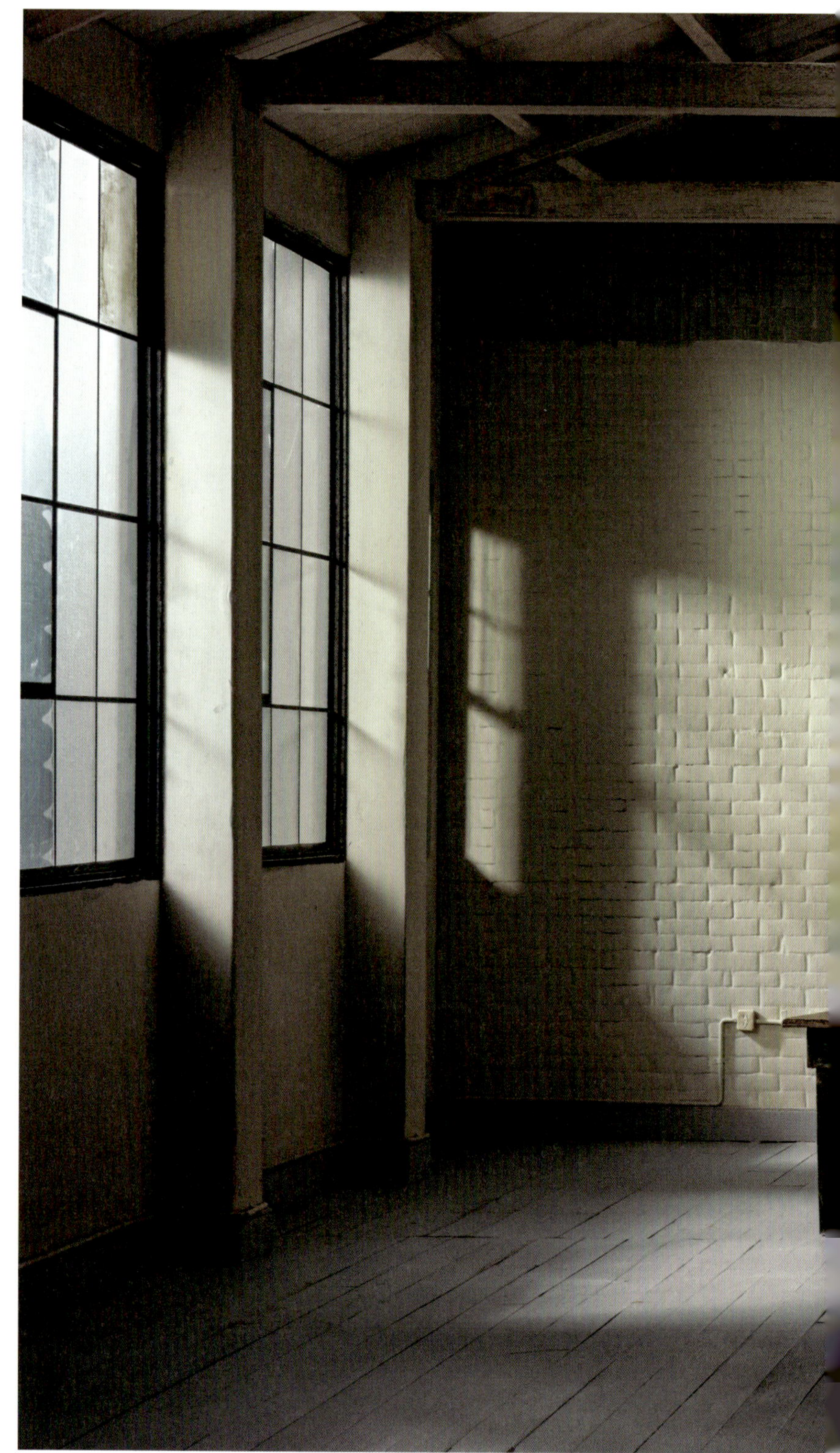

7. Eben Haines
(American, born in 1990).
Shelter in Place Gallery,
2020. Mixed media,
53.3 × 61 × 80.6 cm
(21 × 24 × 31¾ in.)

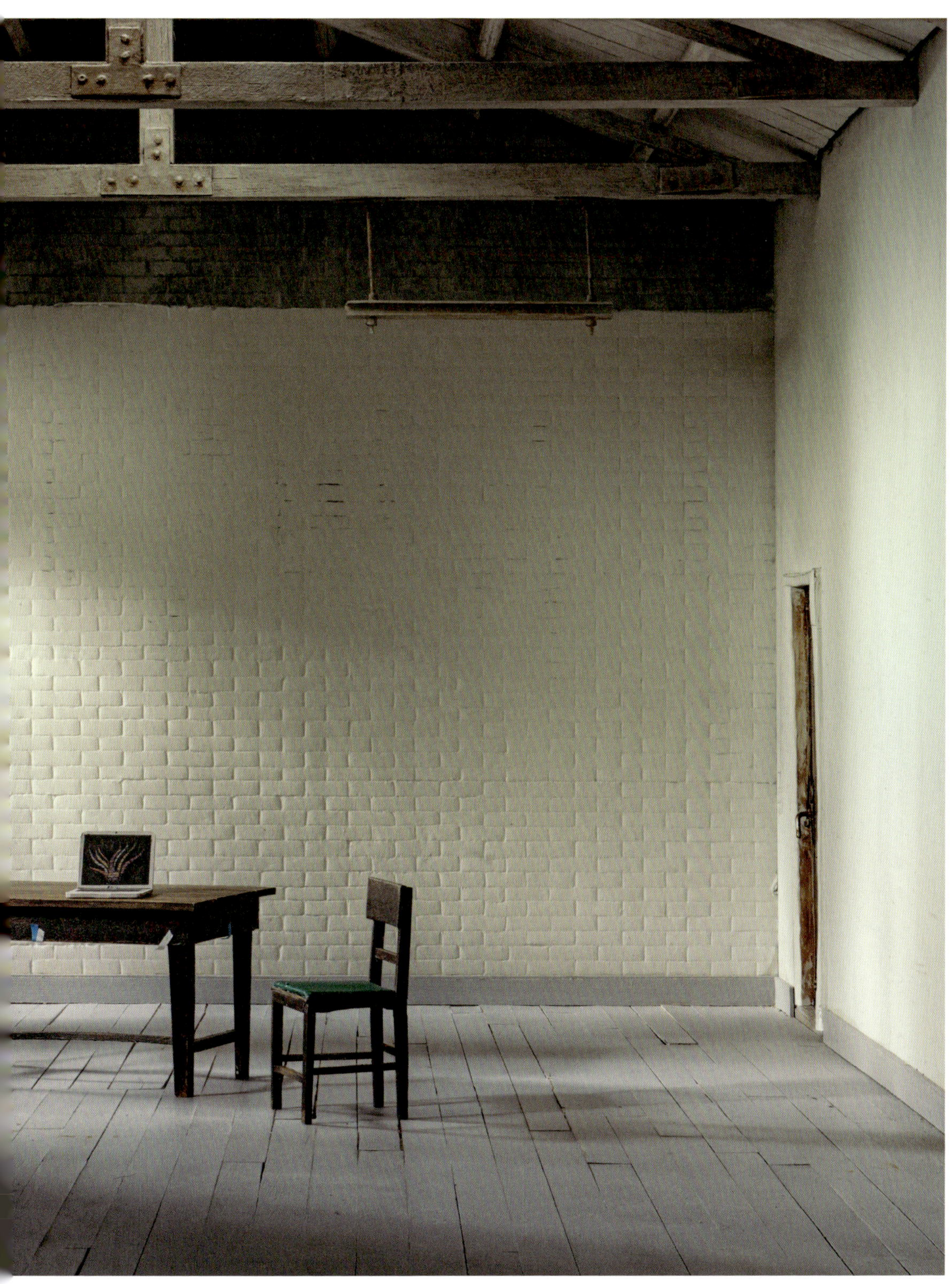

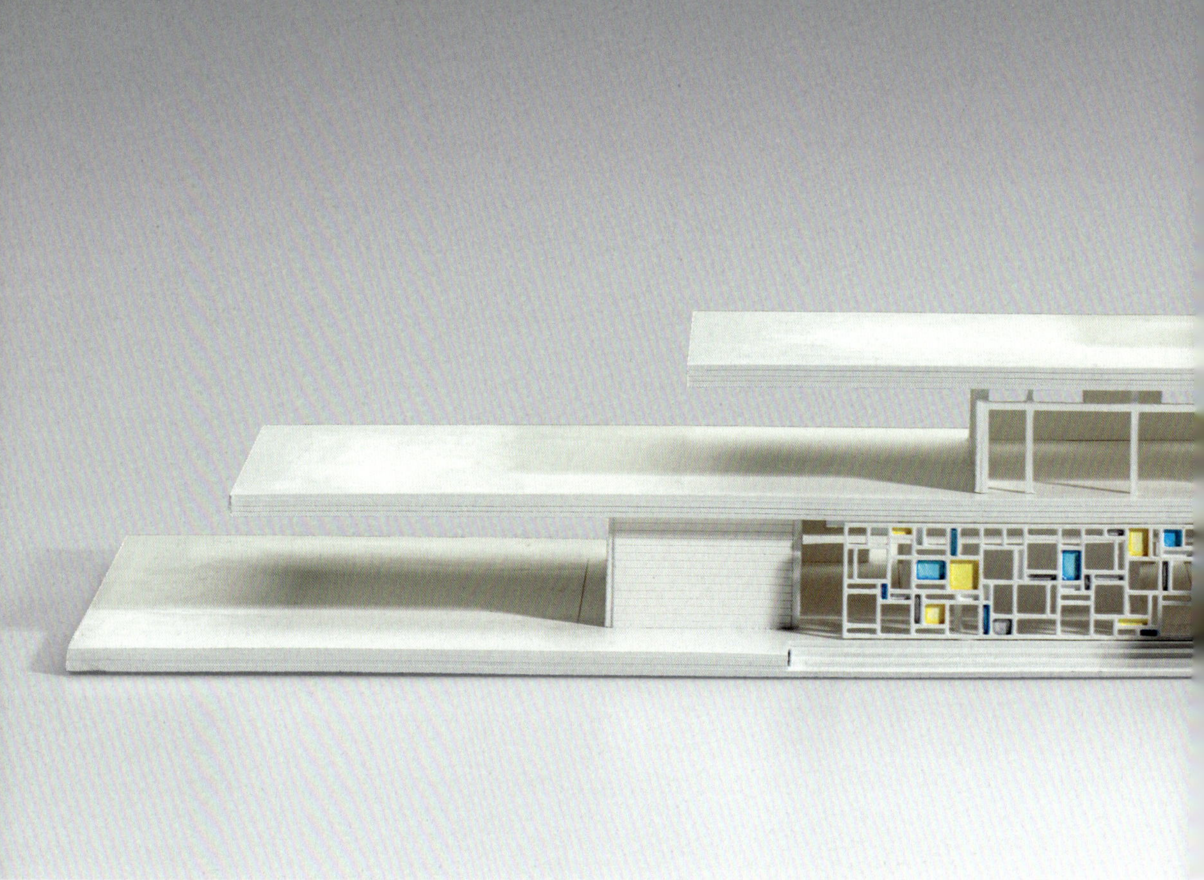

truth to the idea that miniature objects are (usually) quite small, and smallness makes us think of when we were smaller versions of ourselves: young children.

Childhood also brings to mind images of cuteness and quaintness. A baby is to be tickled and cooed over. A doll, a miniature image of a human being, can elicit a similar response. But if we allow this to be our only reading of miniatures, we miss a number of more substantial meanings.[11] Each of the thematic sections in this volume examines topics that move beyond the idea that miniatures are for children and simply to be admired but not scrutinized. By

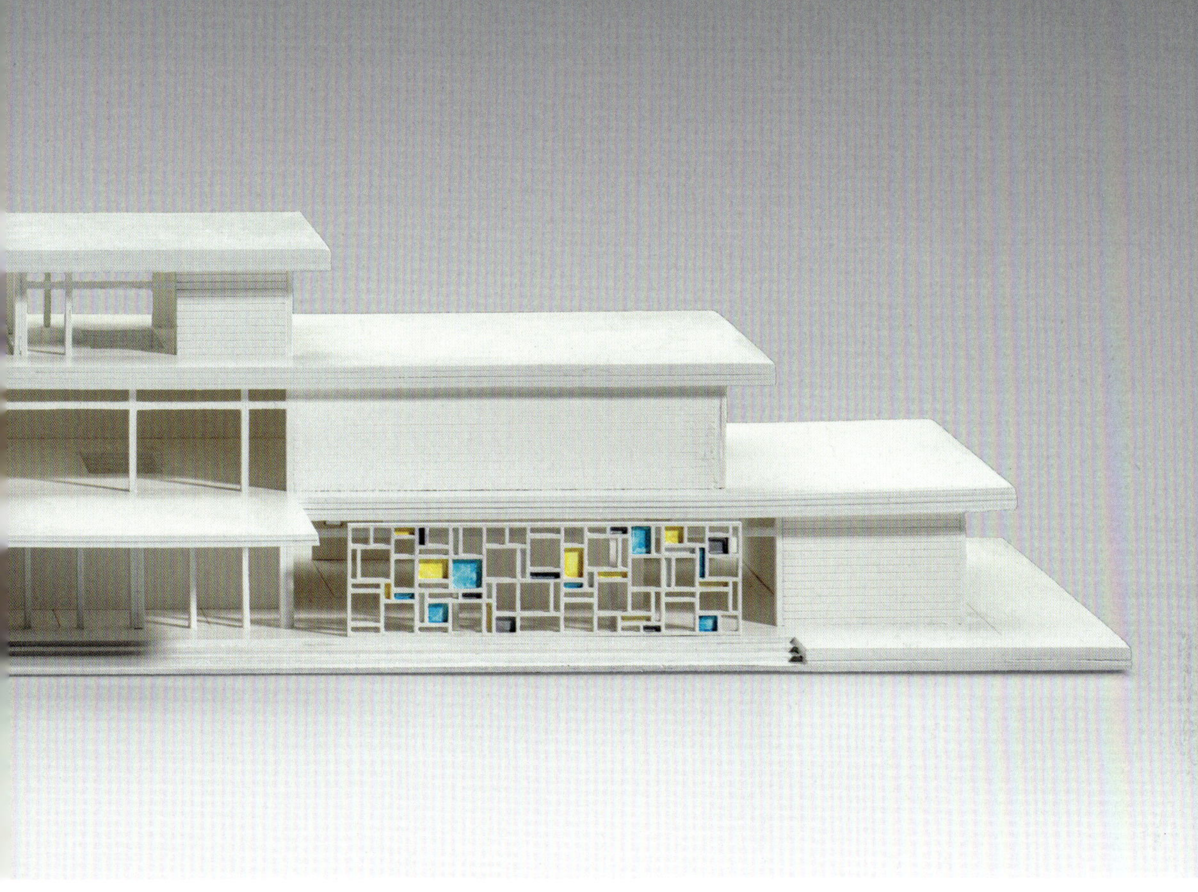

8. Katarina Burin (Slovakian, active in Canada and the United States). *Hotel Nord-Sud model, 1932–34,* 2010–17. Chipboard and paint, length: 61.5 (24¼ in.)

looking closely at different types of miniatures—those that carry powerful, mystical, even ritualistic properties; those that represent everyday objects and the natural world; those that adorn the human body; and miniatures that defy categorization—we can unravel the complex history of why artists and artisans have long made works in miniature. The phenomenon is one that transcends time, place, and culture and therefore must reflect a deep human need.

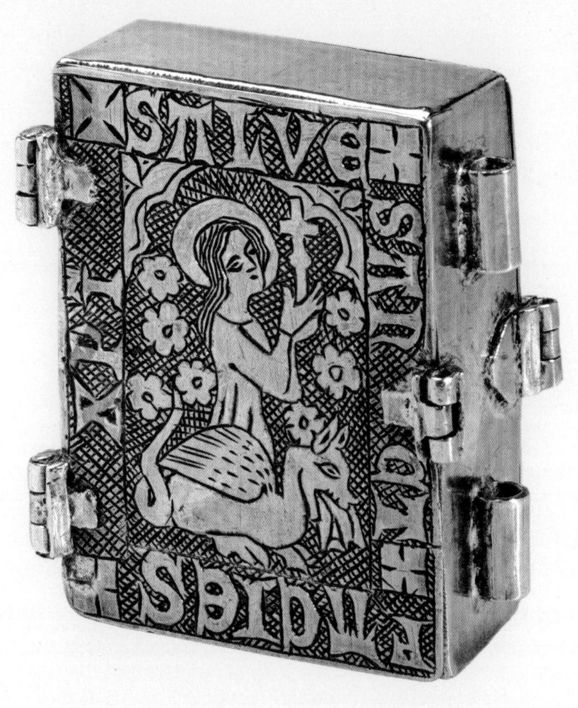

When Small
Is Powerful

What makes most miniatures so appealing is their diminutive scale, which brings with it the value of portability. The desire to wear or carry an object, perhaps as a personal talisman or a religious symbol, opens up many opportunities and reasons for making objects in miniature. Here we consider miniatures that are both portable and powerful, imbued with mystical or spiritual meaning. These objects derive their power from their parent object and stand in for it on a smaller scale, or at a distance. And inevitably, when we think about such powerful objects, we must view them through the lens of religious practice.

Within the Christian tradition, beginning in the medieval period in Europe, people came to believe that replicating a holy image extended and enhanced its power. This often began with an image, such as an icon, perhaps one related to a miraculous event that occurred at a particular site. The holy subject rendered the image mystical and powerful in the eyes of the Church and its believers. As people traveled to visit such an image themselves, they may have wished to take away with them a copy of it, a smaller version that they could keep. When they returned to their homes with their miniature reproductions, they spread the power and influence of the original.

Larger holy images, such as sculptures of the Madonna and Child, were also reproduced, perhaps out of a less costly material (terracotta as opposed to marble) and on a smaller scale. Their size made the replicas portable and more suitable for use in the home, rather than in a church setting. Some types of religious miniatures even look like small altarpieces, recalling the church itself, and were designed to be carried or worn.

A smaller, personal object could help individuals explore their faith in a more intimate way than by worshipping with fellow congregants in a church. In the Netherlands, between 1500 and about 1530, the workshop of Adam Dircksz created a number of intricately carved prayer beads out of soft and delicate boxwood. Ideally suited to small carvings owing to its structure, boxwood also held important spiritual significance, with some scholars at the time

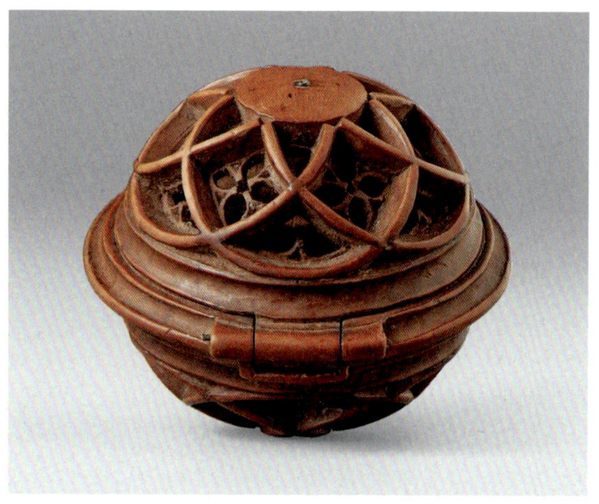

9. Prayer bead with depictions of Saint James
and Saint George, Netherlandish,
about 1500–1530. Boxwood, height: 4 cm (1⅝ in.)

speculating it may have been the wood used for Christ's cross.[1]
Opening to reveal two or more detailed religious scenes, these
beads are part of the prayer tradition of the Rosary; worshippers
would meditate on the Passion of Christ, or the trials of various
saints, while holding the bead in the palm of their hand (fig. 9).
Some of the nearly three dozen beads attributed to the Dircksz
workshop also contain small carved elements that rattle when
shaken, adding an auditory element to the physical and spiritual
practice of prayer.[2] The elaborate interior scenes related to contemporary altarpieces and would have helped their owners
recall the spiritual experience of being in the church, even when
in private prayer.

Reliquaries, special vessels that hold objects believed to have
been associated with the saints, are another important category
of items reproduced in miniature. Religious pilgrims would journey
long distances to visit particular churches or spiritual centers to
see and venerate their holy relics, believing that saints could enact

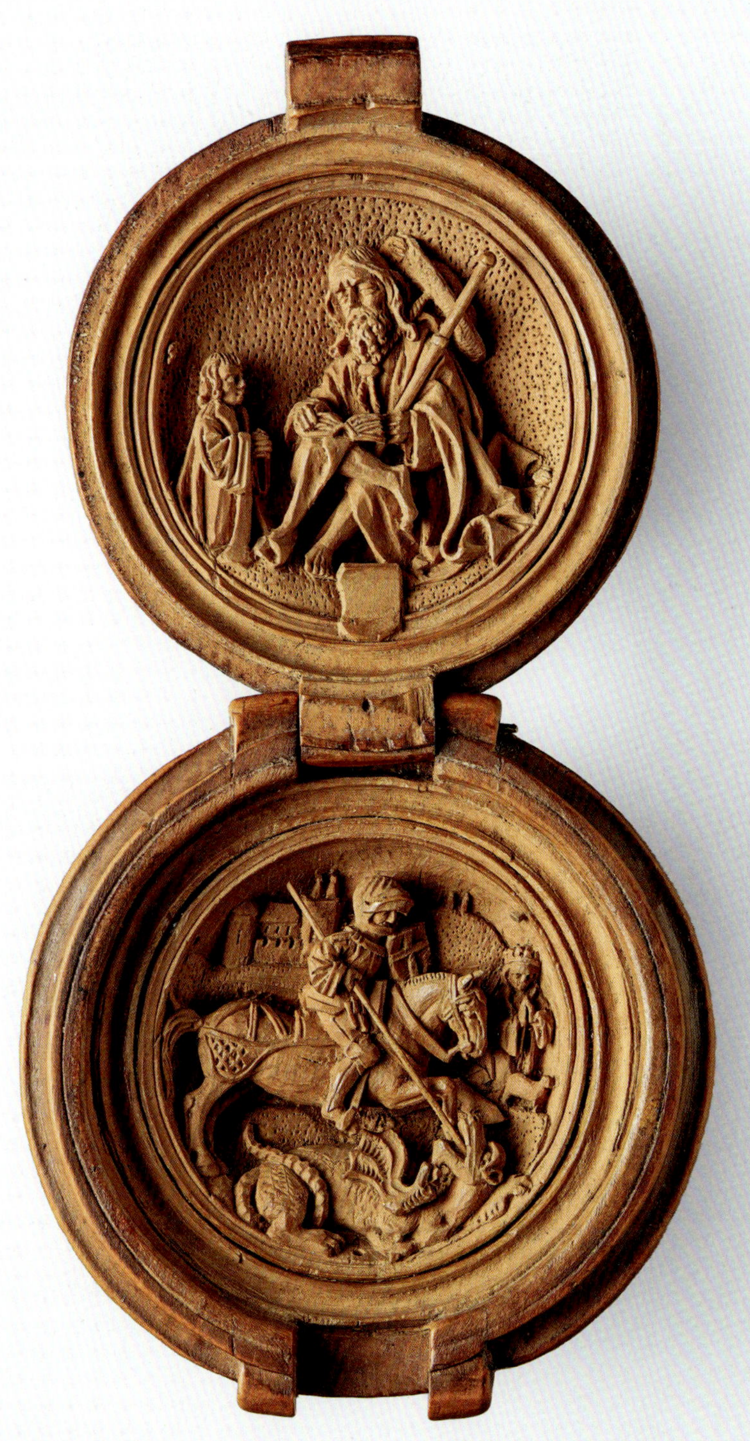

miracles through their physical remains. In many cases the body or bones of a saint would even have been split into multiple small pieces (individual knuckle bones, for instance), creating additional relics to be sent further afield and thus spreading the saint's power beyond the burial site and home shrine.[3]

We find a rare and unusual example of a reliquary in the Emly Shrine, from late seventh- or early eighth-century Ireland, which takes the shape of a house and has champlevé enamel decoration covering its yew-wood box (fig. 10). House-shaped reliquaries like this one, instantly recognizable by their form nearly 1,500 years later, were first created in Ireland in the seventh century and would have held small relics. Though lost on this example, on other surviving house reliquaries (of which there are only nine) one can see that leather straps would have been connected to the gabled roof of the house so that the piece could be worn around the neck, perhaps as protection in battle or when the wearer went on a pilgrimage.[4] Named for its nineteenth-century owner, Lord Emly of Limerick, this reliquary casket bears the word "shrine" in its modern title. Shrines are generally physical places, within a church, a public space, or the home, where worshippers can go to venerate relics, contemplate an image of a saint or deity, and pray. Here, the shrine has leapt from that context onto the body, with its house-like shape a possible reference to safety or protection. On a long journey, whether into battle or on pilgrimage, bearing a shrine in the shape of a miniature house must have been a source of comfort.

Another powerful religious object designed to be worn on the body, likely with leather thongs or strings threaded through the small holes between its two sets of hinges, is a miniature box in the shape of a book (fig. 11). Possibly French, from the mid-fourteenth century, this little box bears the images of two important female saints: Saint Margaret, shown kneeling with the dragon at her feet, and Saint Catherine of Alexandria, with her traditional attributes, the spiked wheel of her martyrdom and a sword.[5] Given such a strong association with female saints and martyrs, it was likely intended to be used by a woman, possibly as a talisman

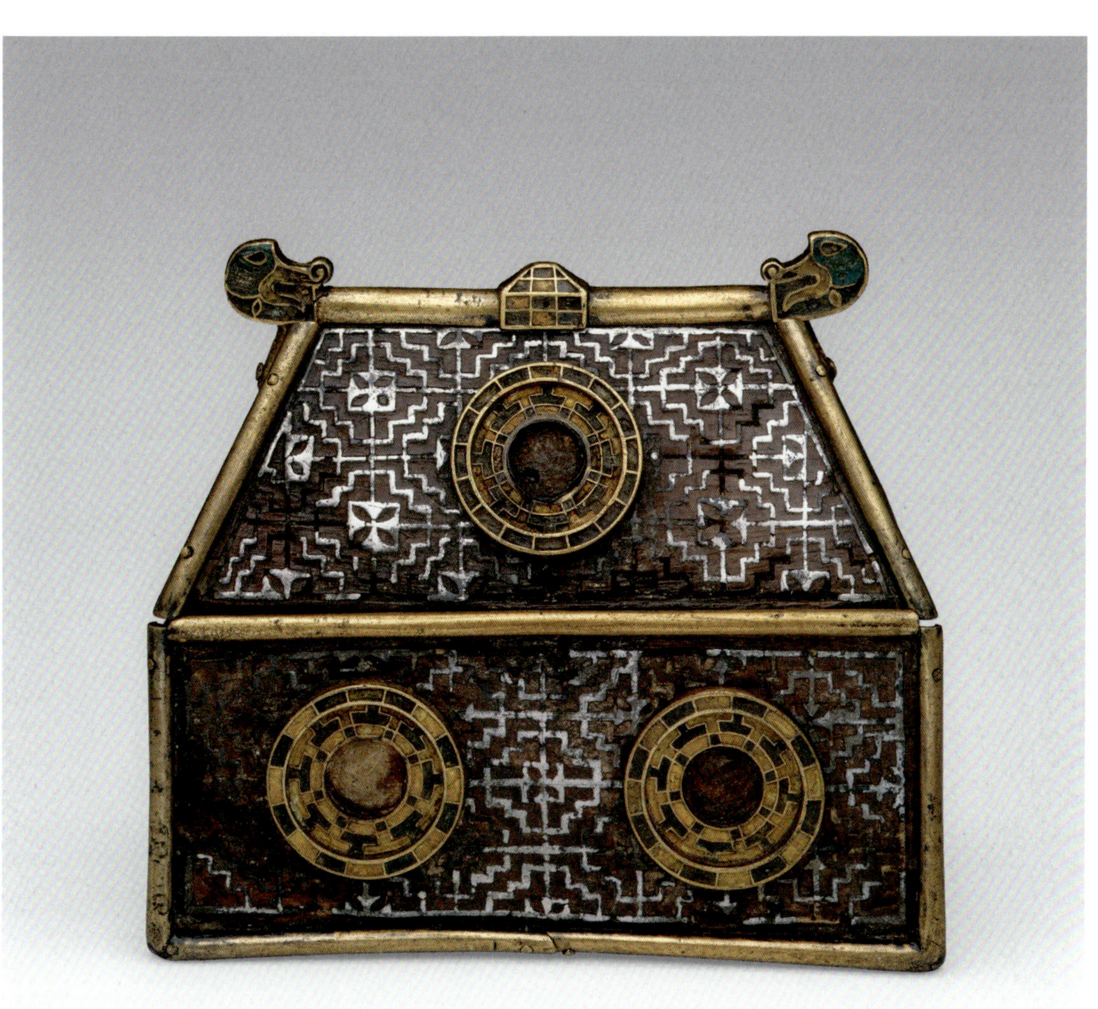

10. Reliquary casket "Emly Shrine," Irish, late 7th–early 8th century. Champlevé enamel on bronze over yew wood; gilt bronze moldings, inlay of lead-tin alloy, height: 9.2 cm (3⅝ in.)

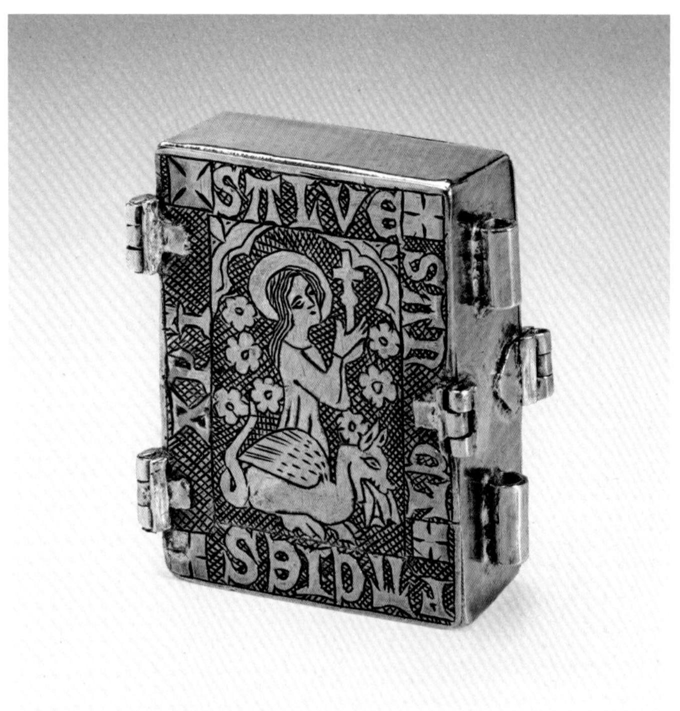

11. Box, Northern European, mid-14th century.
Silver, height: 4.8 cm (1⅞ in.)

during childbirth. With its saintly connections and the way it takes the form of a book, with two hinged covers that open to reveal a small space inside, this box nods toward the life of an educated woman at court. The small void may have allowed the box's owner to conceal within it a short prayer or reflection written out on parchment. Enhanced by the power of the two female saints, the miniature book may have given the woman who wore it the faith that her prayers would be answered.

Some churches would give pieces of relics to visiting dignitaries to take away with them, or miniature versions of the reliquaries that held them. Common pilgrims, to mark their visit to a holy site,

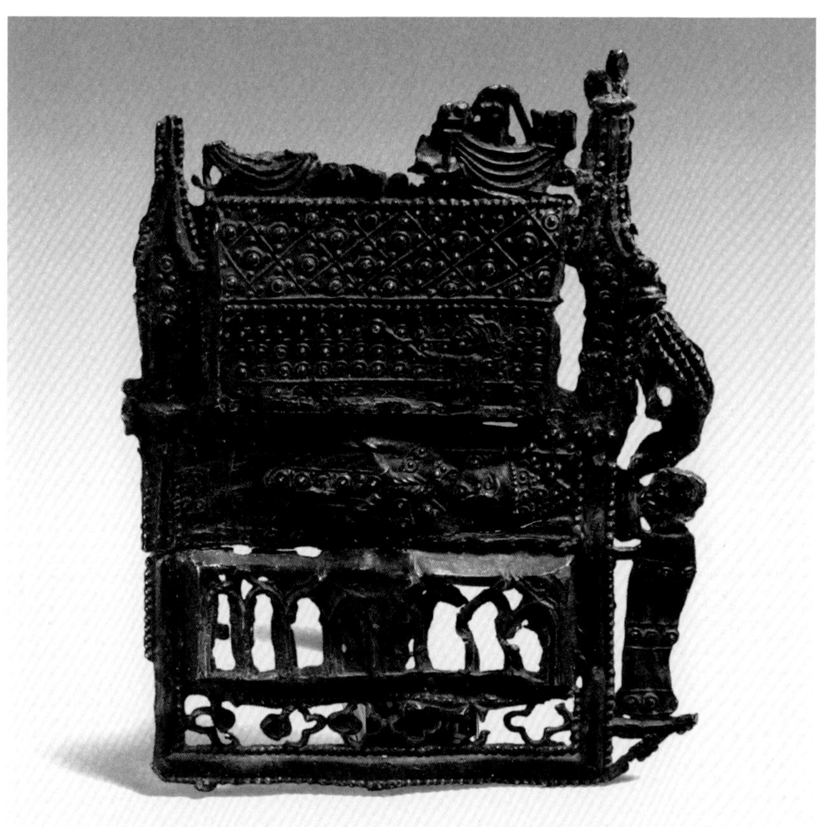

12. Pilgrim's badge of the shrine of Saint Thomas Becket at Canterbury, English (Canterbury), 1350–1400. Cast tin-lead alloy, height: 7.9 cm (3⅛ in.)

could sometimes purchase a "pilgrim badge."[6] The sale of such badges by a shrine would support the upkeep of the saint's burial place. For the travelers who bought them, the badges showed that they had made the pilgrimage, signifying their social status and faith to others they met on the road. Furthermore, pilgrim badges could be touched to the saintly remains at the shrine, essentially transferring the power of the saint to the badge.[7]

One extraordinary surviving example of a pilgrim badge is an English tin-lead badge from 1350–1400 depicting in miniature the shrine of Saint Thomas Becket at Canterbury, (fig. 12). This badge is in excellent condition, considering that it was likely worn by its

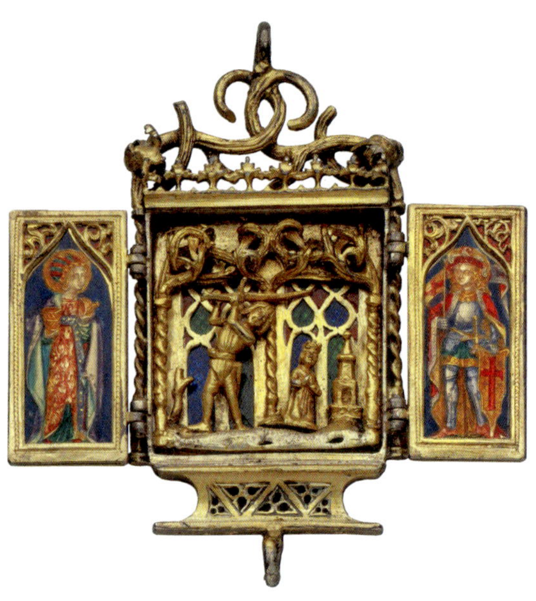

13. Triptych Pendant depicting Martyrdom of Saint Barbara, Mary Magdalen, and Saint Gereon, German (Cologne), 1504. Basse-taille enamel and gilding on silver, height (open): 7.2 cm (2⅞ in.)

owner on a long homeward journey. It shows in striking detail the tomb of the English saint and the gabled shrine atop it. Thomas Becket, brutally murdered in Canterbury Cathedral in 1170, was canonized shortly after his death, and the church decorated his tomb with an elaborate shrine to create a fitting destination for the many pilgrims who came to venerate him. With its image of the tomb, which was relatively unusual— most pilgrim badges bore simpler designs—this badge essentially brought the holy site into the world and spread its power wherever the pilgrims went along their journeys home.

Portable, wearable items like the pilgrim badge could thus transfer their mystical religious power from a source site or object out into the world. A triptych pendant in the form of a central scene flanked by two folding wings recalls the large altarpieces that were common in churches throughout Northern Europe in the medieval period (fig. 13). The iconography of the central scene and the one at the right help us to associate this piece with the German city of Cologne. At center, Saint Barbara is pictured kneeling, about to be beheaded by her father, who did not support her Christian faith, and at right we see Saint Gereon dressed in armor. In Cologne there is a basilica dedicated to Saint Gereon, built in the first quarter of the thirteenth century, and Saint Barbara appears within a triptych altarpiece, *The Virgin and Child with Saints*, from the

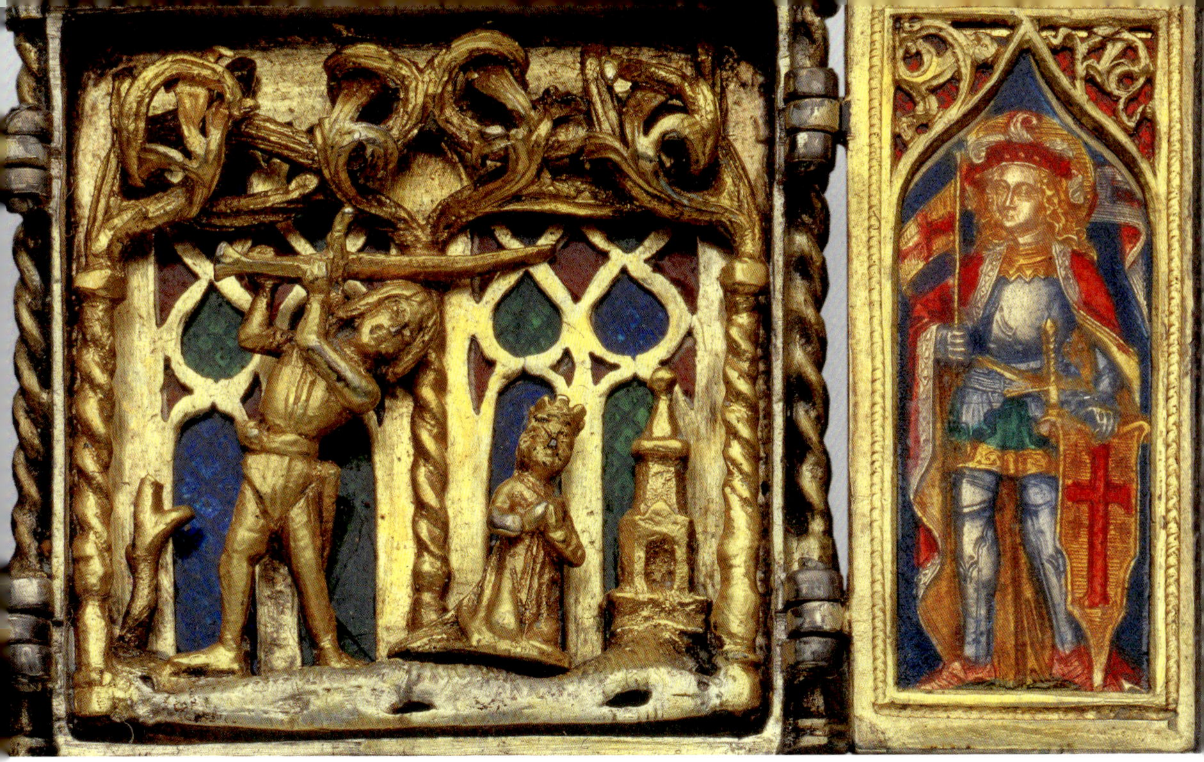

Church of Saint Katherine, also in Cologne (the triptych is now in the National Gallery of Australia). The altarpiece was created in Cologne around 1510, shortly after this pendant, which is inscribed with the date 1504.[8] The wealthy patron who commissioned the pendant, and may have worn it as a necklace or hanging from a belt, likely wished to refer to those important sites in Cologne and drew strength and protection from the favored saints.

Nearly two thousand years earlier, amulets in ancient Egypt and Nubia carried a similar power, derived from their materials, shape, inscriptions, and the gods or goddesses that they represented. Often incorporating a loop that would have enabled them to be worn on a cord of some kind, these ancient vessels were generally small and portable, like the tiny and delicate Bastet amulet inscribed for Pamay, which, at less than two inches tall, would have required close looking to read the inscription on the underside (fig. 14). While some ancient amulets were used purely in a funerary context, those depicting gods or goddesses, like Bastet (daughter

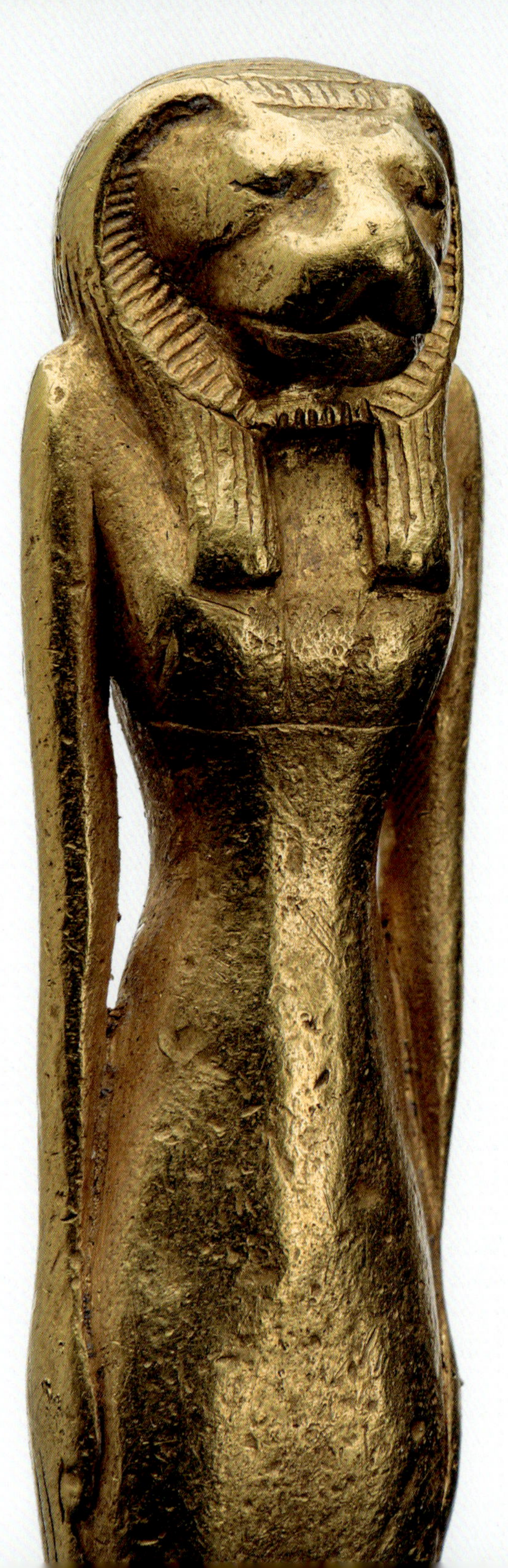

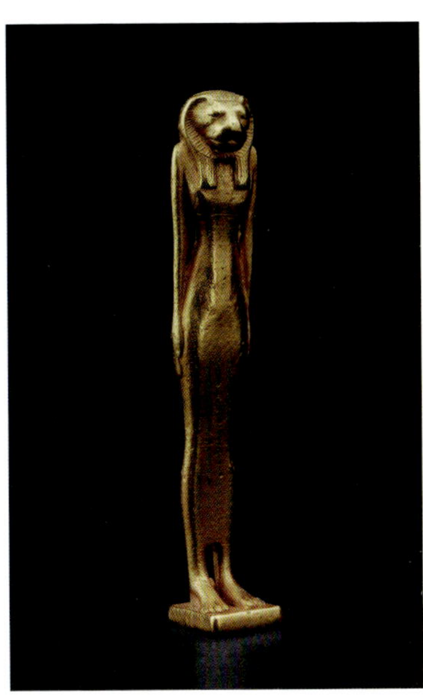

14. Bastet amulet inscribed for Pamay, Egyptian, 724–712 BCE. Gold, height: 4.7 cm (1⅞ in.)

of the sun god Ra), could have been used by a living owner and then later in a burial, reflecting the dual role that the deities played in life and the afterlife.[9]

Life and afterlife also come into play in more recent objects designed around memory and memory making. At first glance, a nineteenth-century gold bracelet appears simple: a plain, rigid bangle with a single ball-shaped decoration dangling from it (fig. 15). However, closer examination reveals that the ball is actually a locket, within which is a glass ball containing four sets of braided hair identified as "Father," "Mother," "George," and "Robert," and an inscription, "RCB to HMW, 1864." While we do not know for certain who this family was, or indeed where they lived (most likely England or the United States), this bracelet is a powerful stand-in for the memory of an entire family. It is interesting to speculate why someone would have gathered together the hair of four family members in this one locket. Perhaps they all perished from the same disease at one time and are being memorialized in death; a happier idea would be that the bracelet's owner simply moved or emigrated overseas and wished to remember the family that they left behind. Whatever the reason, this is a very personal, intimate object, with the wearer controlling when the little ball is opened to reveal its contents. Was it opened for friends or only in private? What did it mean to the wearer to carry their family with them in miniature form?

This kind of memorializing jewelry was common in the nineteenth century, particularly in England and in the United States, when Victorian sentimentality around death contributed to a culture of mourning, or performative grief.[10] The bracelet is a lovely

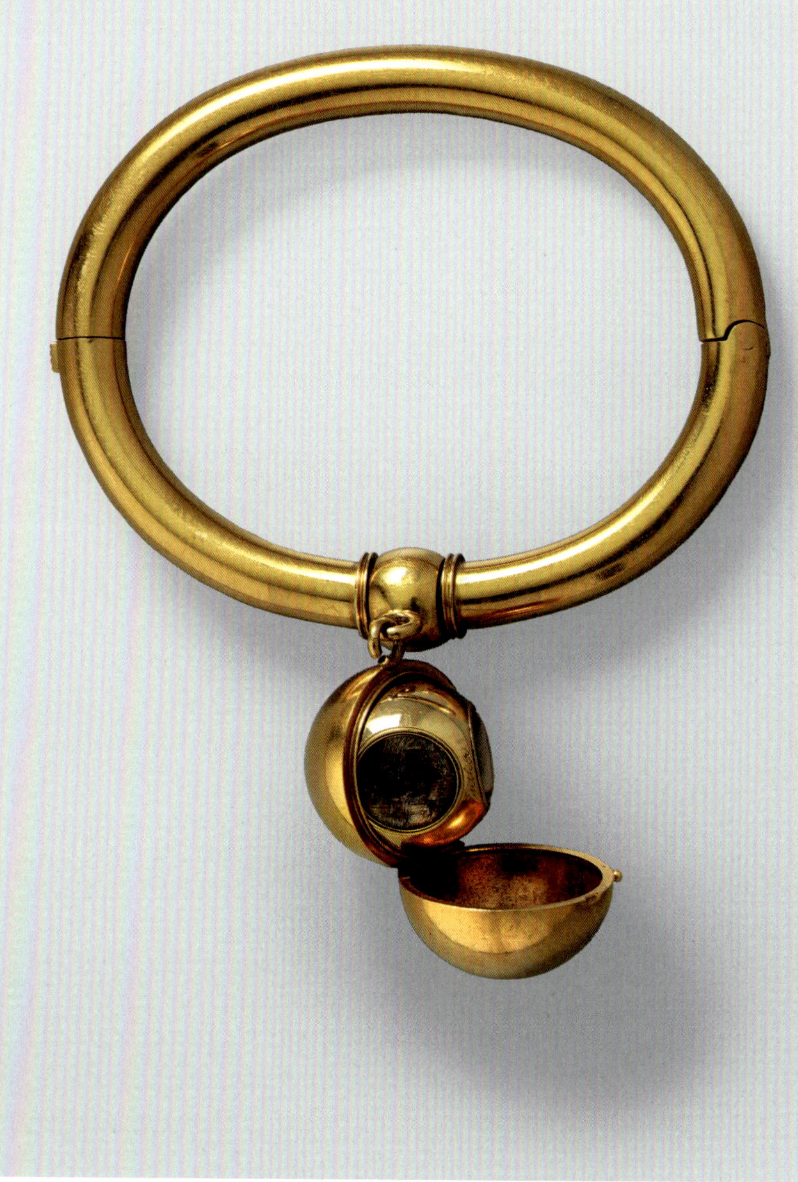

15. Bracelet, American or European, 1864.
Gold, glass, and hair, width: 9.5 cm (3¾ in.)

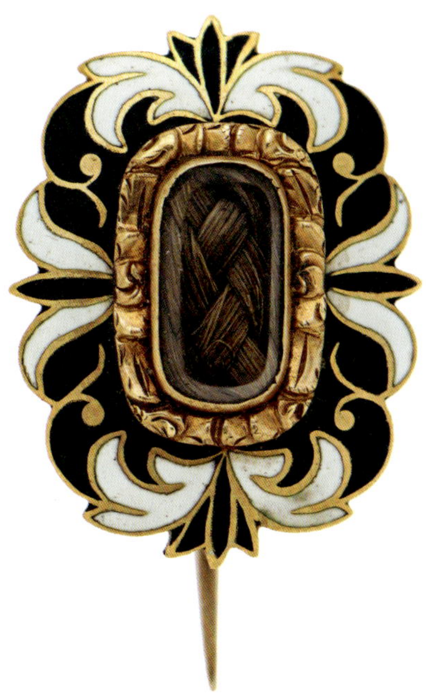

16. Brooch, American,
19th century. Enamel, gold,
crystal, braided hair,
height: 1.8 cm (¾ in.)

example that offered the chance to express both private and public grief: the wearer could decide whether to release and experience the memory or not. Other examples of nineteenth-century memorial jewelry, such as a white and black enamel and gold brooch, are more overt in their incorporation of an intimate memento like a braid of hair, which forms part of the design of the brooch and is prominently featured (fig. 16). This piece seems to claim that the act of memorializing can make something beautiful, if sad.

Referred to as secular relics, memorial jewelry played an important role in life and literature throughout the Victorian period, finally falling out of fashion by the turn of the century. The idea of a secular relic was a uniquely nineteenth-century one, when an

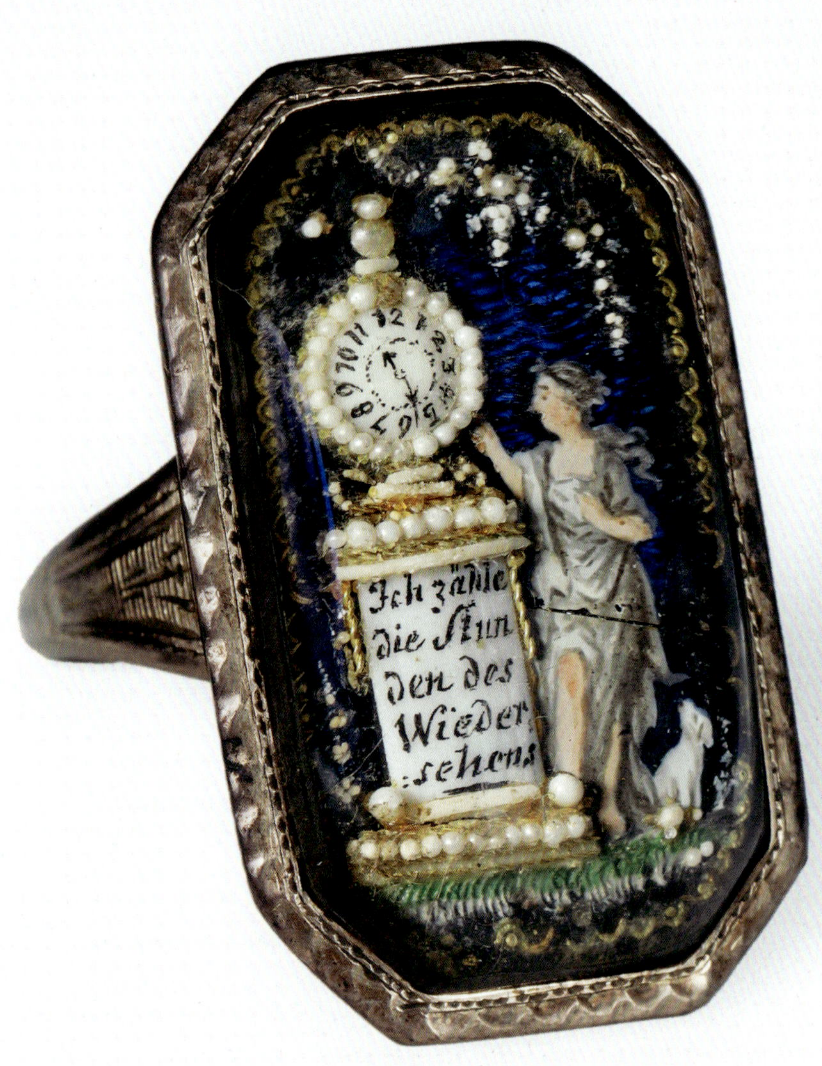

Ich zähle
die Stun
den des
Wieder
:sehens

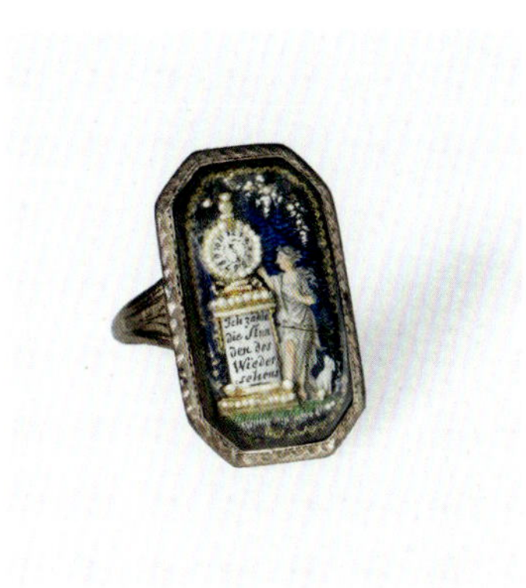

17. Memorial ring, Central
European, late 18th century.
Gold, pearls, paint, enamel and
glass, height: 2.8 cm (1⅛ in.)

object could be meaningful not because of its relationship to a saint, a deity, or even a royal or well-known figure, but purely through its connection to a regular human being.[11] Rather than acting as a memento mori, or a reminder of death, a locket or brooch containing a lock of hair was an actual physical, and therefore spiritual, link to the body of the deceased. The small part that remained, memorialized in a piece of jewelry, acted as a miniature representation of the soul of the dearly departed person.

While hair jewelry created a physical tie to the body of the deceased, other pieces evoke the memory of a loved one through an image of a grave or burial site. These works recall earlier religious objects that represent shrines or the burial site of a saint, such as the pilgrim badge from the tomb of Saint Thomas Becket in Canterbury. A memorial ring, probably from Germany in the late eighteenth century, dates from just before the Victorian era and its obsession with death. Instead of linking its wearer to the deceased though his actual hair, this ring depicts the person's burial place (fig. 17). An elegantly dressed woman, clothed in garb inspired by ancient Greece and Rome, stands alongside a memorial sculpture, likely a tomb, which has a clock on it—a reference to the passing of time. The German inscription, "Ich zähle die Stunden des Wiedersehens" (I count the hours until we meet), indicates the ring owner's longing to be reunited with her beloved. An ever-faithful dog, perhaps the departed gentleman's loyal companion in life, stands beside the grieving woman. This ring becomes a symbol for the burial site, which might have been located far away, and so allows the wearer to carry with her the site of mourning.

Much like the German ring, an American brooch from 1792 depicts deep personal sorrow and grief in miniature form (fig. 18). The owner of the brooch, a woman named Ruth McConnell, is

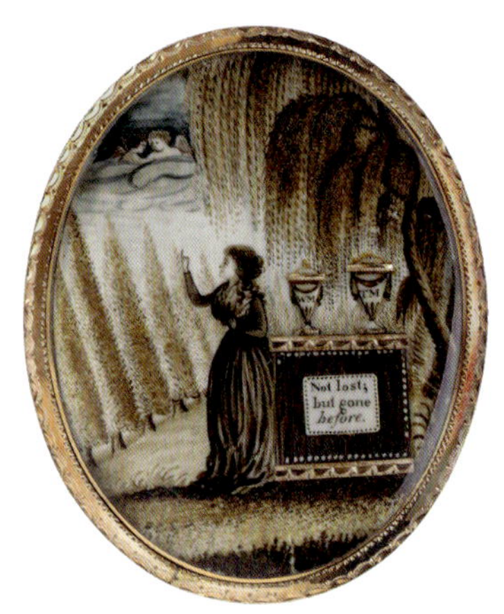

18. Rowland Parry (American, active about 1790–96). Mourning pendant brooch, 1792. Gold, watercolor on ivory, hair, glass, height: 5.7 cm (2¼ in.)

shown in dark mourning attire, standing alongside two funerary urns bearing the initials of her young sons, "WM" and "TM," above the inscription "Not lost; but gone before."[12] This very maternal image with its nostalgic sentiment makes the boys' gravesite portable and wearable, symbolizing the mother's private contemplation as well as her public, performative grief.

These memorial objects serve to condense or transfer power, converting something larger and more public, like a saint's tomb, an altarpiece, or the burial site of a loved one, into a private and contemplative experience. The miniatures derive their power from the person or place they depict and pass it on to the owner or wearer for their personal meditation on the memories they represent.

While private prayer, memory, and devotion are important features of spiritual life, public religious ceremonies also play an important role. Like the portable shrines and reliquaries, miniature versions of objects used in Jewish and Christian rituals speak to their owners' desire to possess and possibly carry with them the ceremonial instruments of worship. A Hanukkah lamp possibly from Italy and a pair of Sabbath candlesticks, both from the twentieth century, are small-scale versions of important objects used for worship in the Jewish home. The Hanukkah lamp would be used to celebrate the festival of lights, falling in November or December, which commemorates the rededication of the Temple in Jerusalem after the defeat of the Seleucid kingdom by the Maccabees in the second century BCE (fig. 19). During that time, a small amount of consecrated oil burned miraculously for eight days. Today the miracle is celebrated by lighting a new flame on each night of

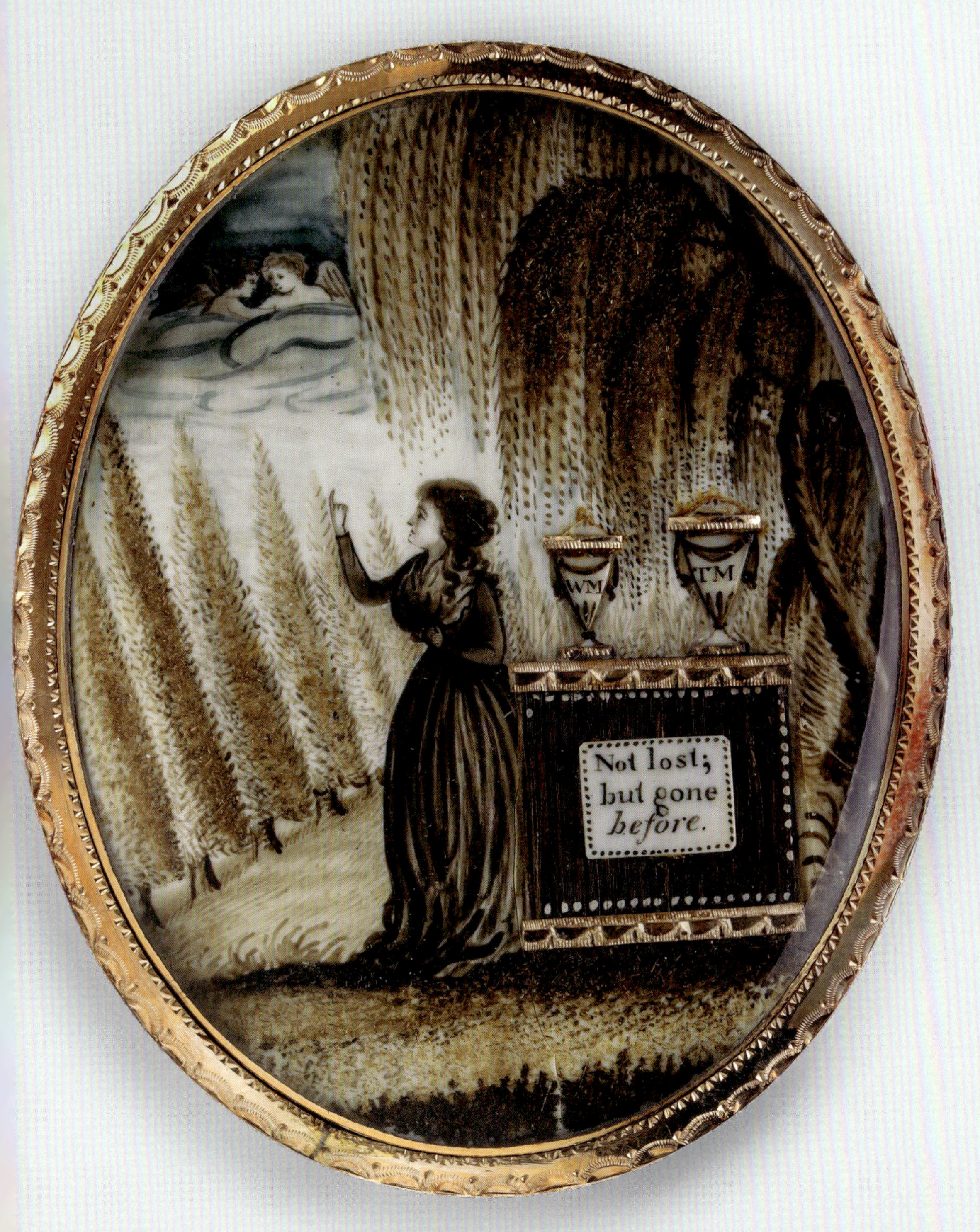

WM
TM
Not lost;
but gone
before.

19. Miniature Hanukkah lamp, possibly Italian, 20th century.
Silver, height: 6.8 cm (2½ in.)

the holiday. The miniature Sabbath candlesticks were made in the
1920s in Israel at the silver workshops of what was then the Bezalel
School of Arts and Crafts, using applied filigree work and etched
decoration (fig. 20). The candles they held would be lit each week
as part of the Sabbath ritual, beginning at sunset on Friday and
running until sunset on Saturday, to mark the holy day of rest.

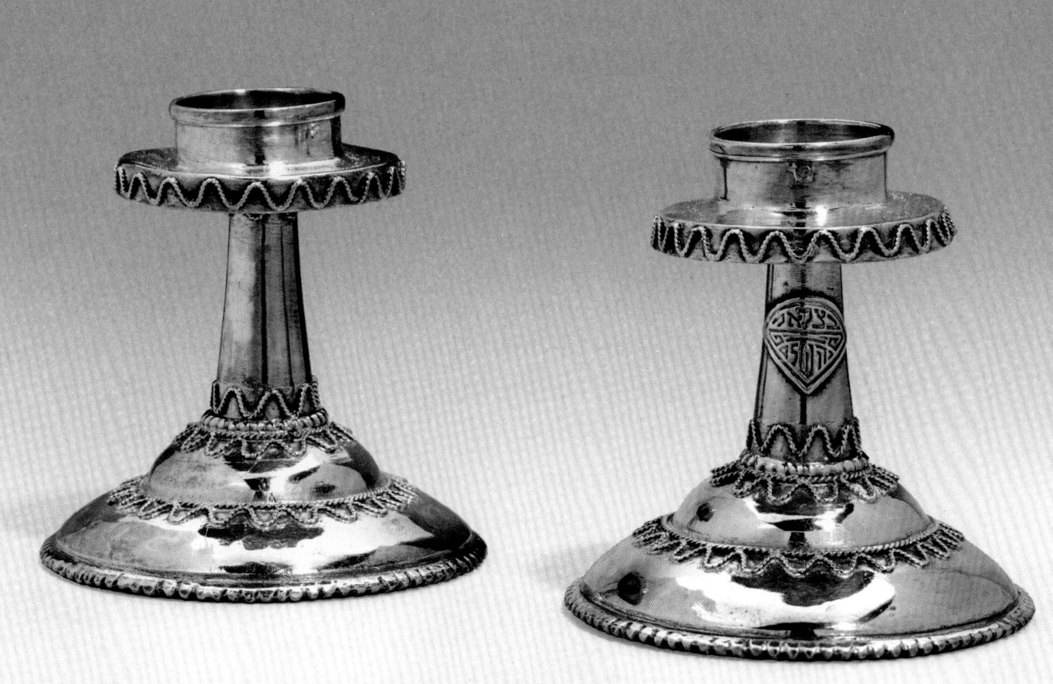

20. Made at Bezalel School of Arts and Crafts, Jerusalem (British Mandate Palestine).
Sabbath candlesticks, probably 1920s. Silver, each, height: 6.5 cm (2½ in.)

Because of their miniature size, one might assume that both of
these items were made for children, but their ritual significance
makes that unlikely. Given their important roles in religious ceremonies in the home, and their quality of craftsmanship, particularly
with the Bezalel examples, these may have been produced on a
small scale for use when traveling.

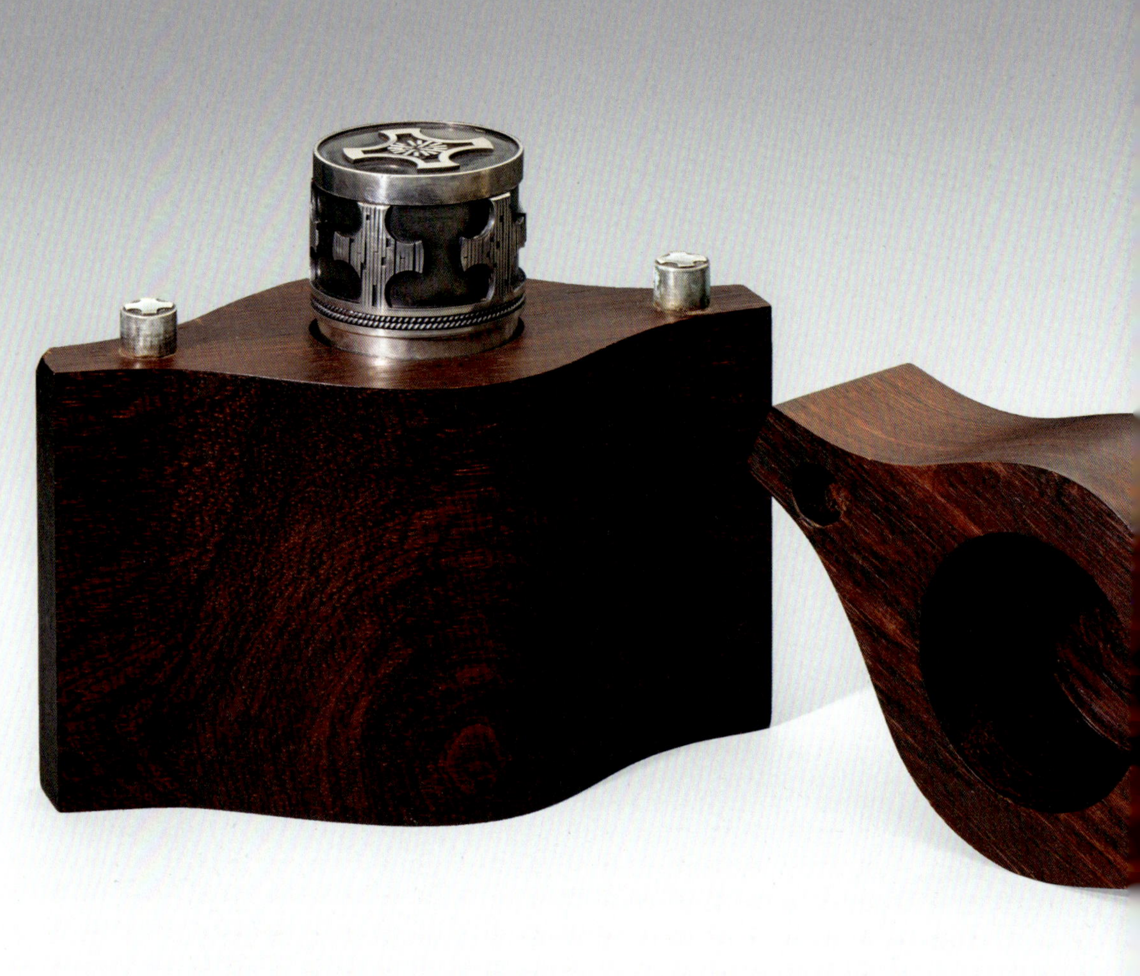

21. Robert W. Ebendorf (American, born in 1938). Traveling communion service, 1967. Silver vessel with rosewood and silver box, vessel height: 11.8 cm (4⅝ in.)

Another example, a simple, modern rosewood box with a gently undulating shape, conceals a set of portable items for a Christian ritual. When the tightly fitted lid is opened, the box reveals a cylindrical vessel fitted into an interior hollow (fig. 21). Inside this vessel are a cup and a small circular dish, and a hidden container at the base of the cylinder. The cup and dish, the container for wafers, and the small decorative crosses decorating the pieces reveal that this is a portable set for the celebration of communion, the ritual of the Eucharist, in which bread and wine, representing the body and blood of Christ, are consecrated and consumed by members of the church community. If a priest or minister were to travel with this communion set, it would provide everything needed to perform the fundamental Christian rite. It is essentially communion in a box, and for that reason can be understood as a miniature version of a church.

As we can see, "miniature" is a flexible term. All of these objects that are viewed as mystical or spiritual perform some sort of condensing and distilling: making bigger things and ideas smaller for portability, for memorializing, and above all, to increase their power.

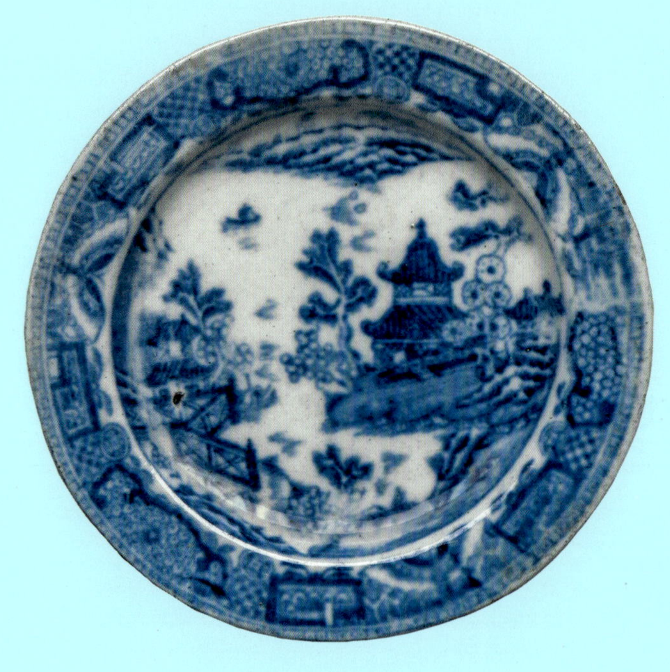

The Miniature at Home

Perhaps the most common misconception about historical miniatures from the domestic world is that they belonged to the realm of children. Certainly many children did play with various sorts of miniature objects in their nurseries and playrooms, including small houses, child-size tea sets, and dolls and toy soldiers, among others. However, it would be wrong to assume that, in earlier periods, miniatures imitating household goods were exclusively intended for children.

One case in point is the important tradition of miniature houses, such as the *pronk poppenhuisen*, or "showpiece dollhouses," made in the Netherlands from around 1600 to 1710. Five surviving dollhouses, all in public collections in the Netherlands, offer us immediate evidence for their use not by children but by wealthy women. For instance, they were made using costly materials, including fine silver, embroidered linens and textiles, and imported Chinese and Japanese porcelain—everything created on a miniature scale and meticulously arranged in elaborate wooden boxes decorated like rooms. The caliber of the objects within the surviving dollhouses makes it clear that the *poppenhuisen* were not children's playthings.

A well-known example from 1686–1710 is the dollhouse once owned by Petronella Oortman, now in the collection of the Rijksmuseum in Amsterdam. A contemporary visitor to Amsterdam, German diarist Zacharias Conrad von Uffenbach, saw Petronella's dollhouse in 1718 and estimated that it had cost between 20,000 and 30,000 guilders, roughly the price of a fully furnished home in a prestigious location along one of the city's canals—perhaps an exaggeration but still a shocking figure.[1] No child would have been playing with something of such value. Instead, these dollhouses can be seen as a hobby, perhaps, for wealthy female collectors like Petronella Oortman.

Much like men of means who assembled collections of books, prints, or paintings, the women who owned display dollhouses would have patronized various craftspeople to acquire the miniature furnishings for their collections. A great number of such miniature works in silver survive today, as can be seen in an example of an interior display with nine rooms (fig. 22). Many of the silver

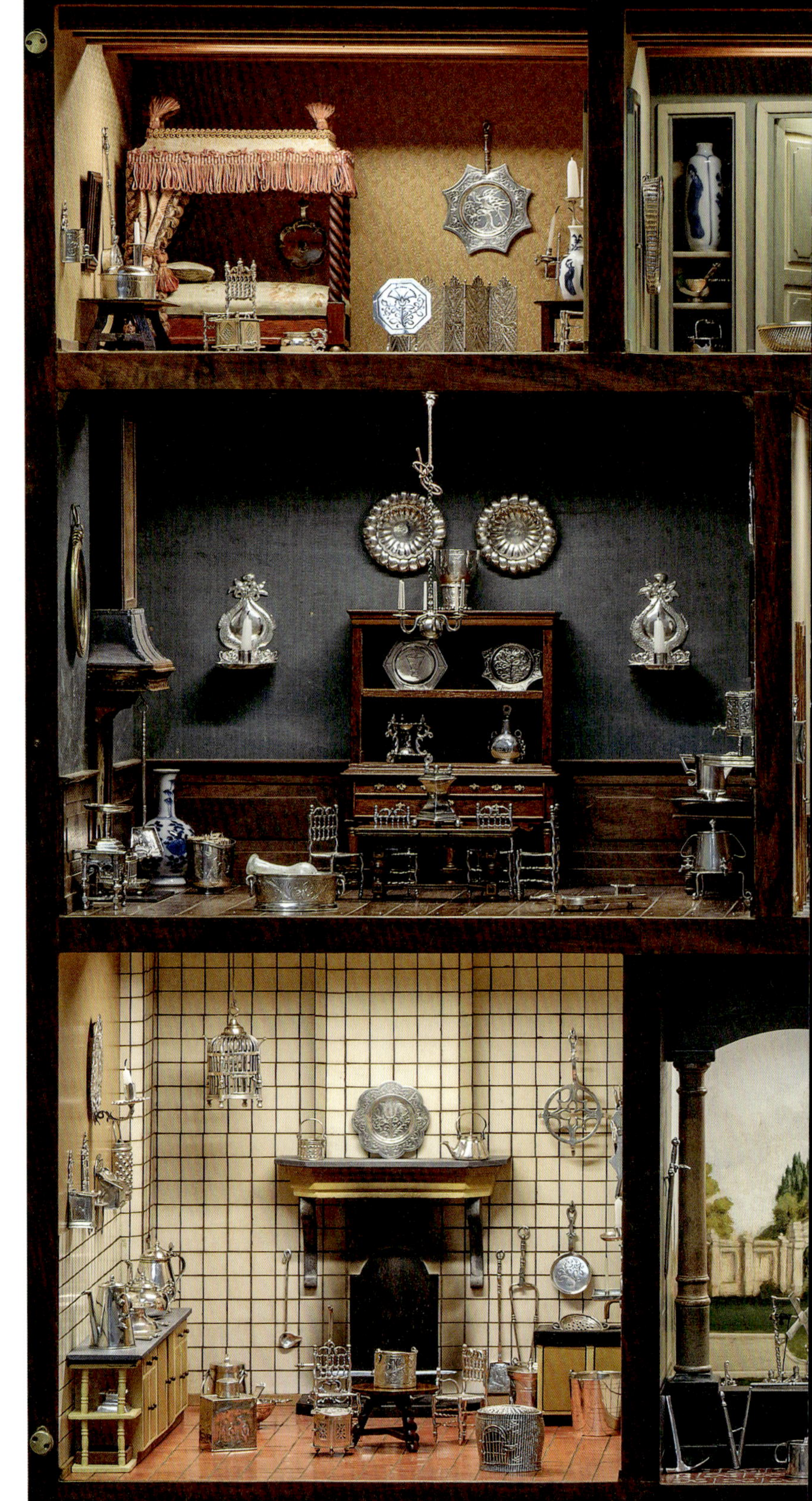

22. Dollhouse, Dutch, 17th–18th century. Wood and mixed media, height: 196 cm (77⅛ in.)

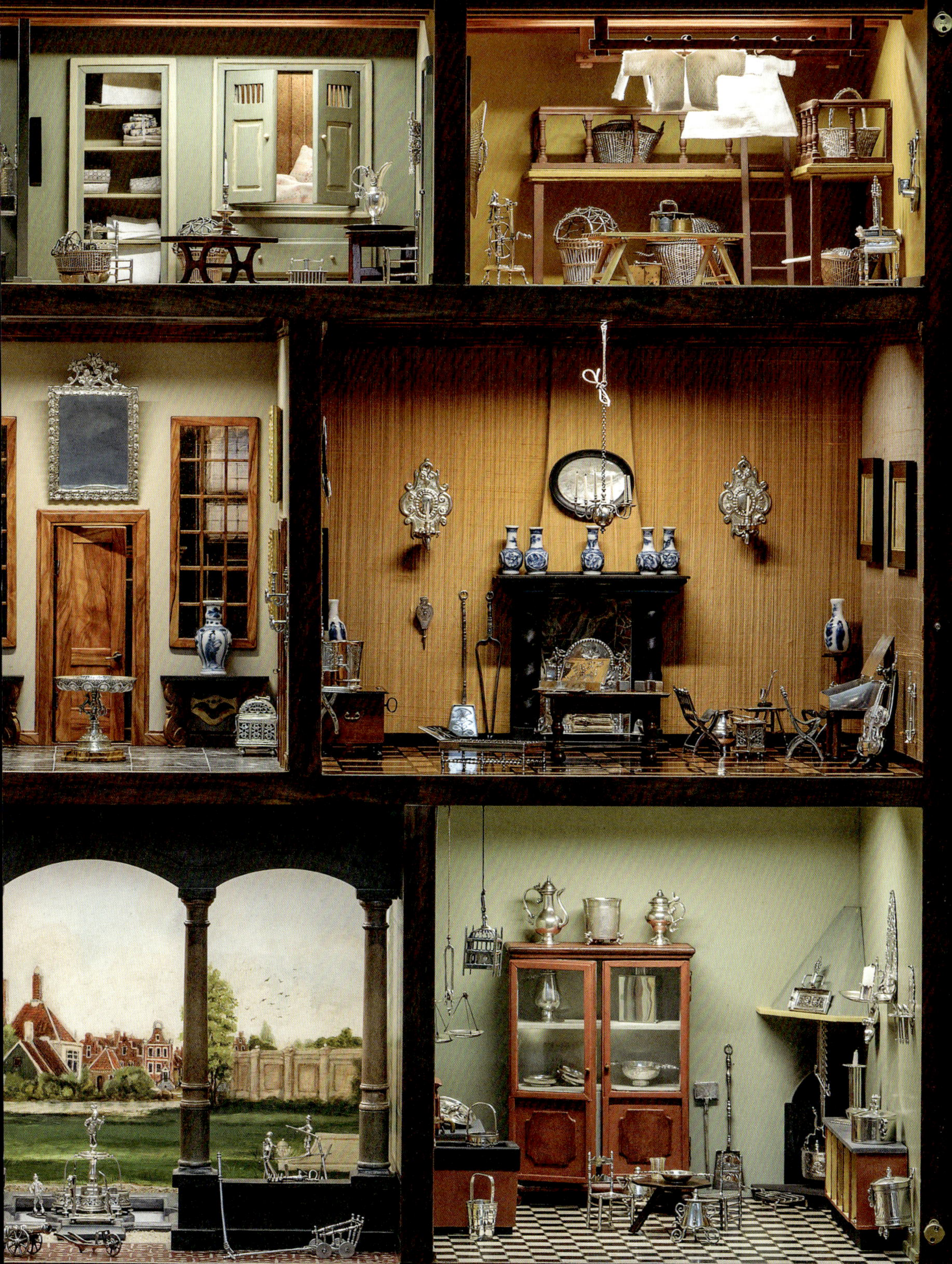

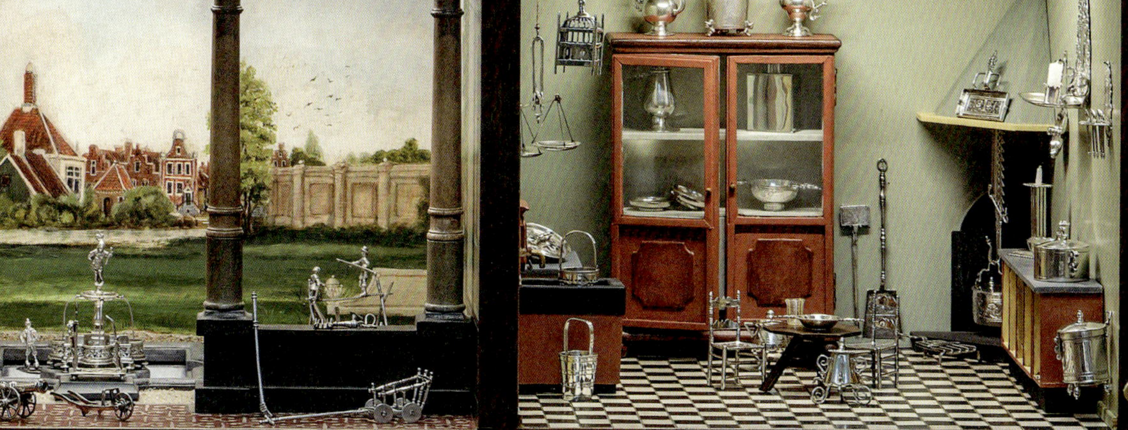

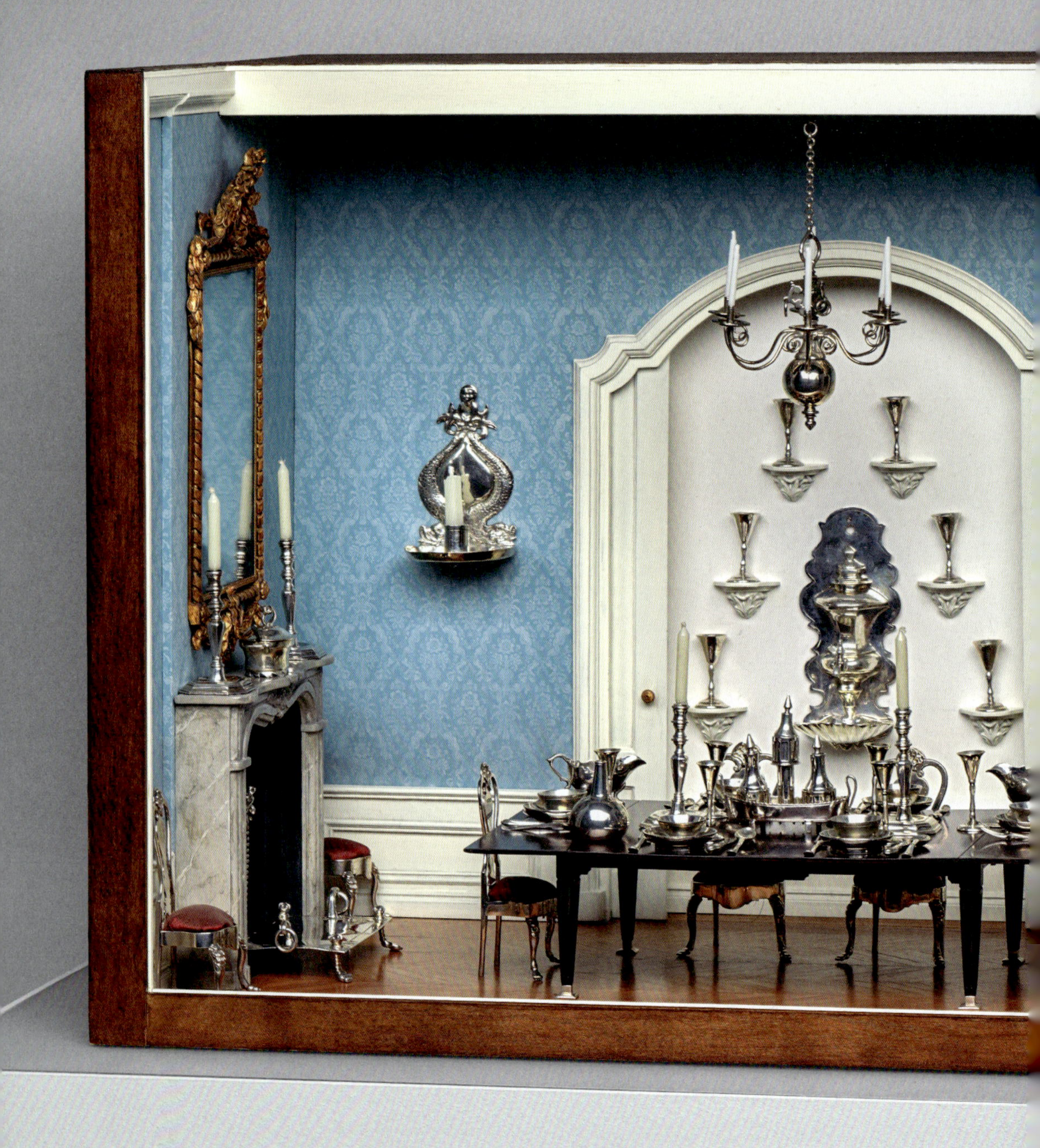

23. Arnoldus van Geffen (Dutch, 1728–1769). Dining room with silver miniatures, second half of the 18th century. Mixed media, width: 48 cm (18⅞ in.)

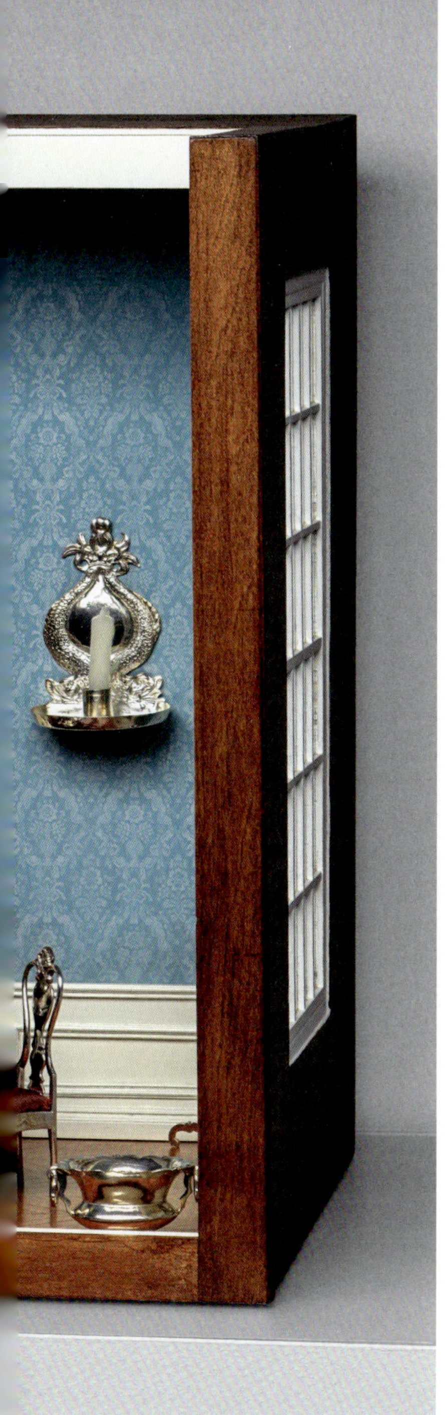

miniatures bear hallmarks identifying them as the work of specific silversmiths, some of whom produced full-size wares as well. The best-known specialist in silver miniatures, Dutch silversmith Arnoldus van Geffen, was active in the first half of the eighteenth century and made all sorts of miniature objects, including chairs, windmills, dining room settings, even Jewish ritual objects (fig. 23). The rooms in these dollhouses would be fully furnished, with elaborate wall coverings, floor treatments, and interior fixtures, such as chandeliers—particularly rooms like the dining room shown here, where visitors would have dined by candlelight reflecting off silver and mahogany furnishings.

The tradition of furnished dollhouses seems to have been strongest in the Netherlands, although lesser-known examples survive in Germany and England. The English miniature houses tend to date from the eighteenth century, and often were designed to replicate exactly the homes of their owners, such as the miniature copy of the English country house known as Nostell Priory, in Yorkshire, which was once attributed to the renowned furniture maker Thomas Chippendale. Interestingly, artisans and collectors in the Protestant countries of Northern Europe tended to create elaborate dollhouses, whereas in Southern European Catholic countries, such as France and Italy, the preference was for crèche or nativity scenes, complete with miniature people and animals, which were displayed during the Advent and Christmas seasons each year.

More recent works in the miniature-house genre are the sixty-eight miniature rooms created by the artist Narcissa Niblack Thorne, now in the collection of the Art Institute of Chicago. Thorne was interested in interior design and wanted a way to show people different design movements, such as French Louis XVI, Pennsylvania Dutch, American Arts and Crafts, and so on, without having to decorate full-size rooms.[2] She landed on the idea of creating miniature replicas, which she produced at a scale of 1:12, complete with wallpaper, flooring, furnishings, lighting, and even exterior scenes in the windows. She worked with woodworkers and other craftspeople, creating the miniature rooms throughout the 1930s. In their setting at the Art Institute, they offer visitors a quick overview of trends in interior design, mostly European and American, through the past three hundred years. Some of the rooms are questionable in their accuracy, as Thorne sought above all to convey the feeling of the spaces and design movements, rather than re-creating them in exact historical detail.

Other miniature objects, for example copies of the sorts of lesser-quality silver pieces made in large quantities in England, may have in fact found their way to a child's nursery, such as a miniature teapot on a warming stand (fig. 24). The advent of mass-production techniques for patterned ceramics also made it possible for factories to cater to the miniature and dollhouse market with tiny tableware—plates, bowls, dishes, cups, and saucers that looked like fine china. Patterns were achieved by means of a process called transfer printing, in which a metal plate was used to print a design onto paper, which was then pressed onto the surface of the ceramic object. Developed in England in the 1750s, this process allowed factories to replicate the quintessential hand-painted decorations popular throughout the early eighteenth century, resulting in less precise but still visually appealing designs. A specialty of the Staffordshire region of northern England, long a center for ceramic innovation, some transfer-printed miniature ceramics

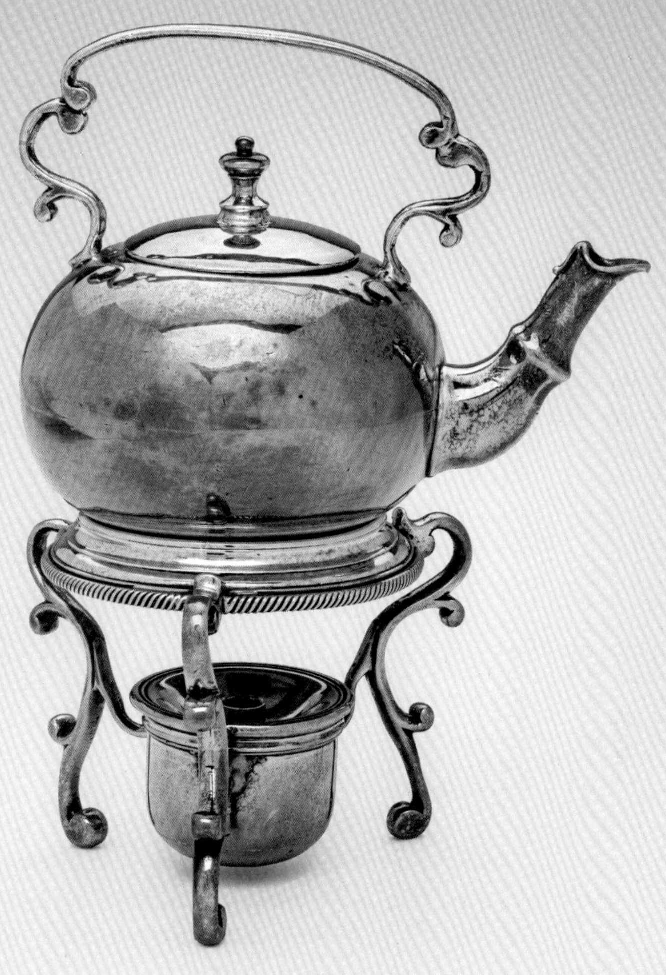

24. Miniature teapot and stand, English (London), about 1730.
Silver, height: 9.7 cm (3⅞ in.)

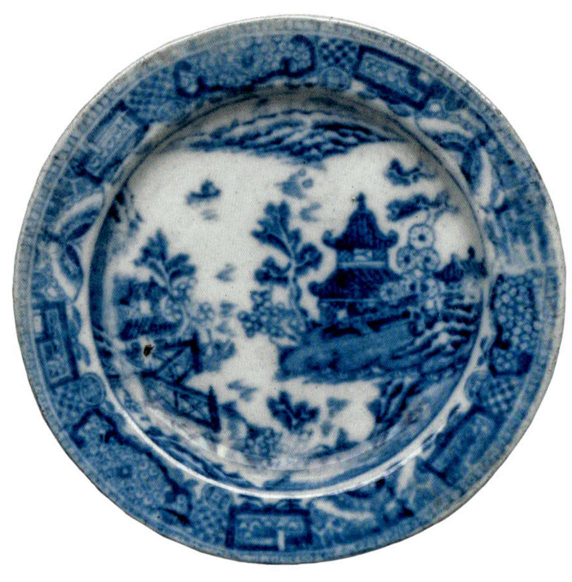

25. Miniature plate, English (Staffordshire), 19th century.
Lead-glazed earthenware, diameter: 7.6 cm (3 in.)

even feature the Willow pattern that is recognizable to many as a popular design on full-size tableware (fig. 25).

An English-born craftsman, Arthur Stone, became known for making miniature tableware and toys in silver. Stone was a prominent silversmith, active around 1900 in the United States. In addition to producing full-size silver works for patrons, he developed a specialty in miniatures, which were sold by J. P. Howard & Company of New York as well as in his own shop.[3] Some of Stone's silver miniatures, including this elegant covered cup as well as more mundane domestic items like toast racks, tea caddies, and candlesnuffers, appear as finely wrought as their full-size counter-

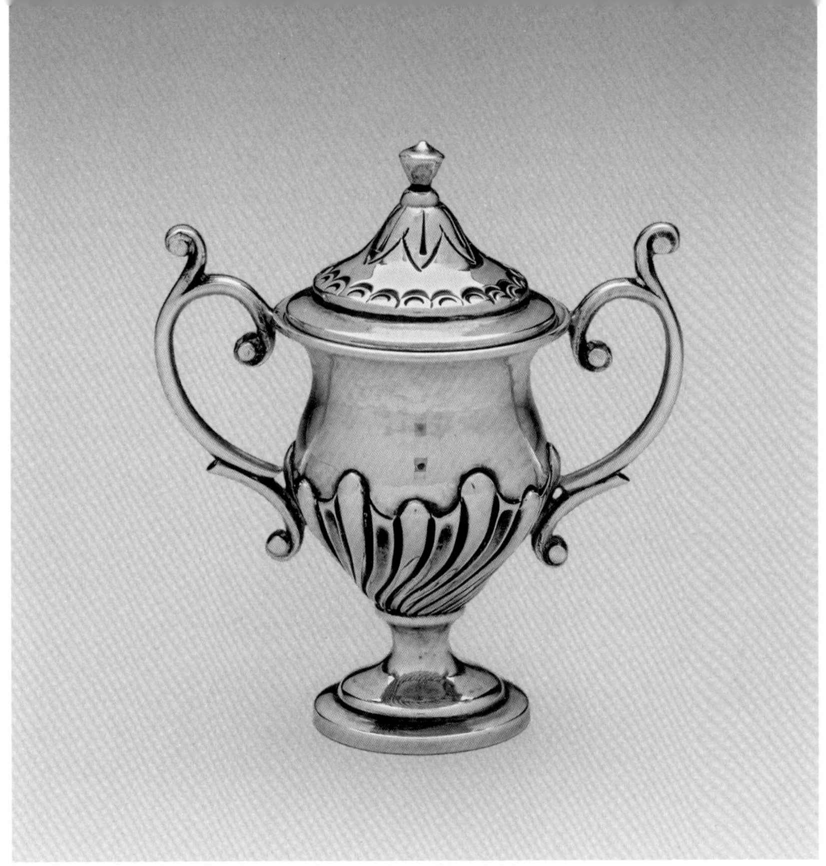

26. Arthur Stone (American, born in England, 1847–1938). Miniature
two-handled covered cup, 1895–97. Silver, height: 5.5 cm (2⅛ in.)

parts, complete with movable parts (fig. 26). Achieving detail
and quality on such a small scale was no small feat, and Stone's
miniatures were highly prized.

While miniature dishes and silverware are familiar as dollhouse
furnishings, other miniature household items can be harder to con-
textualize. If they were not intended as playthings for a toy house, we
may wonder why some miniatures of everyday objects were made.
Good examples are miniature German ceramic stoves, which
almost exactly replicate actual stoves, made of many ceramic tiles,
that were used to heat German, Austrian, Finnish, and occasionally
Russian houses and castles in the early seventeenth century. Some

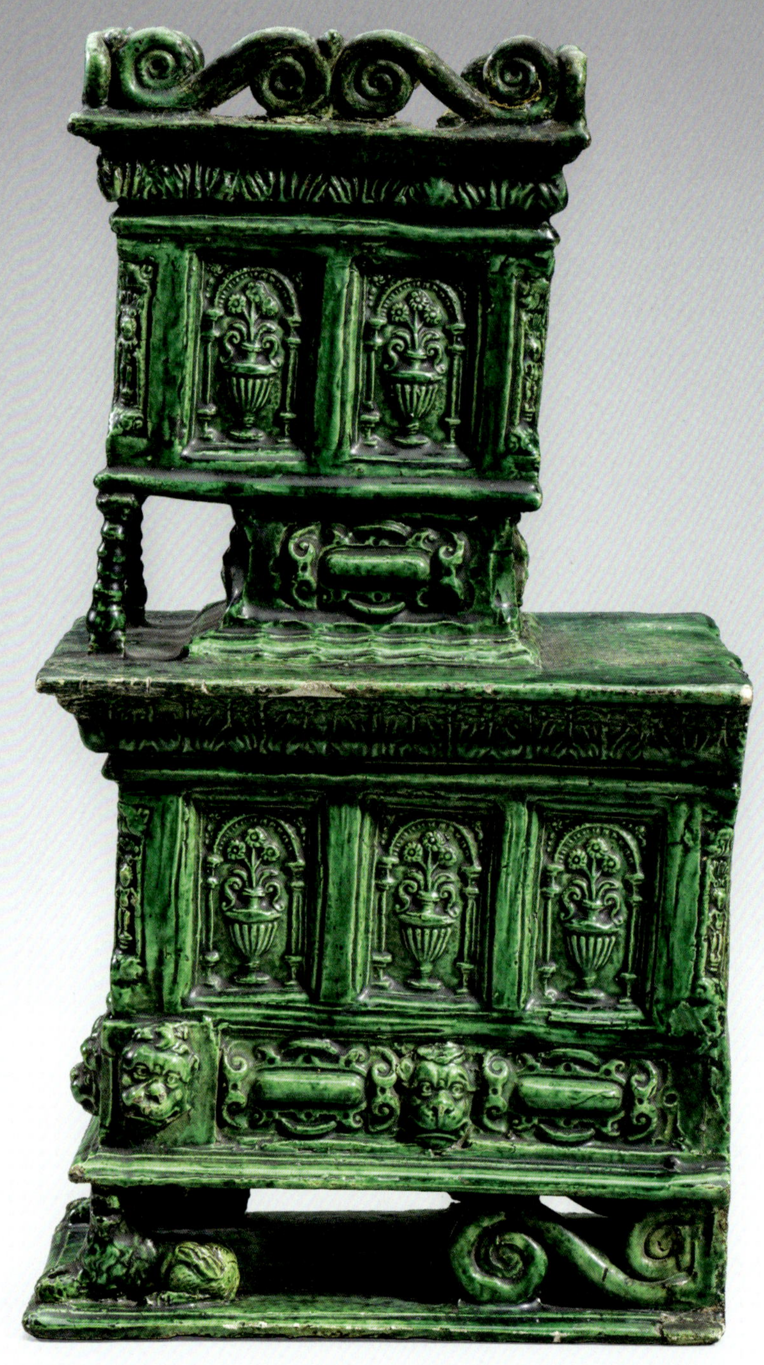

27. Miniature stove, Southern German, late 16th century.
Lead-glazed earthenware, height: 80.5 cm (31¾ in.)

of these elaborate full-size stoves still exist in their original locations in historic houses and palaces throughout Eastern Europe; others are now found in museum collections.[4] With their intricate angled surfaces, the stoves were designed to provide the maximum surface area for heating the surrounding space. One unusual miniature version follows the stoves' general shape and color (they were almost always made of green-glazed tile) but differs in its construction. Instead of being made of individual tile panels constructed over a core, this miniature stove is one solid piece of earthenware covered in a thick tin glaze (fig. 27).[5] Could it have been used as an advertisement for a craftsman's skill? Or perhaps it was created to model a different layout for the tiles on the surface, using far less of the valuable clay and glaze than a full-size example would require. We cannot discern for certain why an artisan would have gone to the trouble to make this miniature version.

In thinking about the reasons for making a miniature version of a practical household item, let us jump forward nearly 350 years and across the Atlantic Ocean to consider another miniature stove: a wonderfully realistic model made by the Wrought Iron Range Company of Saint Louis, Missouri, for use by its traveling salespeople. The company specialized in goods for the home, including refrigerators and stoves. To give its representatives a way to show potential customers the company's products without having to transport a big heavy appliance around the region, the company created portable miniature versions. The "Home Comfort" sample range is a delightfully scaled down version, complete with full oven, stove-top range, exhaust pipe, handles, dials, and the company logo (fig. 28). The sample range came in a travel box also prominently labeled with the company's name and trademark. At most one-fifth the size and weight of the full-size range, this miniature would have helped homeowners imagine how Wrought Iron's "Home Comfort" stove would look and work in their own kitchen.

While the miniaturization of the ceramic stove may be somewhat baffling, and the iron range clearly practical, a miniature chair by inventor and furniture maker Augustus Eliaers was created out

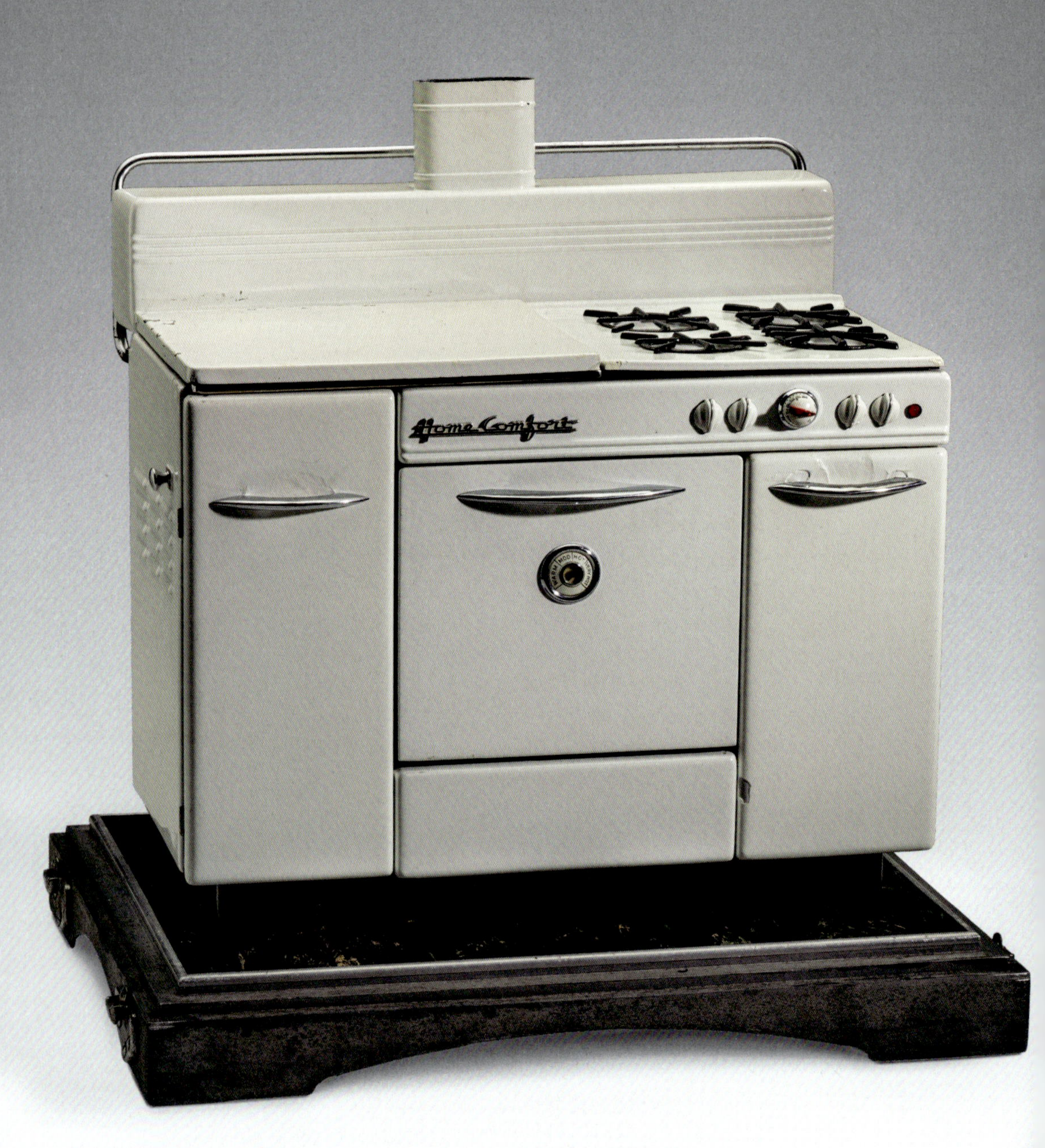

28. Wrought Iron Range Co., St. Louis, Missouri, 1864–1960.
"Home Comfort" salesman sample range and travel box, about 1940.
Iron and enamel, height: 40.6 cm (16 in.)

of financial necessity. In the mid-nineteenth century, modernization and invention were driving forces in society. Coming up with new ideas—and how to sell them—preoccupied European and American designers and engineers in the middle part of the century. Eliaers, who was born in France, was active in Boston in the 1850s and worked primarily making chairs for people who had been injured or were otherwise unable to walk.[6] He submitted a number of patents, or proofs of invention, which entitled him to proceeds from sales of his work. In addition to functional "lounging chairs," he also created a new kind of library chair that could convert into a stepstool to help users reach books on higher shelves.[7] As part of his patent application, which Eliaers submitted on October 25, 1853 (and was granted), he created a miniature version of his chair to demonstrate the hinge on the front legs that users could activate by pressing their foot on a spring bolt (fig. 29).[8] A drawing of the library step-chair, also submitted to the US Patent Office, focuses on the mechanism by which it converted from chair to stepladder (fig. 30). When compared with finished examples of the chair, which survive in good numbers in museum collections, we can see that the final products included embellishments such as carved figures on the chair shoulders, scrollwork on the seat rail, and curved arms (fig. 31). For a work that derived its uniqueness from its functionality, including a small-scale model to demonstrate his invention must surely have contributed to Eliaers's successful patent application.

Making a small version of a product is a smart way to conserve valuable materials while modeling a new design. Conserving materials, and thus being able to make more works with less, motivates artisans the world over, including, for example, Indigenous and Native artists who make miniature works for the tourist trade. Compare, for instance, two types of miniature baskets made in recent decades, for which the decision to go small came from a desire to sell more works. A miniature basket by Emerita Membache (Wounaan) from around 2003, woven from dyed nahuala and chunga plant fibers, resembles full-size, functional baskets (fig. 32). However, even the larger baskets are never used by the Wounaan,

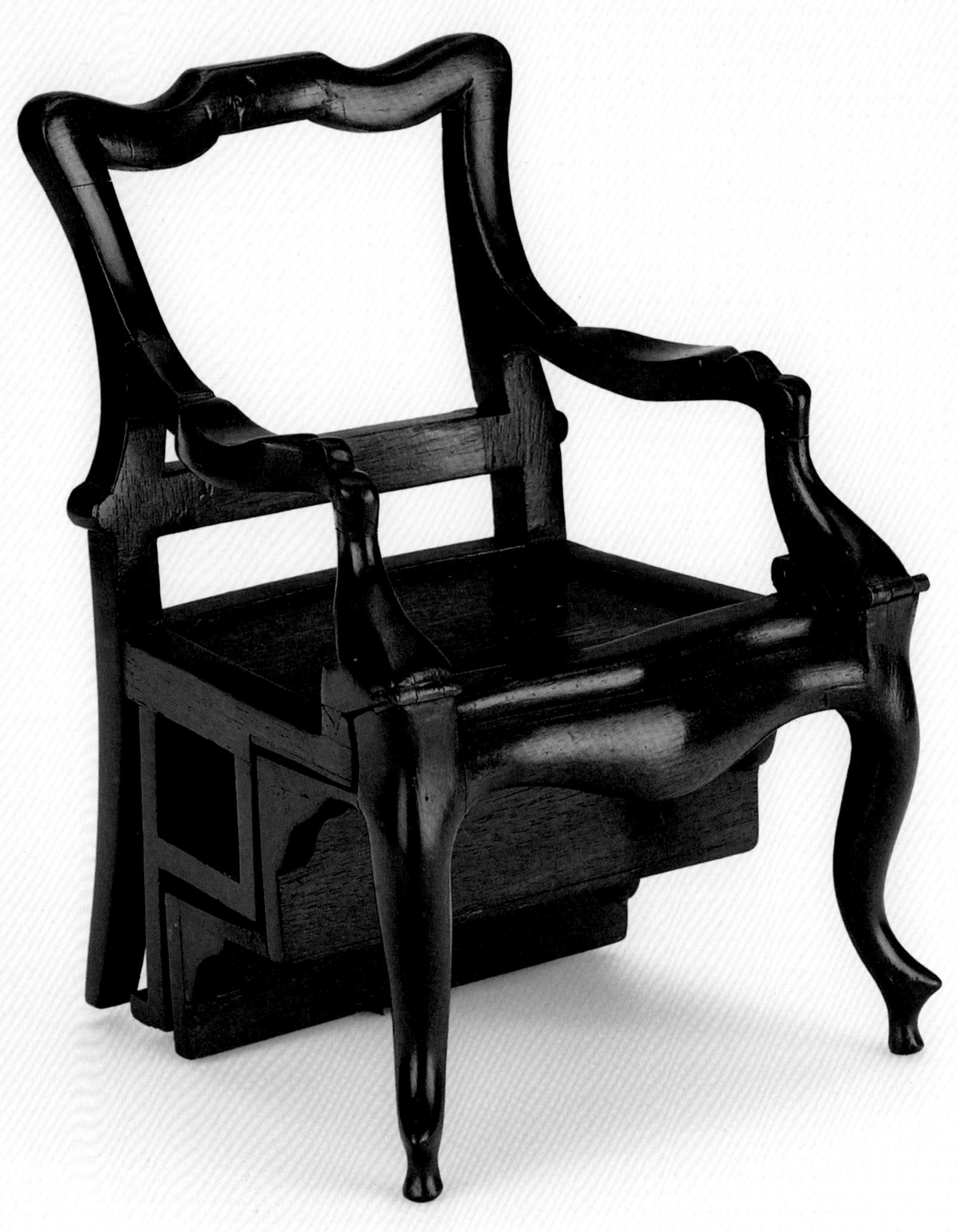

29. Augustus Eliaers (American, active 1849–65). Patent model for library step-chair, 1853. Mahogany, height: 17.8 cm (7 in.)

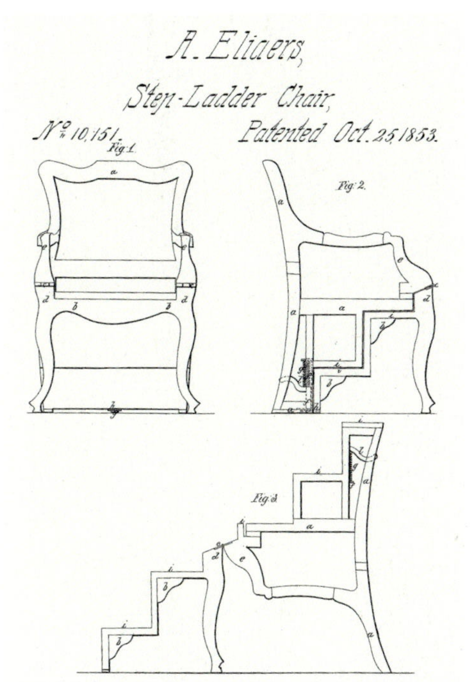

30. Augustus Eliaers (American, active 1849–65). Library step-chair patent drawing, U.S. Patent 10,151, issued October 25, 1853

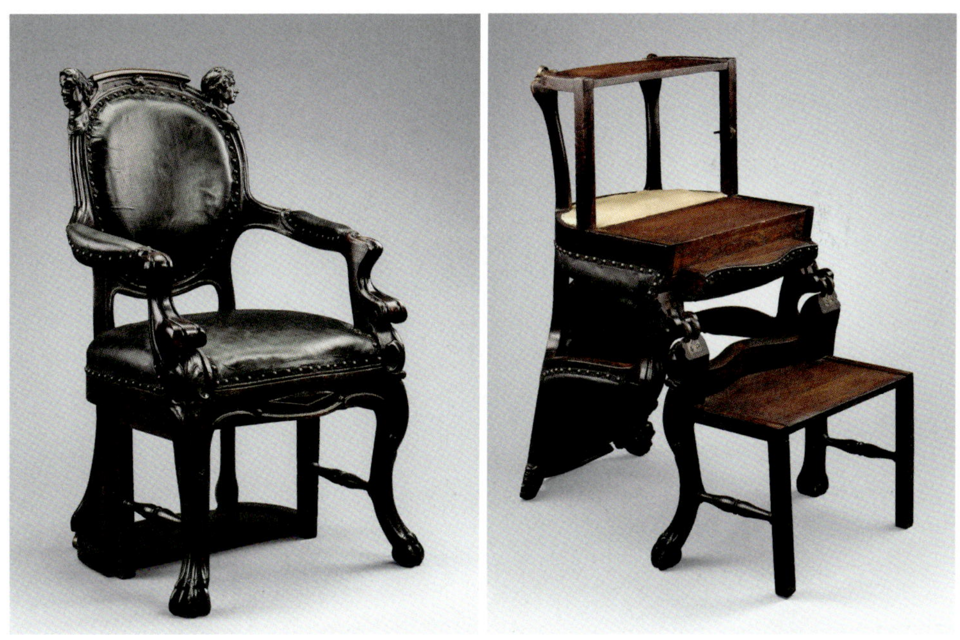

31. Augustus Eliaers (American, active 1849–65). Library step-chair, about 1854–60. Oak, brass, original oilcloth upholstery, height: 101.6 cm (40 in.)

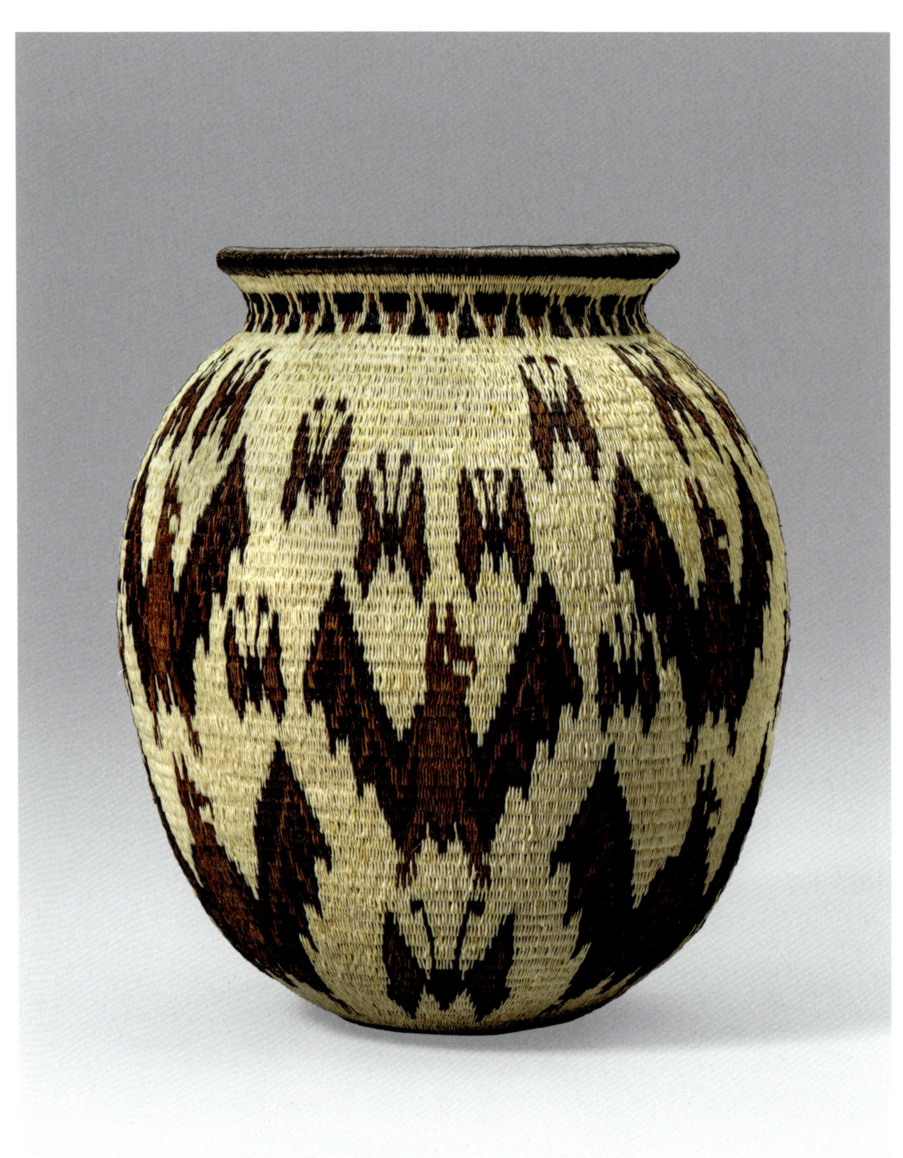

32. Emerita Membache (Wounaan, active late 20th–early 21st century).
Pictorial basket, 2003. Nahuala and chunga plant fibers,
natural and artificial dyes, height: 10.3 cm (4 in.)

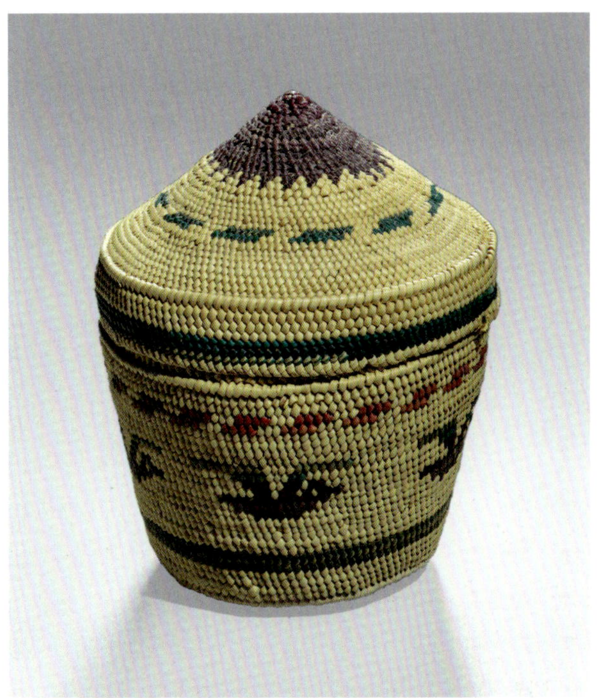

33. Francis Williams (Nuu-chah-nulth, 1919–1996).
Miniature basket, about 1990. Woven reeds or grass,
dyed, height: 5.7 cm (2¼ in.)

an Indigenous community in Panama, but are produced solely for
the tourist trade. By contrast, miniature baskets by Francis (Fanny)
Williams (Nuu-chah-nulth), made of dyed reeds or grass, do represent full-size baskets actually used within the community in the
Canadian Pacific Northwest (fig. 33). This distinction may not have
been significant for tourists purchasing the baskets, but it is an
important one for scholars and collectors who wish to understand

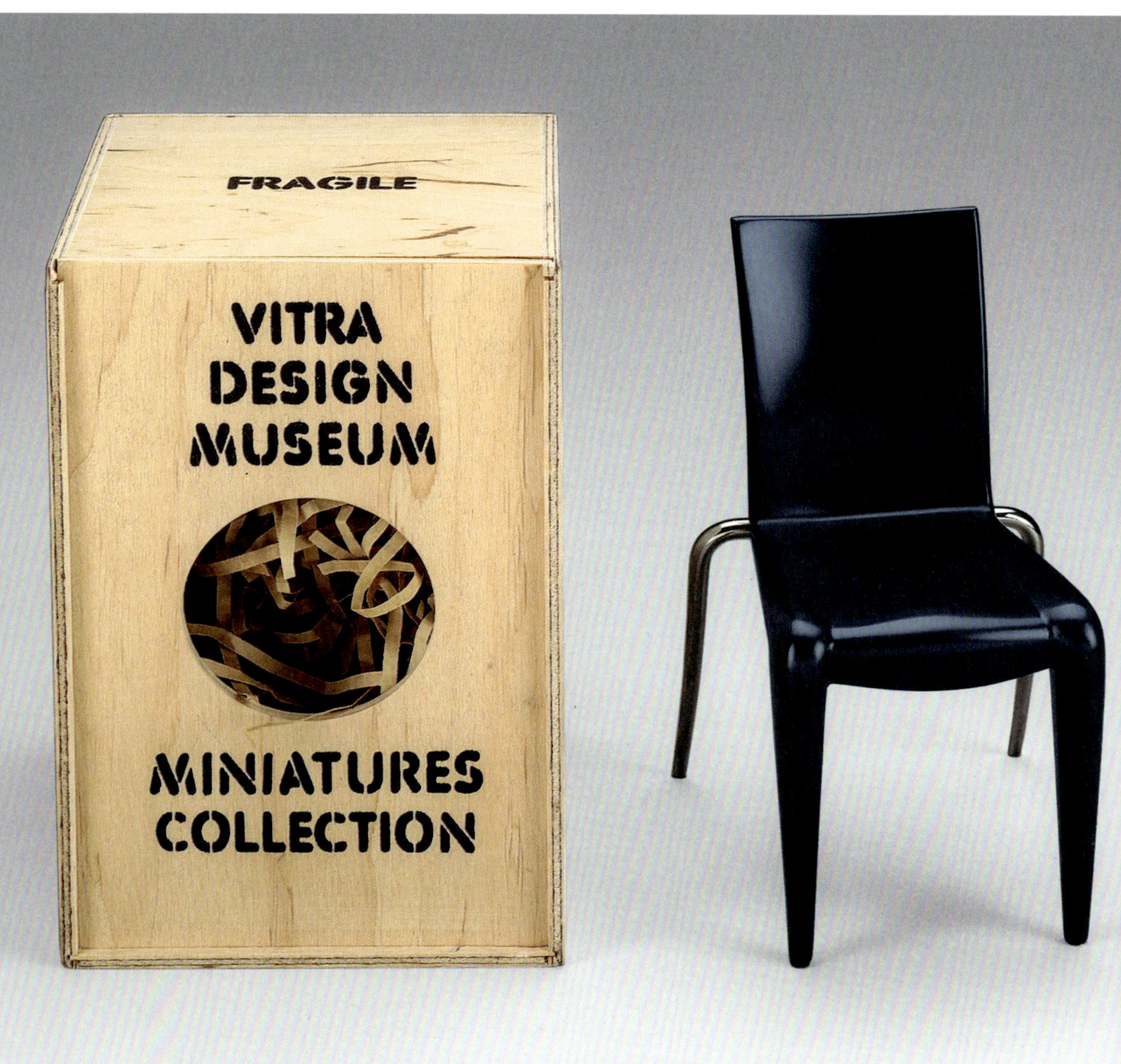

34. Designed by Philippe Starck (French, born in 1949), manufactured by Vitra International AG (Swiss). Miniature of "Louis 20" chair and crate, designed 1992. Blown polypropylene body; aluminum rear legs, chair height: 14 cm (5½ in.)

the ways in which these miniature baskets relate to objects used in Indigenous communities.

Unlike the step-chair model and miniature souvenir baskets, other domestic miniatures, such as tiny versions of iconic pieces of modern furniture, seem neither functional nor practical. From the mid-twentieth century onward, well-known architects, interior designers, and furniture makers active in Europe, Asia, and America began to develop recognizable "brands" and styles that have become famous in and of themselves. We may know their pieces from magazines or books, and their designs have also trickled into spaces such as restaurants, offices, public buildings, and so on. The distinctive look of certain chairs and tables, in particular, became very popular. For collectors and others who enjoy the sleek, modern furniture in its collection, the Vitra Design Museum in Germany has produced replicas in miniature of some of the seven thousand pieces in its collection. These miniatures range from 1870s Viennese designs, such as Josef Hoffmann's *Sitzmaschine* ("machine for sitting") of 1905, to examples by Bauhaus designers Mies van de Rohe and Marcel Breuer, to Charles and Ray Eames office furniture. Each miniature chair (and they are all chairs—it seems everyone designed a chair) comes in a small packing crate into which it fits snugly (fig. 34). These museum replica chairs may serve as gifts or inspiration for those interested in modern design. In other instances, design companies themselves have produced furniture in both full-size and miniature versions. The furniture company Herman Miller, for example, produces both full-size and small-scale versions of the famous coffee table designed by the artist Isamu Noguchi (fig. 35). Many miniature objects certainly deserve to be taken seriously, but sometimes miniatures like these are purely whimsical and fun.

Making miniatures also offers artists a chance to combine and represent things in a way that they cannot in real life and at real size; a miniature can act as a model or provide a new space for an artist to explore different ideas and themes. In a work from 1992, the Chinese American artist Ron Ho combined elements of his Chinese heritage with a traditional American household scene including a television set. Using objects associated with Chinese household shrines, such as offerings of fruit, red candles, and incense sticks in various silver and gold vessels, he created a miniature tableau representing his own merging of cultures. Depicting the offerings and the TV set placed together on a narrow table with minimal decoration, Ho's domestic scene is actually a pendant, meant to be worn around the neck and thus hanging on one's chest (fig. 36). As a portable "home," the piece allows its wearer to proclaim the importance of these two traditions existing in one space together.

Contemporary artists approach miniatures and their relationship to dollhouses, interiors, and domestic goods in many different ways.[9] Argentine artist Liliana Porter uses miniature figures and household items in compositions that explore questions of labor. Often in her works, miniature figures stand isolated, overwhelmed by their task, which is depicted on a huge and monstrous scale: sweeping an enormous pile of straw, mopping up a spill, and so on. The juxtaposition of the solo figure with the immense quantity of labor to be completed is a poignant one. In her work *Untitled with Fallen Chairs*, miniature figures, as well as domestic objects we might associate with the home—chairs, a ladder, wagon wheels—are all caught up in a deluge of white paint that traps them against the canvas (fig. 37). Although in some ways calm and still, with the luminous white of the paint, the overall effect of the piece is disconcerting and disturbing.

The word "home" may mean different things to different people, and the concept of a domestic object varies by culture. Here we have explored what it means to make miniature versions of objects that are most

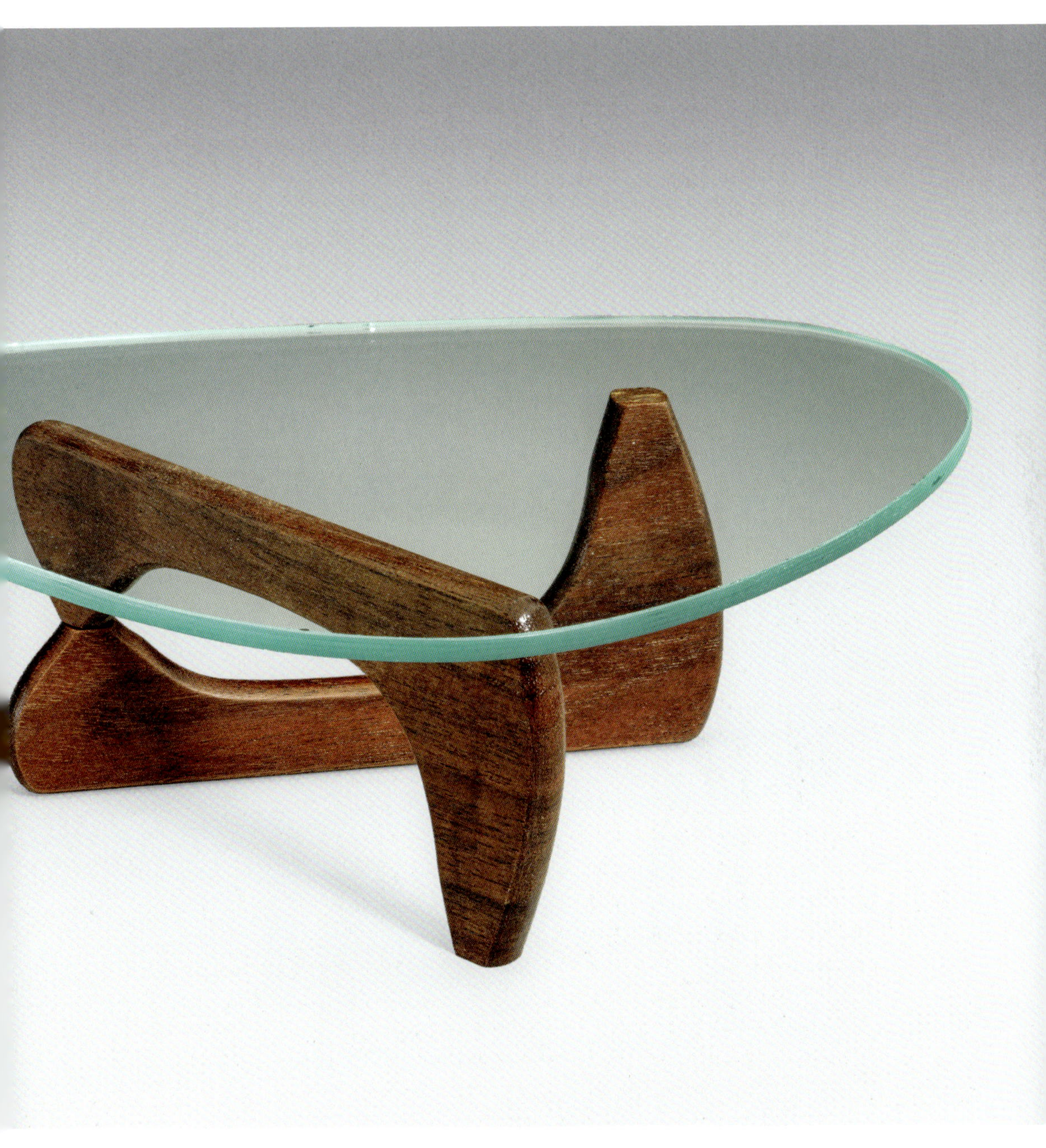

35. Isamu Noguchi (American, 1904–1988). Miniature coffee table, second half of the 20th century. Glass and wood, width: 20.3 cm (8 in.)

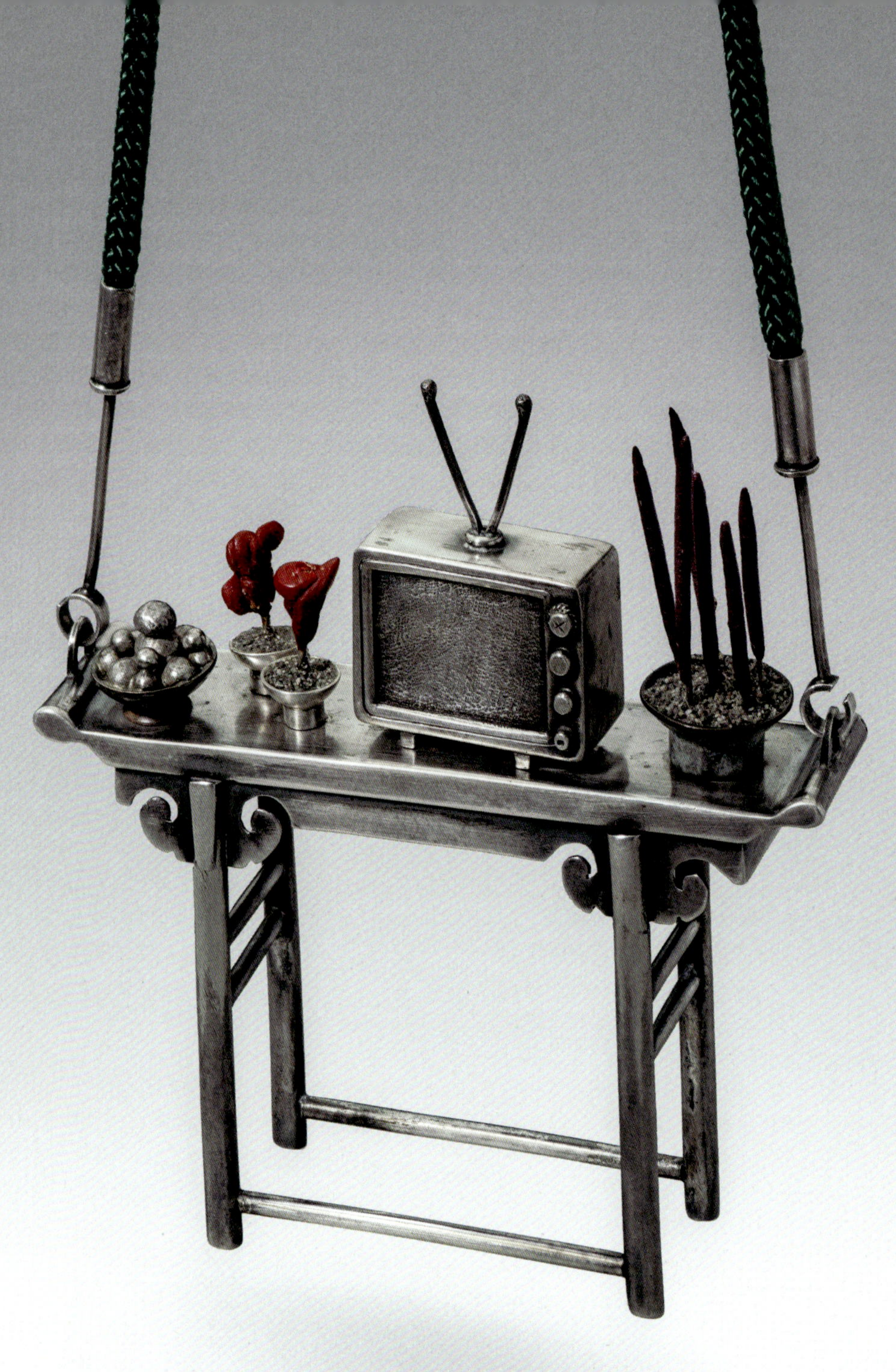

familiar to us: things we live and work with on a daily basis, and that, in their full-size versions, are usually practical and functional. When made miniature, some retain an element of functionality, like the sample range that saves space and heavy lifting and still demonstrates the company's product. Other miniatures, like the patent chair and design models, actually precede their full-size complements and derive their utility from the way they lead to a fully realized object. And still others live up to the common stereotype of the miniature by being cute, fun, and purely for enjoyment.

36. Ron Ho (American, 1936–2017). *TV Guide*, 1992. Silver, patinated copper, polymer clay; silk cord, height: 10.8 cm (4¼ in.)

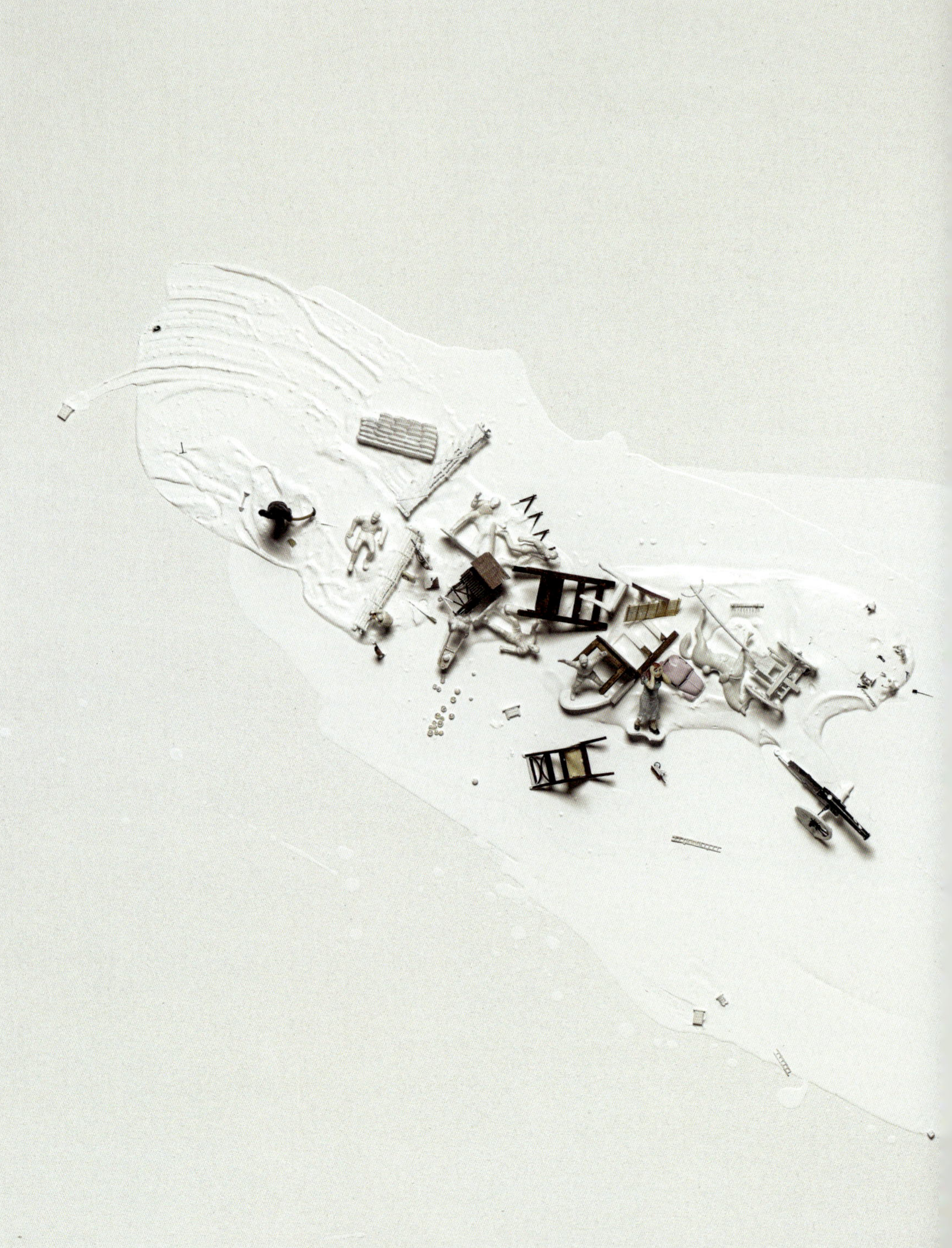

37. Liliana Porter (Argentine, active in the United States, born in 1941). *Untitled with Fallen Chairs*, 2009. Acrylic and assemblage on canvas, width: 152.4 cm (60 in.)

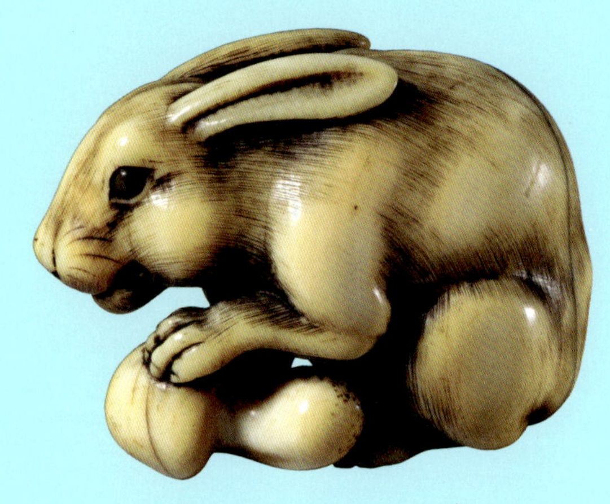

Miniature Worlds Observed

While the home is our domain, furnished with objects made to human scale, the natural world contains an impossible variety of sizes and scales, ranging from the tallest mountains to tiny bacteria. Coming back to the idea of what makes a miniature, it is important to note that something in nature that is small is not in itself a miniature: a fruit fly is not a miniature of something else, it simply *is* small. As we look at the way in which artists depict, represent, and approximate nature, including plants, animals, and natural phenomena, it will become clear that miniaturizing the world around us is a way of achieving dominion over it.

Creating a miniature of something from nature can be a method of ordering the world and gaining knowledge about it. Many of the miniature images in this group condense a view or vista that, in reality, would fill the entire field of vision. Made miniature, it becomes more consumable and even more palatable, perhaps less wild and more tame.

With the development of photography in the early nineteenth century, the medium's initial subjects were people and photographers' images almost exclusively portraits. But once photographs became more common and easier to make, artists turned to nature for inspiration. Perhaps one of the best-known examples of early landscape photographs are stereo photographs, or stereographs, which record a view from two ever so slightly different angles that, when viewed through a special stereoscope, appear as a single three-dimensional image.[1] This example is a poignant view, by an unidentified English artist, of the ruins of Rievaulx Abbey in Yorkshire in northern England (fig. 38). The double image of the abbey shows the large stone structure in disrepair, covered in creeping ivy. A single figure lounges on the lawn in the foreground. Similar to the memory-making objects of mourning discussed earlier in this volume, this recording of nature overtaking a ruined manmade structure is tied up with nineteenth-century Victorian nostalgia. By creating a stereographic image of the place, the photographer takes the view and its sentiment a step further, making a miniature version easily accessible to people around the world who may never visit Yorkshire themselves.

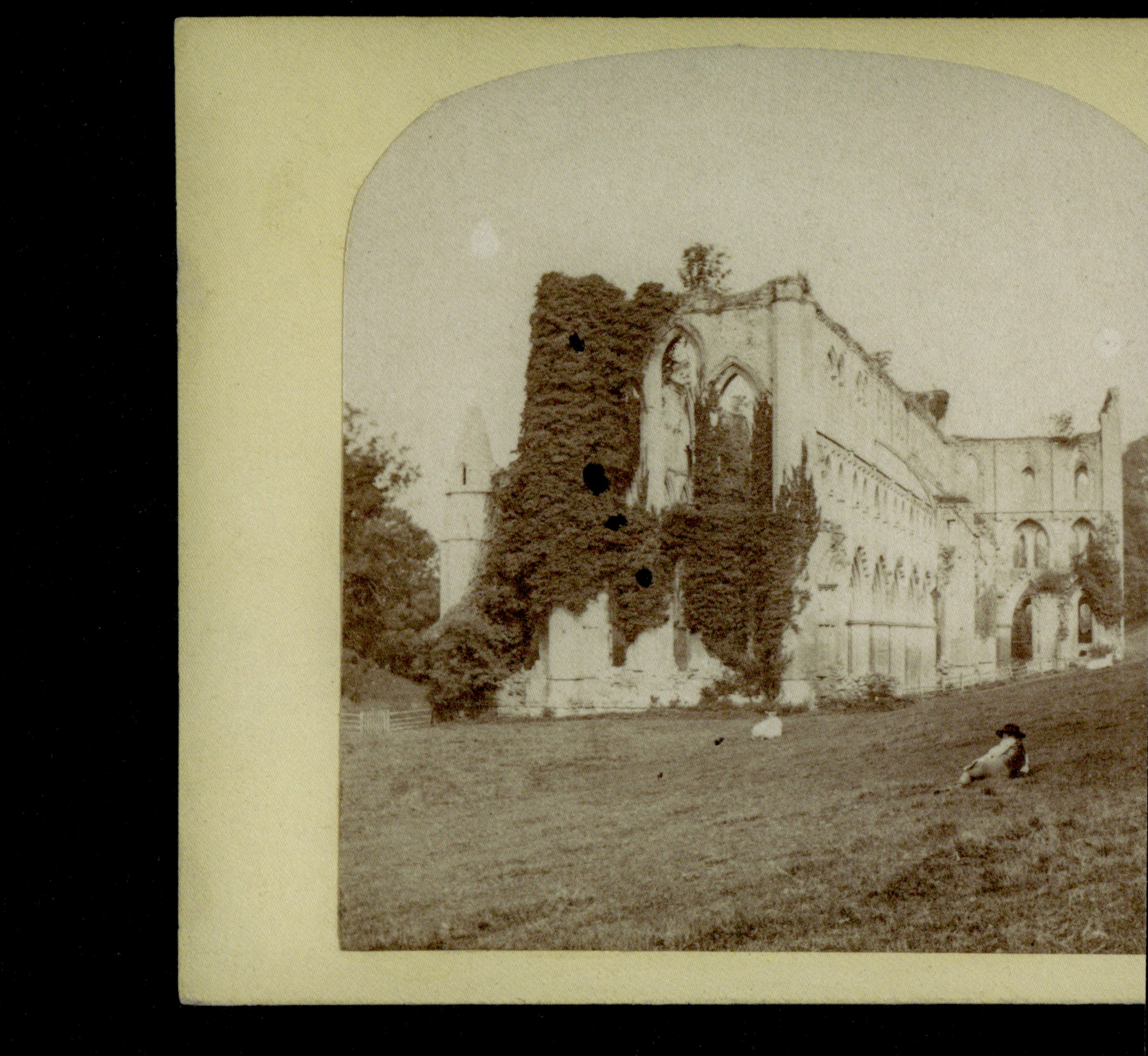

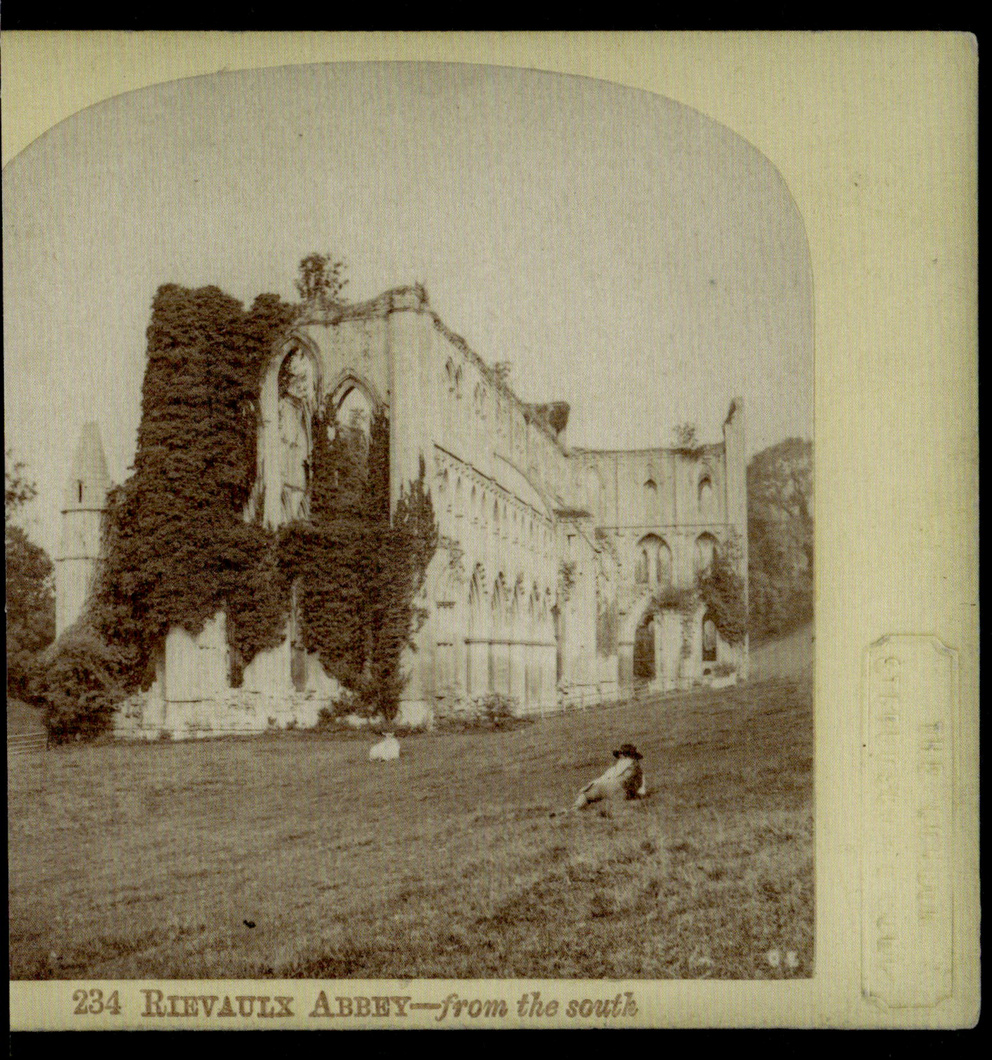

38. London Stereoscopic Company (English, active 1854–early 20th century). *Rievaulx Abbey from the South*, 1850s. Stereocard, 8.4 × 17.4 cm (3¼ × 6⅞ in.)

The handheld stereoscope allowed viewers to fill their entire visual field with an image that seems amplified to appear realistic. Other types of miniatures related to nature set out to do the opposite: they condense and distill a larger object and bring it down to a human or smaller-than-human scale. Japanese-style gardens, for example, and the practice of bonsai—cultivating small, manicured trees that are grown in pots indoors or in a courtyard—represent a mastery of nature through growing something in a controlled, artistic way and creating manicured landscapes on a miniature scale. A woodblock print shows a bonsai grower tending to one small tree, carefully trimming or rearranging the leaves, while his other wares, in a variety of small pots in varying shapes, are on offer displayed beside him (fig. 39). A forest or even a full-size tree may be impossible to cultivate with perfect control, but a small, perfectly designed garden or a bonsai tree only 1 to 2 feet tall allows this bonsai seller's customers to tame a sliver of the natural world.

In the European tradition, gardens offered the aristocracy a chance to design spaces on their own property that were ordered and regular, as they envisioned the world around them. Gardens were spaces for pleasure, for dalliance, and for passing the time. A model for a garden pavilion made in the style of Balthasar Permoser, a leading Baroque sculptor, speaks to the miniaturization of nature through gardens and to the importance of model-making for sculptors (fig. 40). The model, made of painted pine, was likely designed to show wealthy patrons what they might expect the finished pavilion, built of stone (probably marble), to look like on the grounds of their estate.[2]

Another impetus for miniaturizing natural objects is to observe and record them. Artists have done this in multiple ways, through drawing, painting, and sculpture. French painters of the late nineteenth century were particularly drawn to observing nature

39. Katsushika Hokusai (Japanese, 1760–1849). *Bonsai Grower*, 1803. Color woodblock print (*surimono*), 19.2 × 12.7 cm (7½ × 5 in.)

三筋

売りや根笹れ
うも床の上

妻みや夕露も
まつ寿む
樹屋の庭

絶えしや
何こそ生きて
ひおり

風簸

画工人
北斎画

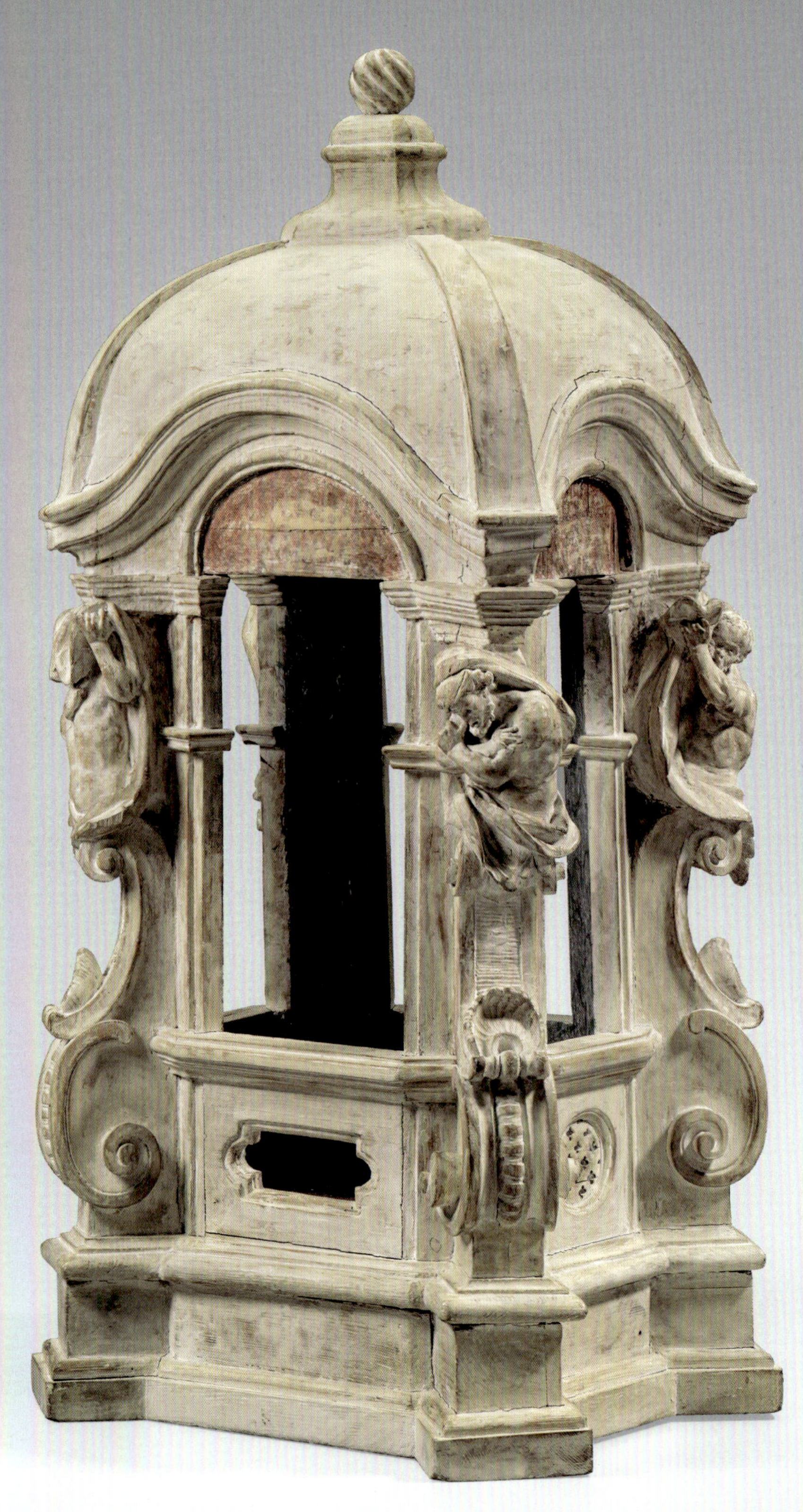

firsthand and showing how they saw it in their works. Painting outdoors while looking directly at the natural scenery, known as plein air (or open-air) painting, became a popular practice. Often artists would carry a small, portable set of materials with them to the forest, the ocean, or the countryside, and create preparatory drawings or sketches from nature that they would then take back to the studio to work up into full paintings.

Two small mid-nineteenth-century works, a watercolor and pen work by Jean-François Millet and an oil painting by Léon Victor Dupré, are examples of paintings from nature that were not preparatory but finished works in their own right and done on a miniature scale (figs. 41, 42). The Millet is just 4⅛ inches wide and the Dupré only 6¼ inches, although it is accompanied by a much larger frame. The scenery in both works appears fully realized with carefully rendered details, like the rocks in the stream by Millet and the cows resting in the landscape by Dupré. Given their miniature size, viewers would have to scale them up in their minds to imagine the full-size environments that they represent. Perhaps they would have even seen similar vistas and could bring them to mind when looking at these paintings.

Now we shrink our view even further, leaving aside entire landscapes to look instead at just one element, a single plant or flower. Still-life paintings have for centuries depicted flowers gathered in opulent and often unnatural arrangements, but these miniatures narrow the artistic focus in a different form: the tradition of finely crafted miniature flowers, displayed in vases, that remain ever beautiful and never wilt. Peter Carl Fabergé, a Saint Petersburg jeweler who worked for the Russian royal family, was best known for the famous Fabergé eggs, the fanciful, finely wrought confections he created with precious and semiprecious gems, gold, and enameled decoration, but he also answered the czarina's taste for botanical decoration by making little floral works. Many of his flower

---

40. In the style of Balthasar Permoser (German, 1651–1732). Model for a garden pavilion, early 18th century. Painted pine, height: 73.7 cm (29 in.)

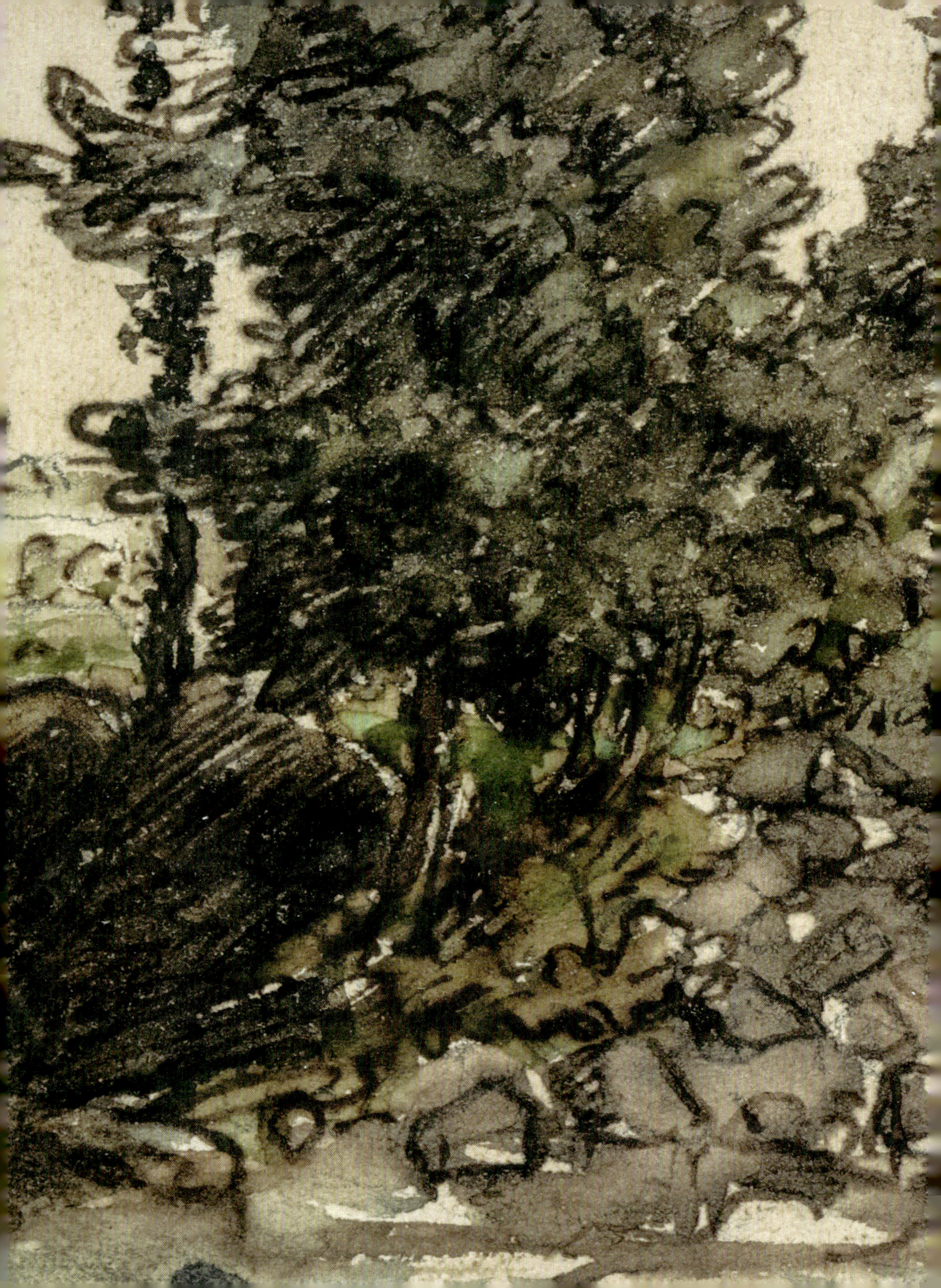

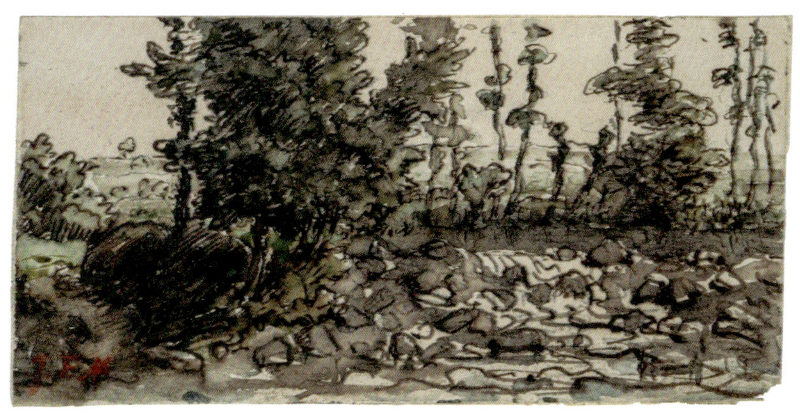

41. Jean-François Millet (French, 1814–1875). *Trees along a Rocky Stream Bed*, 1866–67. Watercolor with pen and brown ink over graphite on paper, 5.4 × 10.4 cm (2⅛ × 4⅛ in.)

Following pages:
42. Léon Victor Dupré (French, 1816–1879). *Water Meadows and Cattle*, mid-18th century. Oil on panel, 8.9 × 15.8 cm (3½ × 6¼ in.)

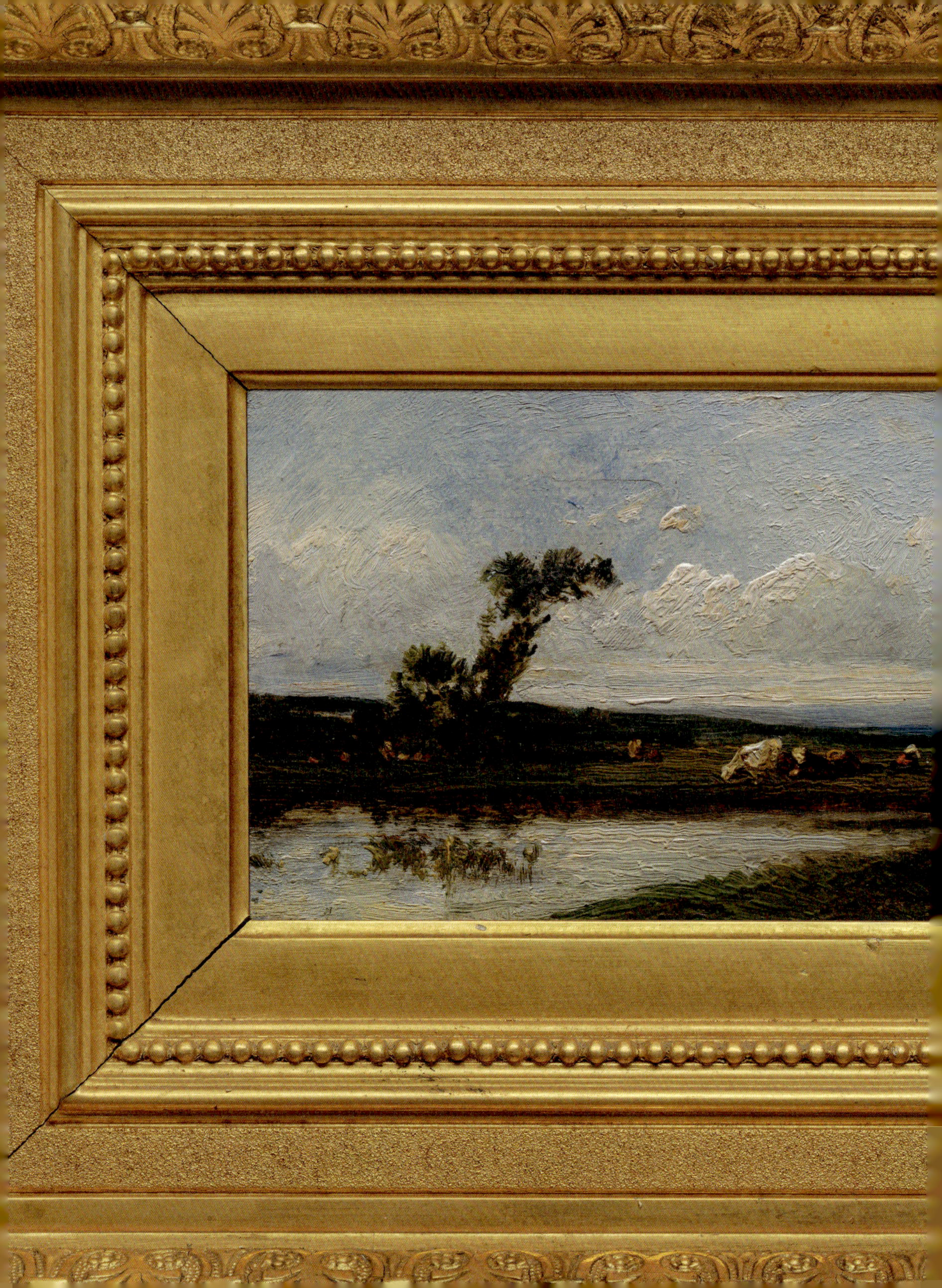

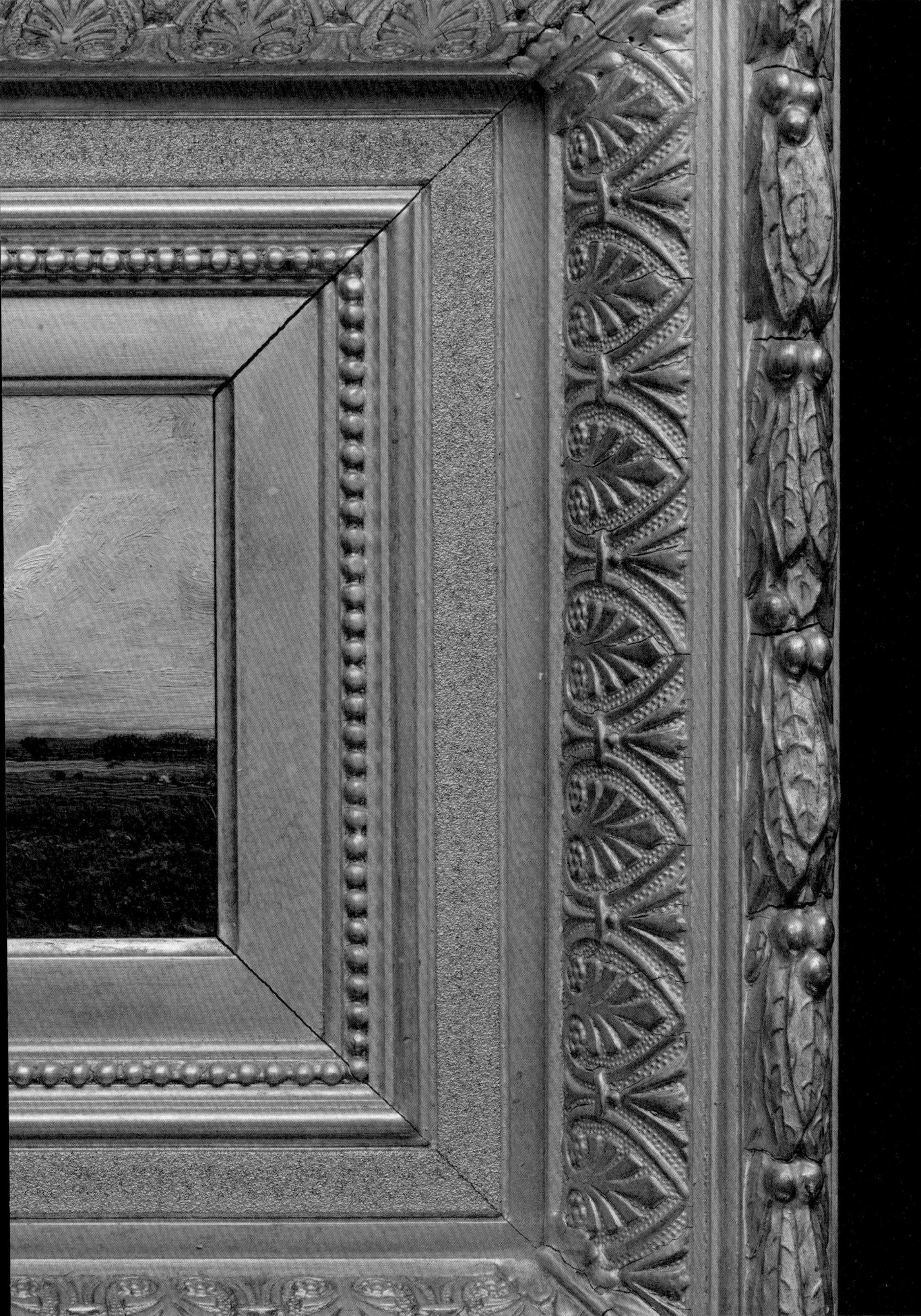

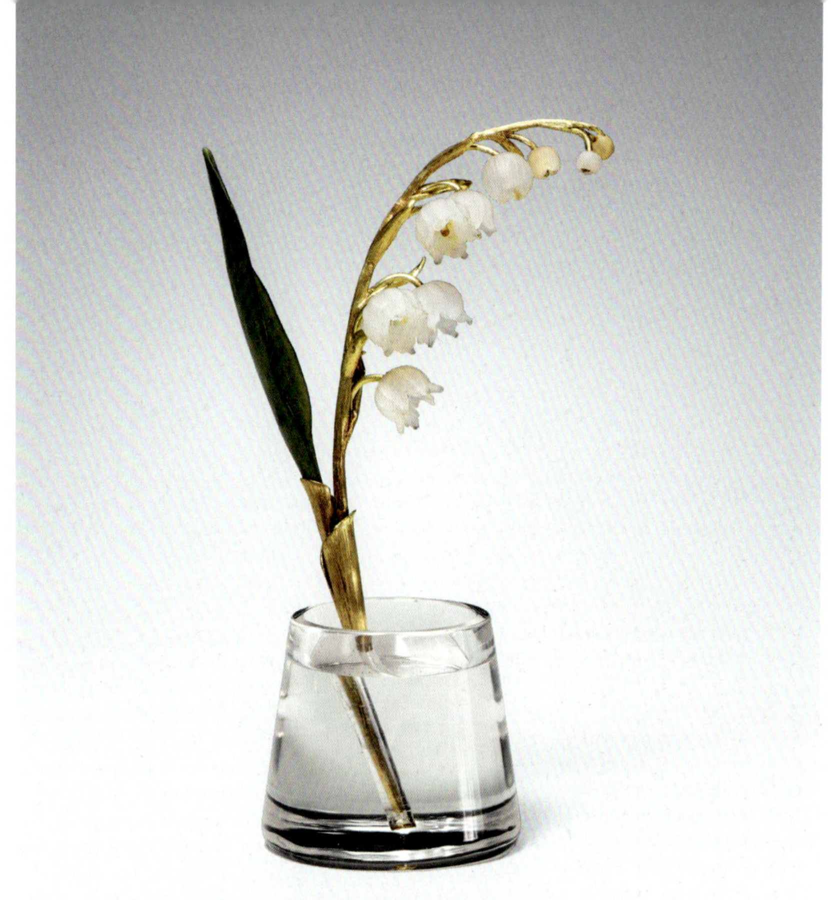

43. Workshop of Peter Carl Fabergé (Russian, 1846–1920). Spray of lilies of the valley, late 19th or early 20th century. Enamel, nephrite, gold in a rock crystal vase, height: 9.5 cm (3¾ in.)

miniatures feature just one type of flower on one or two stems, inserted into a glass vase filled with "water" made of rock crystal (fig. 43). Carefully observed and replicated from nature or botanical treatises, the tiny flowers elegantly preserve—and even surpass—nature, as the beauty of a gold and enamel bloom can never fade.

Among the favorite subjects of collectors are the animals the Fabergé workshop also brought to life as bejeweled miniatures, such as the gold, silver, agate, diamond, and ruby bulldog known as *The Balletta Bulldog* (fig. 44). Rendered in perfect detail and

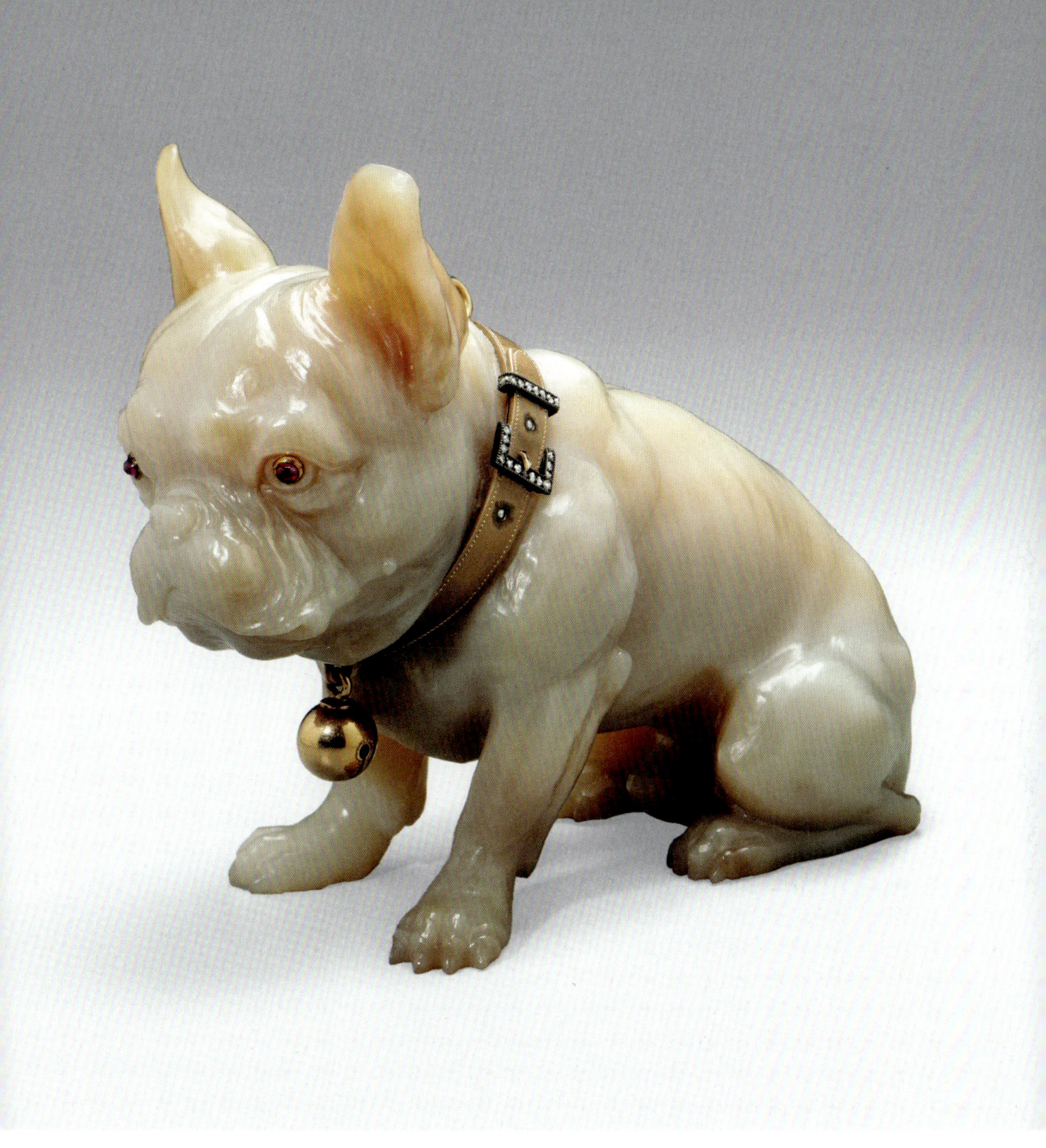

44. Workshop of Peter Carl Fabergé (Russian, 1846–1920). *The Balletta Bulldog*, about 1905. Gold, silver, agate, diamond, and ruby, length: 11.6 cm (4⅝ in.)

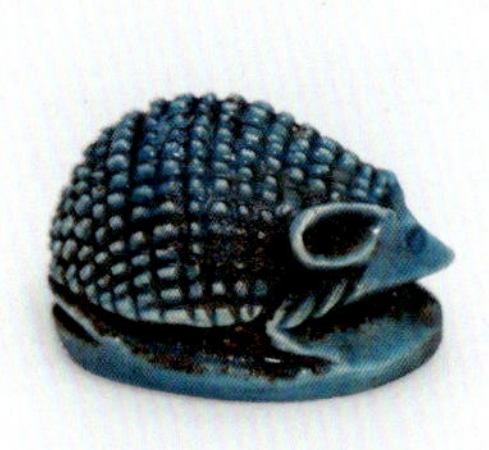

45. Scaraboid of a hedgehog,
Egyptian, 760–332 BCE.
Faience, length: 1.3 cm (½ in.)

with an extremely lifelike expression—we could meet this dog on the street and recognize him—the miniature bulldog was created as a luxurious personal gift. Commissioned by Grand Duke Alexei Alexandrovich around 1905 for the ballerina Elizabeth Balletta, the figure is a tiny likeness of Balletta's beloved pet, Cody. His jeweled collar bears his name, as well as his address in Paris, "Av. Bosquet 9."[3] From flowers to dogs to furniture, Fabergé's workshop carved out a specialty in valuable miniatures around the turn of the twentieth century. The survival of these works in museum collections speaks to their enduring popularity with collectors and visitors alike.

Artists have crafted miniature animals for centuries, as we see with a scaraboid, or scarab, from ancient Egypt's Late Period, around 760–332 BCE. Made of blue faience in the shape of a scarab, or beetle, this amulet actually depicts a hedgehog (fig. 45). The scarab was one of the most popular types of amulets in ancient Egypt, as the beetles were seen as a symbol of rebirth and renewal. The scarabs were used both in life, as seals (an image for stamping a wax seal would be carved on the underside), and in death, for protection on the path to the afterlife. Many ancient scarabs look like the beetles themselves, but this one was crafted to resemble a hedgehog shrunk extremely small. Each individual quill on its back is visible, an artistic achievement in the somewhat brittle material of faience, a glass-like glazed ceramic widely used in the ancient Egyptian world. The scarab in itself is an interesting type of miniature object, and this one is especially so for depicting a different animal altogether.

No survey of miniatures would be complete without looking to Japan and the world of Edo-period netsuke, miniature carvings that were originally designed as anchors or counterweights for small containers hung from the belt or sash of a traditional kimono (fig. 46).[4] The earliest netsuke were fairly simple and practical objects, but over time artists saw them as an opportunity to depict increasingly elaborate figures, animals, and even entire scenes. Usually carved from ivory or wood, which could be stained various

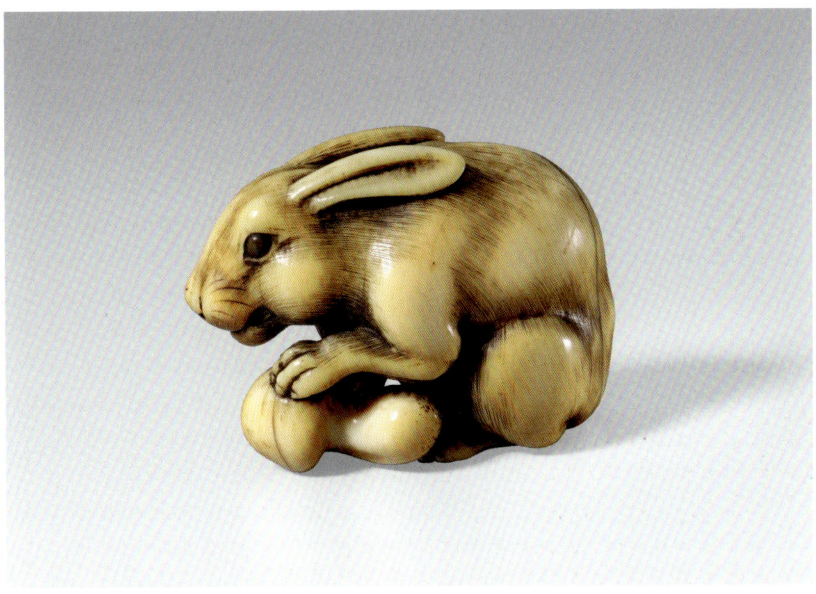

46. Okatomo of Kyoto (Japanese, about 1750–1800). *Hare and Mushroom*, late 18th–early 19th century. Stained ivory and horn, length: 4.5 cm (1¾ in.)

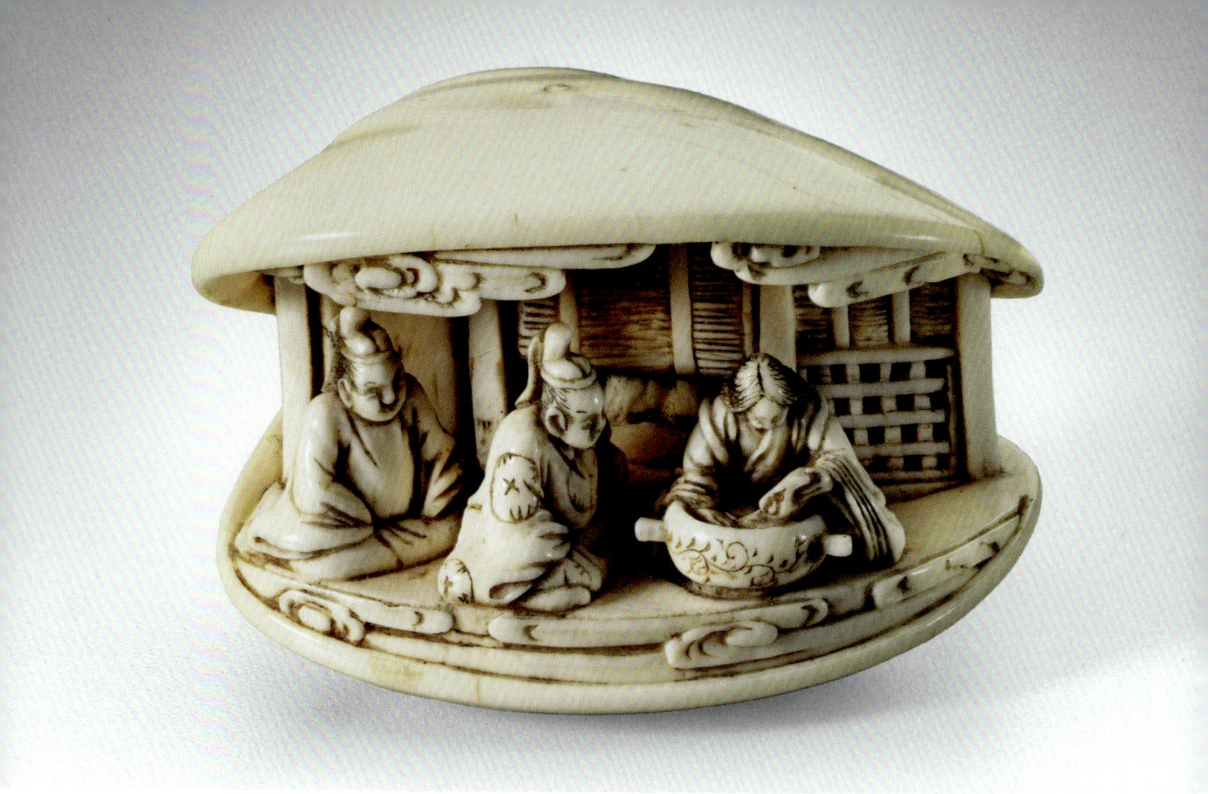

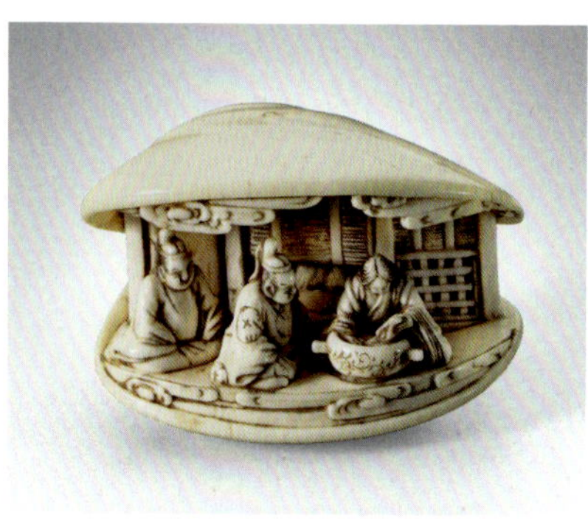

47. Shūōsai Hidemasa (Japanese, active early 19th century). *Clamshell with the Vindication of Ono No Komachi*, early 19th century. Stained ivory, width: 4.4 cm (1¾ in.)

colors or polished to achieve different finishes, many netsuke are fun, whimsical figures and animals; others represent well-known stories or proverbs. One wonderful example in stained ivory, by Shūōsai Hidemasa, takes the shape of an open clamshell, within which is a tiny scene: a woman and two men seated in front of a house (fig. 47). The woman is washing a book in a large decorative basin, a reference to a well-known episode in the life of the ninth-century poet Ono No Komachi.[5] Hidemasa used staining in the folds of the poet figure's

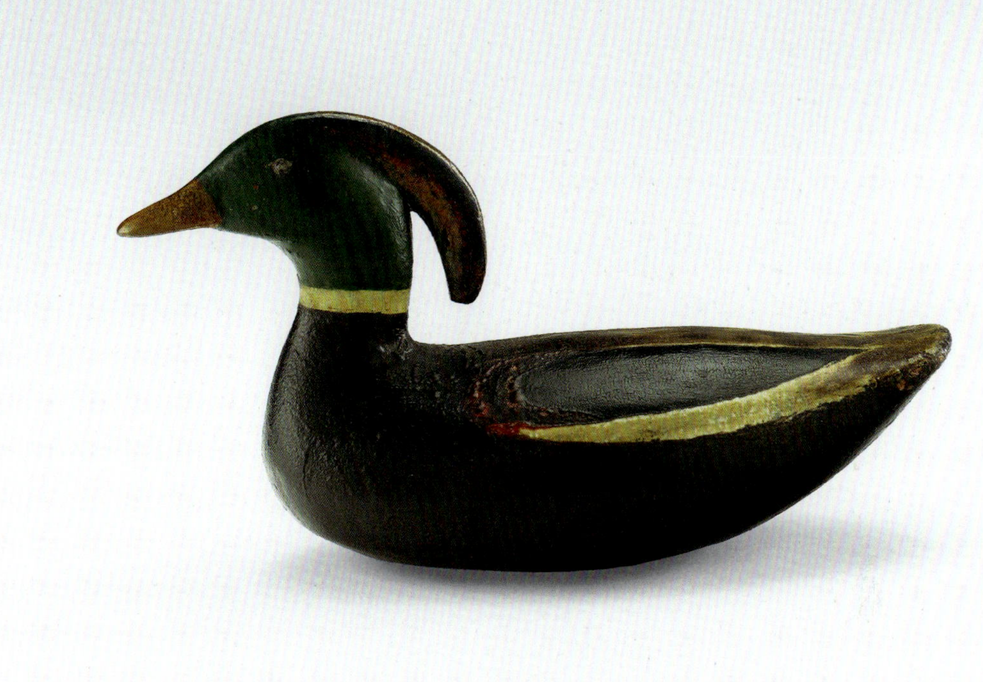

48. Duck decoy, possibly a male wood duck, American, 19th century.
Painted wood, length: 10.8 cm (4¼ in.)

drapery, as well as her hair, to create depth and verisimilitude. With its story nestled into the open clamshell, this netsuke speaks both to the tradition of depicting nature and the practice of representing a legend or moral.

A genre of animal miniatures from the United States, far less detailed than netsuke and crafted more simply from humble materials, are miniature wooden duck decoys. The miniature male wood duck is just over 4 inches long, one-sixth the size of an adult duck (fig. 48). Carving miniature duck decoys was a popular pastime among American folk artists and amateur woodcarvers through the nineteenth century, and the craft remains popular today.[6] Unlike full-size wooden decoys fashioned for duck hunting, these miniature ducks serve no purpose other than the enjoyment of the artists and others who create and collect them. They are a lovely

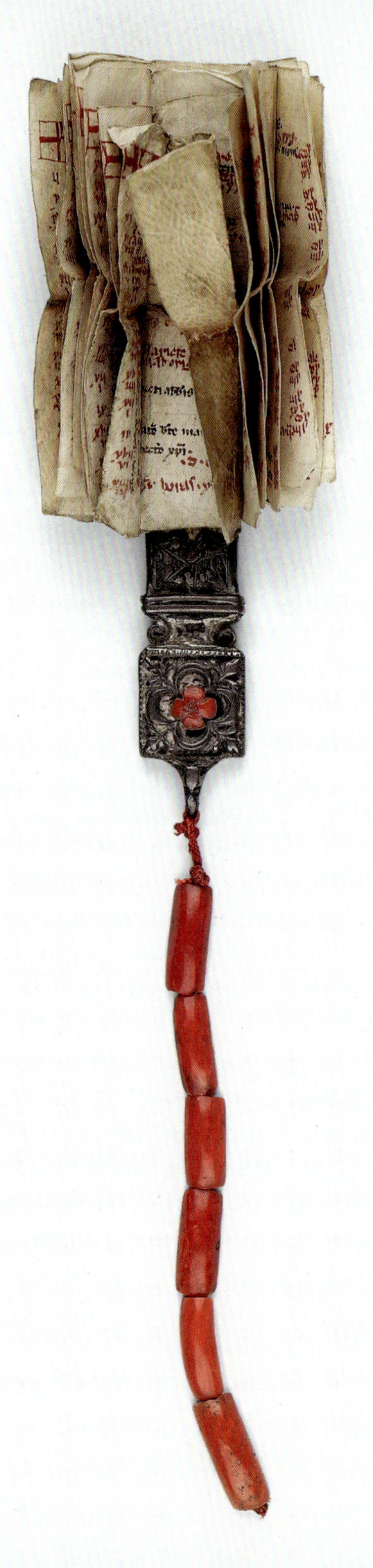

example of how we are drawn to replicate and reproduce nature on a small scale.

Like the stereoscope that could reproduce a wide landscape in a handheld view, a calendar may also be said to take something extremely large—a year and its seasons—and condense it into a small portable object. A tiny medieval calendar from Spain or France is small enough to be hung from the waist on a girdle, or belt (fig. 49). When this now-fragile miniature calendar was new, around 1300–1350, it would have allowed its owner to know the month and date, as well as when to observe astrological occurrences and solstices; a veritable wealth of information about the world would have been at hand at any time. Though it was crafted nearly 250 years before the invention of the microscope, we can already see in this object the driving need to understand the world and to make the intangible, or invisible, into something that could be seen, possessed, and controlled.

In addition to natural landscapes and animals, artists have observed and painted the human figure in miniature. The nineteenth-century French artist Jean Louis Ernest Meissonier is best known as a classical academic painter who specialized in small "cabinet" pictures, paintings often installed in the home in collectors' display rooms, along with other small-scale works. However, a painting of a military officer at a little more than 4 inches high is small even for Meissonier's work (fig. 50). Possibly done in preparation for a scene with many military figures, this painting shows us Meissonier's way of observing the world around him, focused on the officer and leaving his mount shown only by its ear and part of the bridle. We can see his exploration of the way the hat casts a shadow on the figure's face and shoulders, how his arm juts out into space beside him, and the white detailing around the figure's right side, almost like a vibration in space.

---

49. Girdle book calendar, northeastern Spain or southwestern France, about 1300–1350. Ink on parchment, silver handle with six carnelian beads, height (open): 6 cm (2⅜ in.)

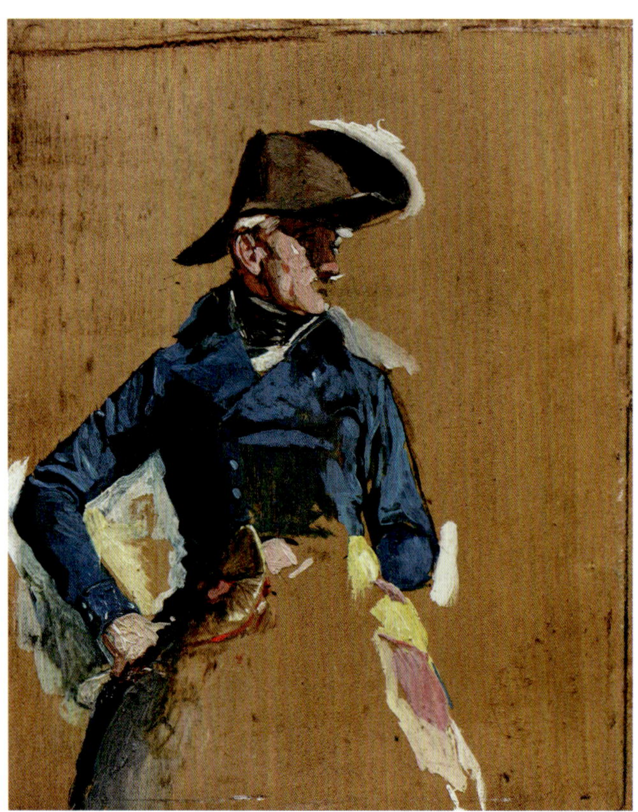

50. Jean Louis Ernest Meissonier (French, 1815–1891). *Officer*,
mid–19th century. Oil on panel, 10.5 × 8.3 cm (4⅛ × 3¼ in.)

Although Meissonier's miniature painting is clearly either
incomplete or preparatory for something larger, another miniature
portrait, *Juif Lisant (Jewish Man Reading)* by Édouard Brandon,
is a highly finished and refined work, just over 5 inches tall (fig. 51).
Every element has been carefully observed, including the slight
highlighting on the hat, the textured pages of the book, and the
gilded silver or brass candlestick in the foreground. Like the

Opposite: 51. Édouard Brandon (French, 1831–1897). *Juif Lisant
(Jewish Man Reading)*, 1870. Oil on panel, 13 × 7 cm (5⅛ × 2¾ in.)

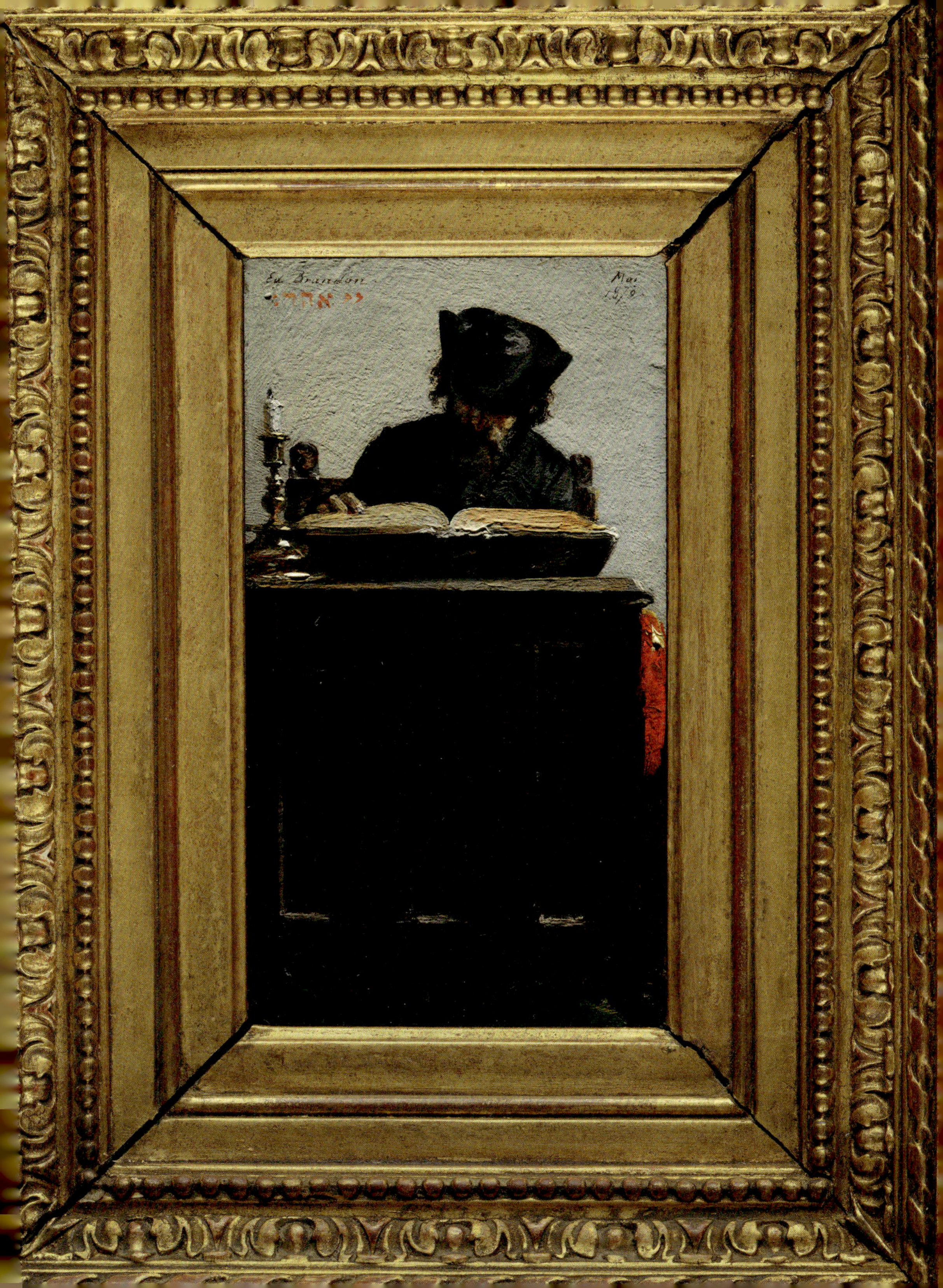
Ed Brandon
ידידיה
Mai
1870

miniature landscape by Dupré, this painting is overwhelmed by its comparatively enormous frame, which makes the image appear even smaller. The repeating moldings of the frame do, however, create a sort of perspectival focus for our eye, zooming us in to rest our gaze on this man in quiet contemplation as he reads.

Artists also observe the world around them by copying the works of other artists, a long-established practice for those trying to learn from the masters who came before them. One such copy was rendered in miniature by the Flemish artist David Teniers the Younger, who worked from a painting by the great Venetian painter Titian, *Parma the Physician* (now in the collection of the Kunsthistorisches Museum in Vienna). Titian's original is more than 36 inches in height, whereas Teniers's diminutive copy is just under 7 inches tall (fig. 52). Besides changing the work's dimensions, Teniers changed the face of the subject slightly and colored his clothing a bit differently. Copying a work like this may have helped him to explore the contrast between areas of light (the face and hair) and dark (the clothes and background). But why did he paint it on a reduced scale? Was he practicing shrinking down a subject? Did he not have enough paint or wooden panel? We cannot know the answer, although from what we do know about Teniers's own oeuvre—he painted small figures in genre, or everyday life, scenes—it is not surprising that he was more interested in making a small-scale work than an impressive prestige portrait the size of Titian's original.

At their core, all of these miniature landscapes, flowers, animals, and human figures display their makers' close and deep observation of the world around them and their desire to find order and depict it in a realistic way. In many examples, the creators also strove to convey the knowledge they had gleaned and, by making it miniature, to make it portable and more knowable.

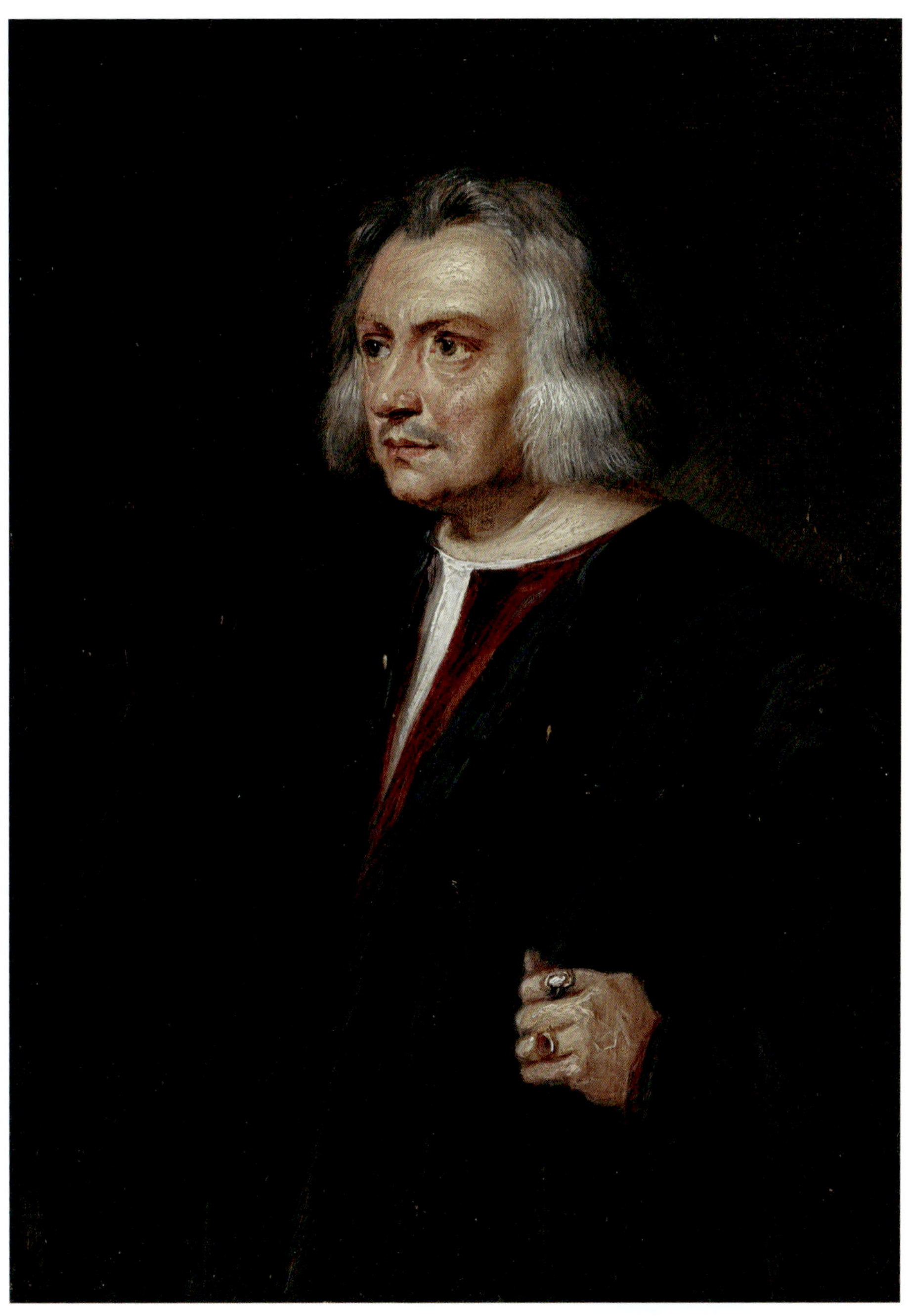

52. David Teniers the Younger (Flemish, 1610–1690), after Titian (Tiziano Vecellio)
(Italian, about 1488–1576). *Parma the Physician*, 17th century.
Oil on panel, 17.1 × 12.1 cm (6¾ × 4¾ in.)

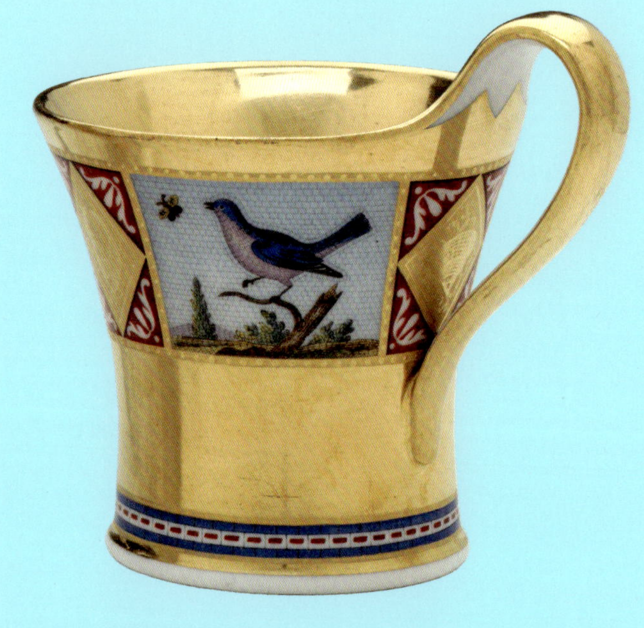

Small Size,
Big Style

Although miniatures need not be small, most are, and with their small size can come not only portability but also wearability. Of interest in this group are objects made on a miniature scale for personal adornment or fashion, as well as those made with materials and techniques that are challenging because of their own diminutive scale, such as micromosaic, *sablé* beadwork, and silver wirework. Both types of miniatures demonstrate the ways in which making miniatures requires extra care and skill on the part of the artist.

Some miniatures are so convincing in their mimicry of their parent objects that they are almost *too* good. A miniature commode, or low cabinet, for example, made by the workshop of the noted jewelry maker Peter Carl Fabergé in Saint Petersburg, is such a good imitation of an eighteenth-century French cabinet that its image in the photograph might fool us if we did not know its actual dimensions: it is just 2¼ inches tall (fig. 53). The body of the commode, with its shaped sides, was made from a single piece of green nephrite. The gemstone was then encased in a pierced and scrolled gold cage, imitating the gilded bronze mounts that would have been applied to a full-size example. Decorated with masks on the front and side ends, its elegant design highlights the contrast between the green body and gold filigree. A tightly fitted lid hinges open to reveal the interior, much like a snuffbox from the previous century. As this box was made in the late nineteenth or early twentieth century, instead of snuff it was more likely intended to hold cigarettes: the interior length is just the right size. And as beautiful as this cigarette-case commode is, it is hard to imagine how someone could have carried it around with them, given its thin and pointy legs. Perhaps it was displayed on a desk, or even on a piece of furniture similar to the one it mimics.[1]

The question of accuracy in miniaturization is a complicated one. Although realistically rendered details can be part of a miniature's appeal, verisimilitude can also be disquieting when it is an illusion—when we are unsure of an object's true size or if it is "real." As objects are shrunk down, their miniature scale may be revealed

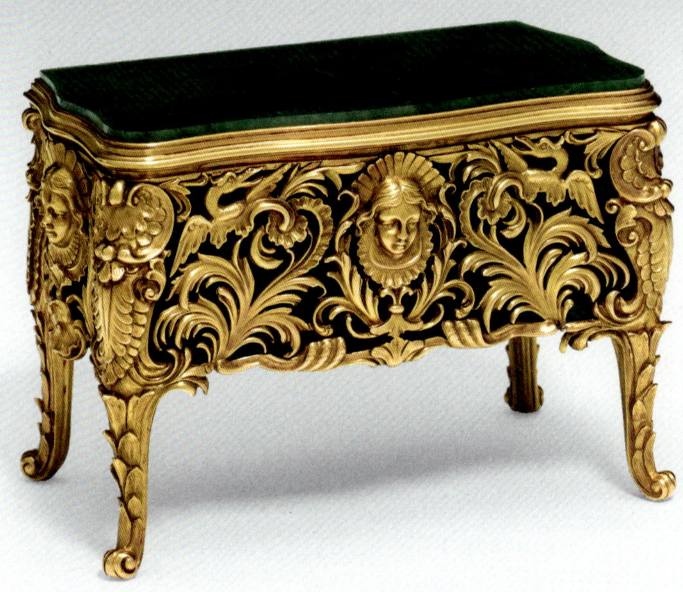

53. Workshop of Peter Carl Fabergé (Russian, 1846–1920). Miniature commode, late 19th century. Gold with nephrite, width: 10.4 cm (4⅛ in.)

by slight imperfections in the manufacturing, in the way the parts relate to the whole. Such imperfections are important clues to recognizing that an object is in fact a miniature. This relates to a phenomenon that designers in the field of artificial intelligence and robotics often encounter, called the uncanny valley.[2] Research has shown that human-imitating robots that come very close to looking like humans tend to be disturbing to us. An almost-human replica inspires a nearly universal negative response, something that designers, animators, and engineers have to navigate and avoid. Similarly, realistic miniatures, particularly when photographed and reproduced without reference to scale, can look eerily like their

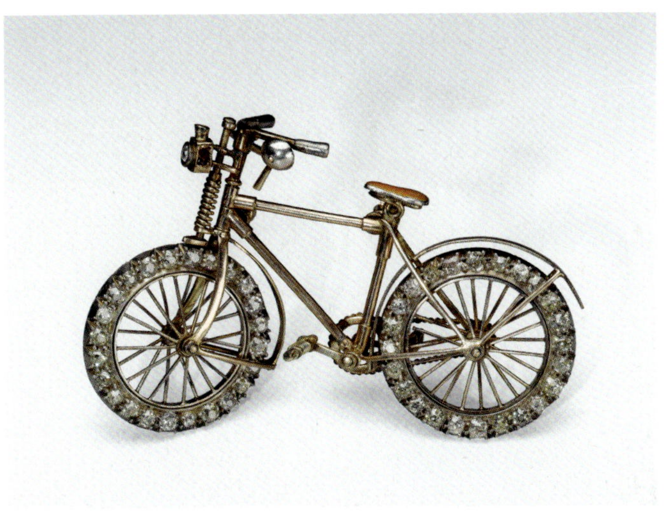

54. Possibly by Streeter & Co. (English). Bicycle brooch, mid-1890s.
Gold, enamel, diamond, and ruby, length: 6.5 cm (2½ in.)

parent objects. Details or imperfections that show their relative size are therefore appealing.

On the other hand, small touches of added realism can heighten the experience of a miniature. In the case of a delightfully glamorous jeweled bicycle brooch, possibly English, from the mid-1890s, the piece is enhanced by the functionality of the pedals, which in turn rotate the two diamond-studded wheels on their axles (fig. 54). Produced at the moment when bicycle mania was sweeping England, this brooch could have made a strong state-ment for its wearer. Bicycles were linked to women's empowerment, as they offered a new mode of transportation and opened up opportunities for women to move about independently. This bicycle bears a resemblance to a specific model, the "cob," which was made for women to ride safely in their long skirts.[3] Wearing this brooch would have perhaps sent a semipolitical message, as

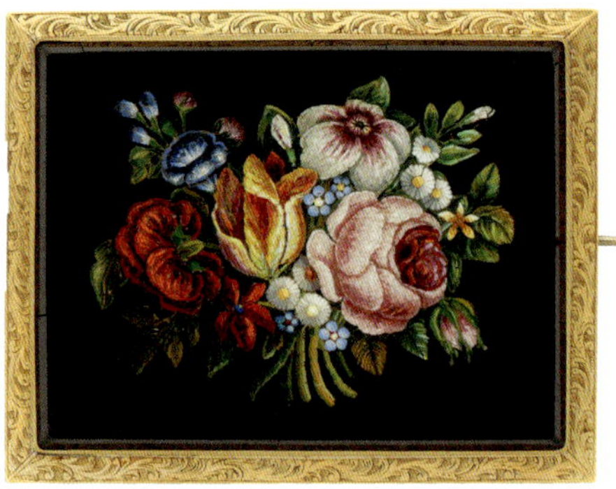

55. Brooch, Italian, about 1870.
Gold, onyx, and glass, width: 5.7 cm (2¼ in.)

women's liberation and independence were tied up in the fight for suffrage, or voting rights. Combining style—with its many diamonds, a ruby, and gold—and functionality, this miniature bicycle is a perfect example of how a small object can pack a punch.

A brooch of a very different style, one that attempts to look not forward to the future but back to an inspiring and ancient past, exemplifies a technique often used in making jewelry, snuffboxes, and decorative items. It is the ultimate expression of miniature materials being employed to make miniature objects: a micromosaic (fig. 55). By the early nineteenth century, artists had turned away from the curving, elaborate shapes of Rococo designs in favor of Neoclassical decoration inspired by ancient art, classical architecture, and the sites that were being rediscovered at the time through archaeological exploration. This brooch, framed to look like a still-life painting of flowers, is made up of many tiny glass tesserae that together create an illusionistic image.[4] Micromosaics, and the related mosaic form *pietra dura*, or elaborate hard-stone inlays, usually on furniture, were popular souvenirs among wealthy, aristocratic tourists on their grand-tour stops in Italy. The glass

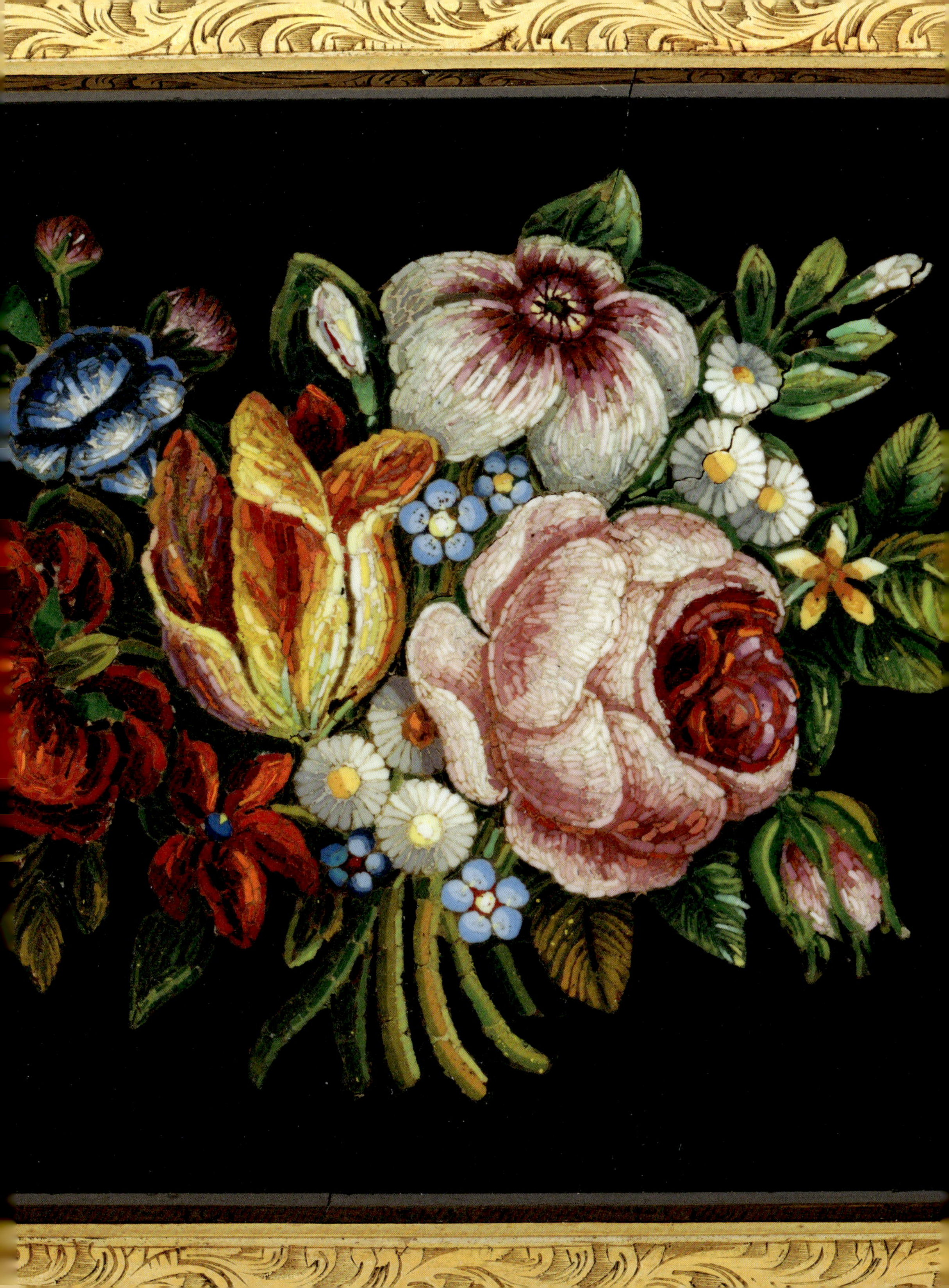

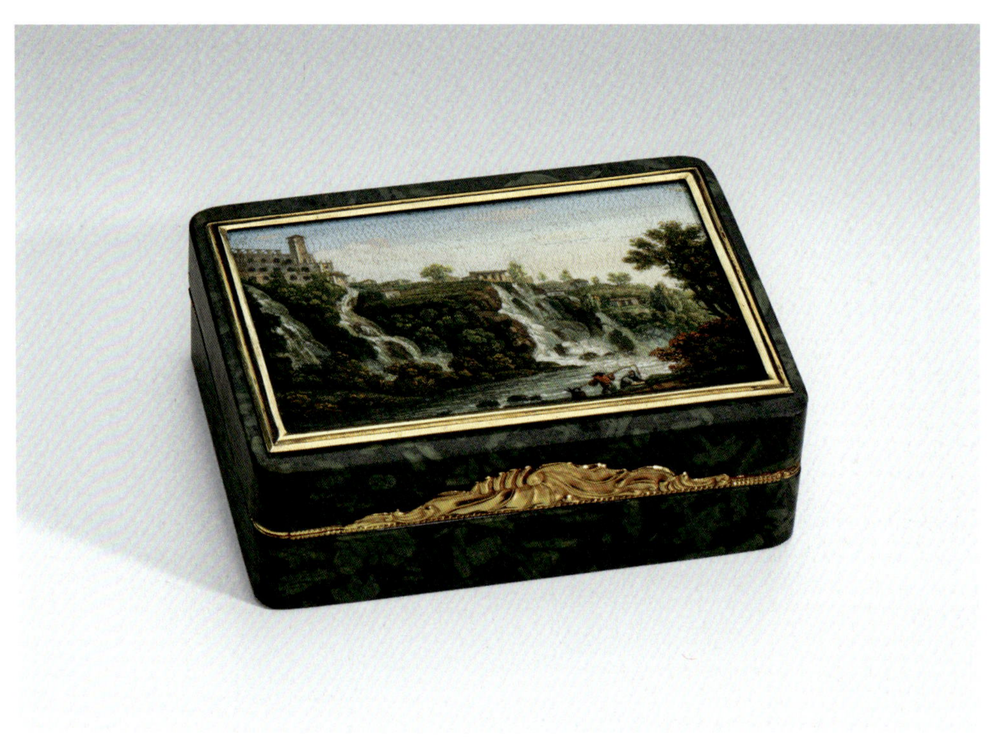

56. Attributed to Giacomo Raffaelli (Italian, 1753–1836). Box, about 1825.
Micromosaic, gold, green porphyry, width: 8.2 cm (3¼ in.)

tesserae of a micromosaic could be set into different small objects,
such as a brooch, as in this case, or a snuffbox (fig. 56). So popular
was the Neoclassical mosaic look that other fields of production
sought to participate in the trend by mimicking micromosaics.[5] A
porcelain cup and saucer from Germany, for example, was painted,
in exquisite detail, to imitate tesserae (fig. 57). As with the miniature
commode, the imitation of something else is part of the object's
appeal: our eye is tricked and we are perhaps pleased to have been
tricked. This sense of wonder and whimsy is inherent in the way
miniatures are viewed and experienced.

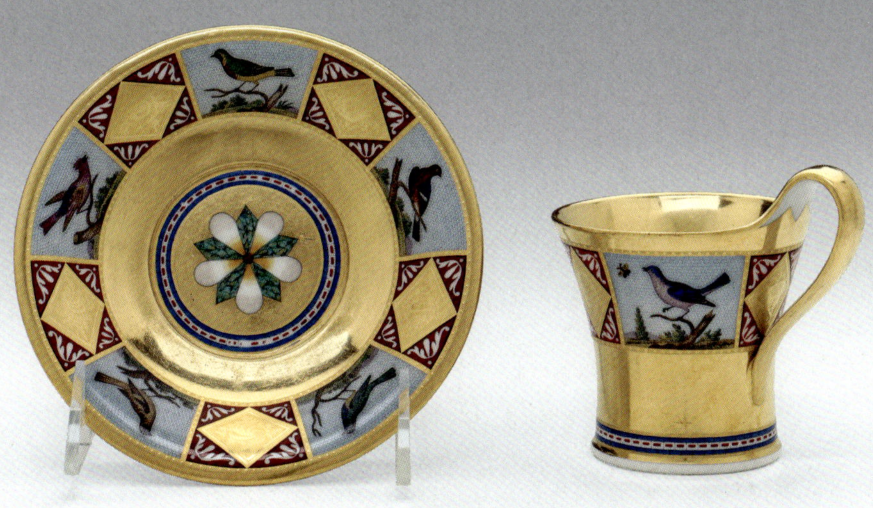

57. Königliche Porzellanmanufaktur, German (Berlin). Cup and saucer with micromosaic decoration, about 1817. Hard-paste porcelain with gilding, cup height: 11.4 cm (4½ in.), saucer width: 13.3 cm (5¼ in.)

Two other techniques that, like micromosaic, require a high degree of technical virtuosity are glass beadwork and silver wire-work. While both approaches can be applied in making larger, full-size objects, they are best suited to miniatures because the materials themselves are small. It also takes extra skill to execute small-scale designs with such tiny beads and fine wire. We cannot know why a French artisan made a miniature eyeglass case, though given that the case and tinted glasses date to the eighteenth century, they may have been intended for a doll or a doll-house (fig. 58). These little eyeglasses and their accompanying

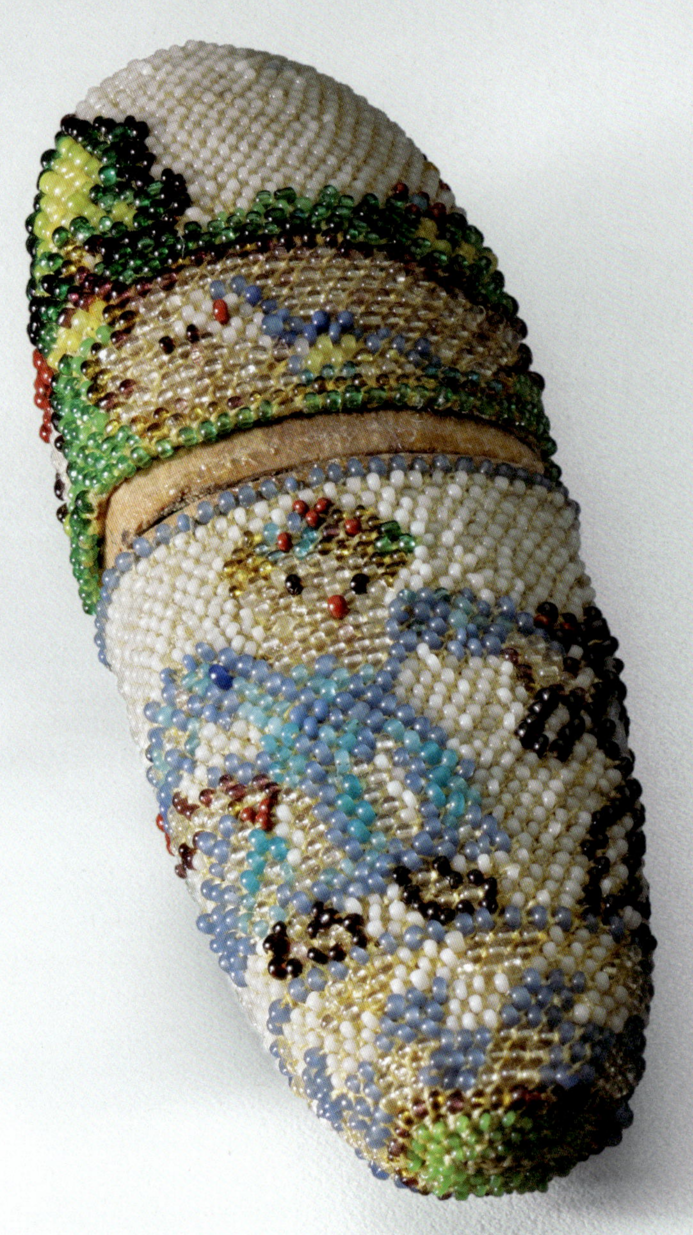

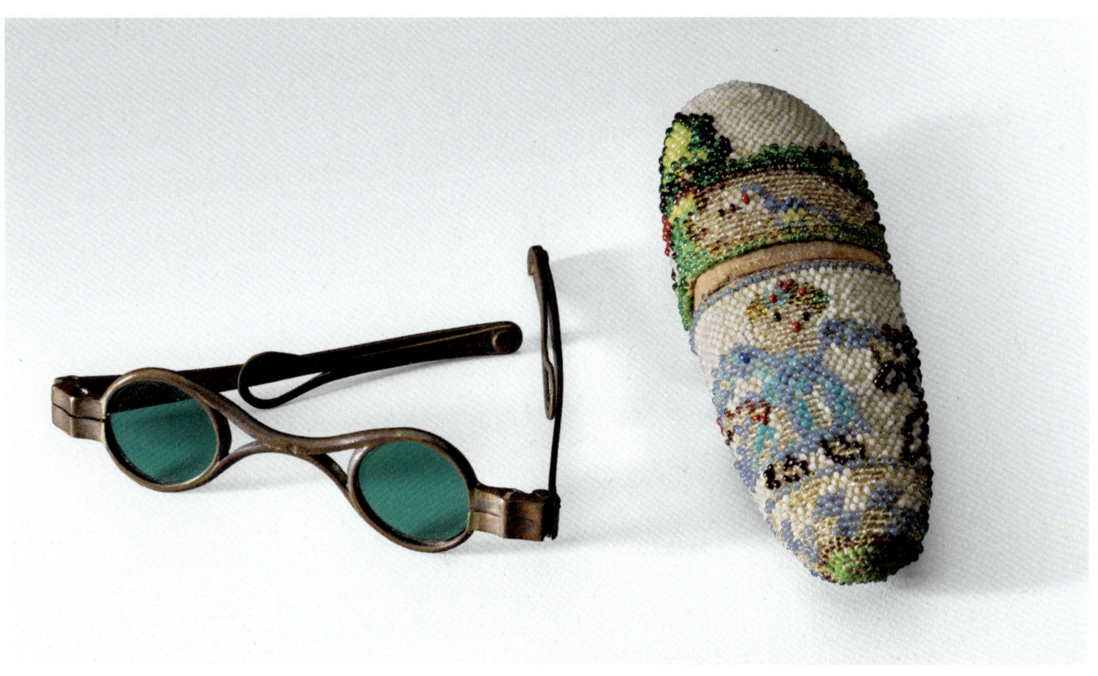

58. Miniature eyeglass case with eyeglasses, French, late 18th century.
Case: beadwork with glass beads (*sablé*), length: 7 cm (2¾ in.)

case are a lovely example of a stylish doll accessory. The choice to decorate the case using very small glass beads in the technique now known as *sablé* surely added to the difficulty of the work, while also enhancing its beauty. *Sablé* takes its name from the French word meaning "grains of sand," in recognition of the minuteness of the beads. Similarly, when an artist makes a miniature work in silver, that is already a challenge in itself—often involving special tools and strained eyesight. Yet some makers of silver miniatures, a specialty of artisans working in The Hague in the late seventeenth to early eighteenth century, stepped up the level of difficulty by choosing to work in delicate silver wire, using thin, rolled strips of silver and weaving them together to create baskets, bins, and similar structures (see fig. 23 for examples). These wirework

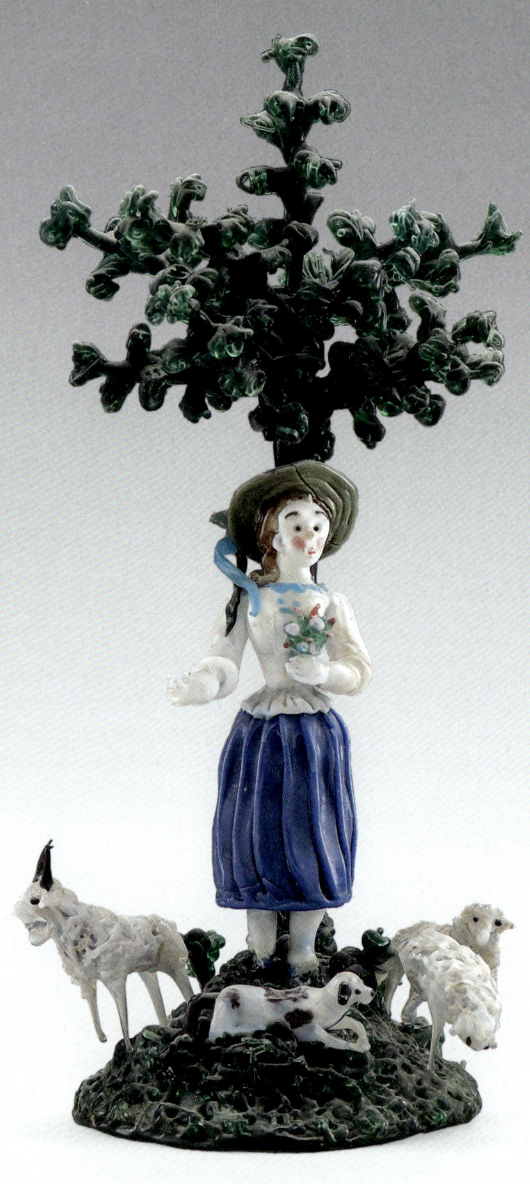

59. Shepherdess, France (Nevers), 18th century. Glass, height: 14.6 cm (5¾ in.)

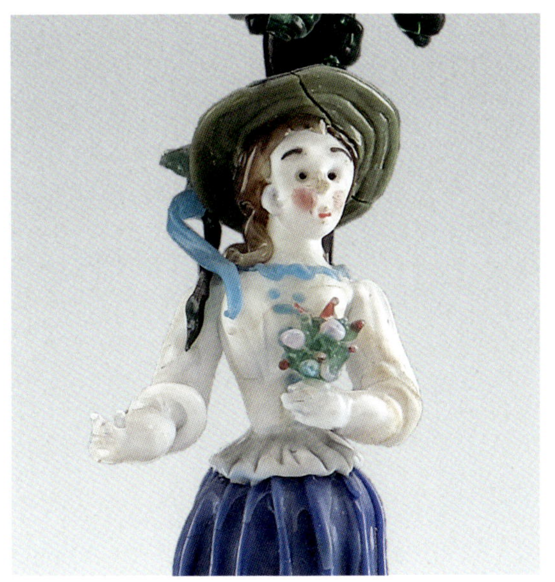 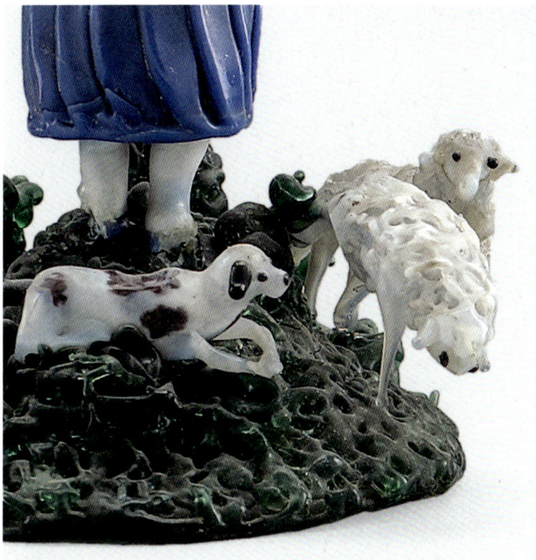

miniatures are admired for both their small size and their technical achievement.

The attraction of working with small materials, as in *sablé* and micromosaic, can seem almost like a madness—making work more difficult just for difficulty's sake. Such a level of painstaking delicacy is nowhere more visible than in the extraordinarily fine work of glassmakers in Nevers, France, who, from the sixteenth to the nineteenth century, specialized in fashioning figurines out of pulled glass. Often inspired by religious imagery, fairy tales, and legends, the miniature figures and elaborate tableaux show the glassmaker's great skill in blowing, pinching, and drawing with the smallest possible pieces of glass. The slightly pinched faces of the figures and often wonky look of the animals adds to their whimsical feeling, making them an endearing and enduring—if fragile—art form (fig. 59).

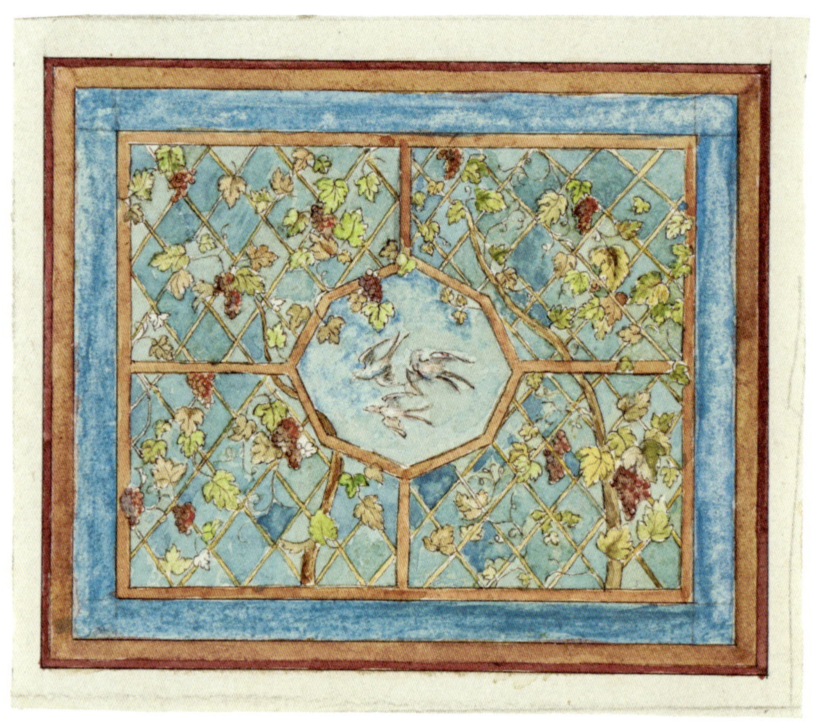

60. John La Farge (American, 1835–1910). *Study for Skylight*, about 1875–1900.
Watercolor over graphite on paper, 9.3 × 11 cm (3⅝ × 4⅜ in.)

Sometimes the purpose or meaning behind a miniature is clear only in the context of its parent object. To explore this, we can look at the works of two radically different artists, the American painter John La Farge and Venezuelan sculptor Jesús Rafael Soto. In the late nineteenth century La Farge created a group of nearly micro-scopically small design sketches for decorative stained glass (fig. 60). Knowing that they are designs to be produced in stained glass, in works large enough, when realized, to occupy an entire window or part of a ceiling, our minds necessarily expand the images before us. Although the tiny La Farge sketches may not scale up exactly—there are small gaps in the painted design—we

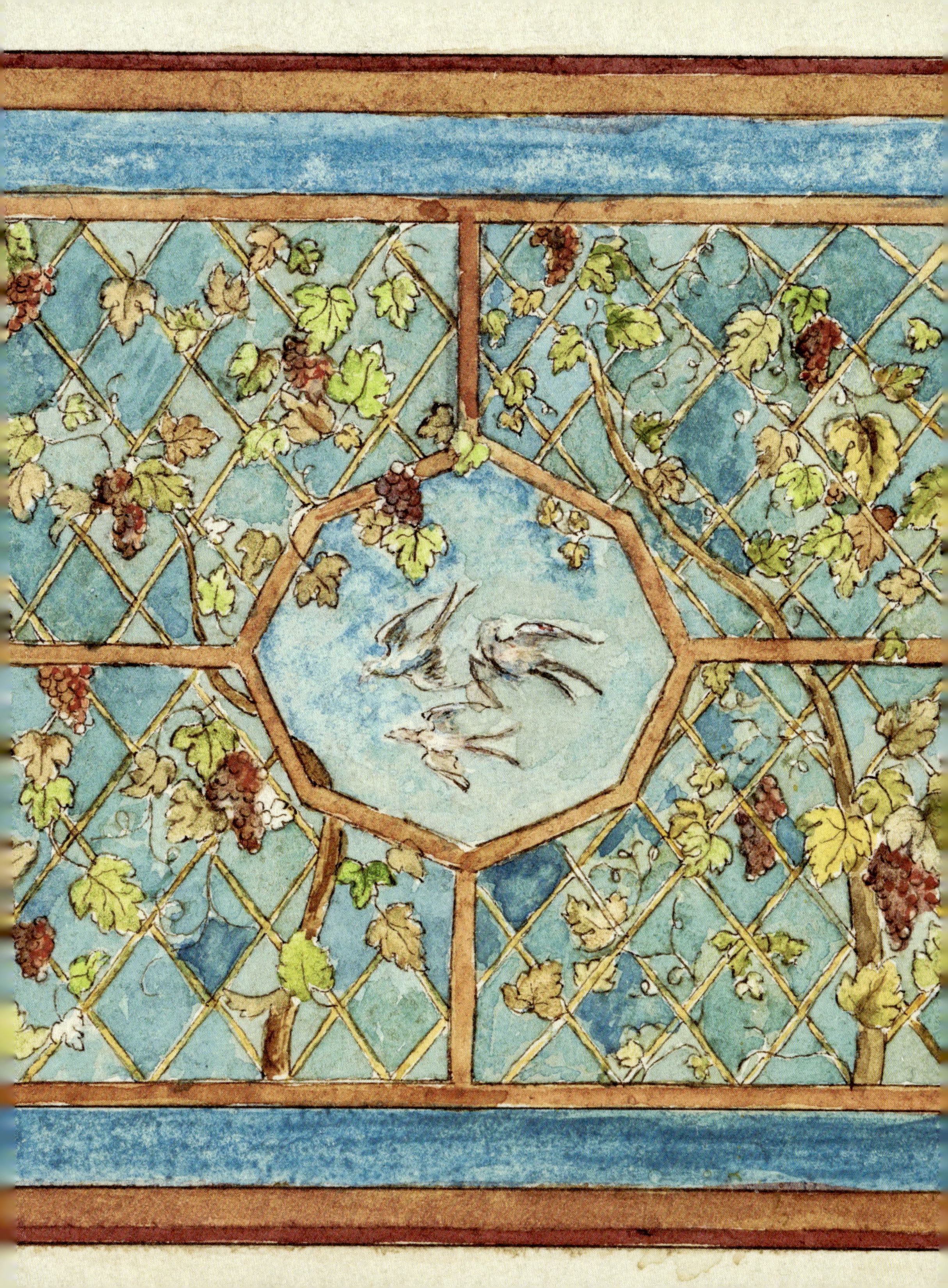

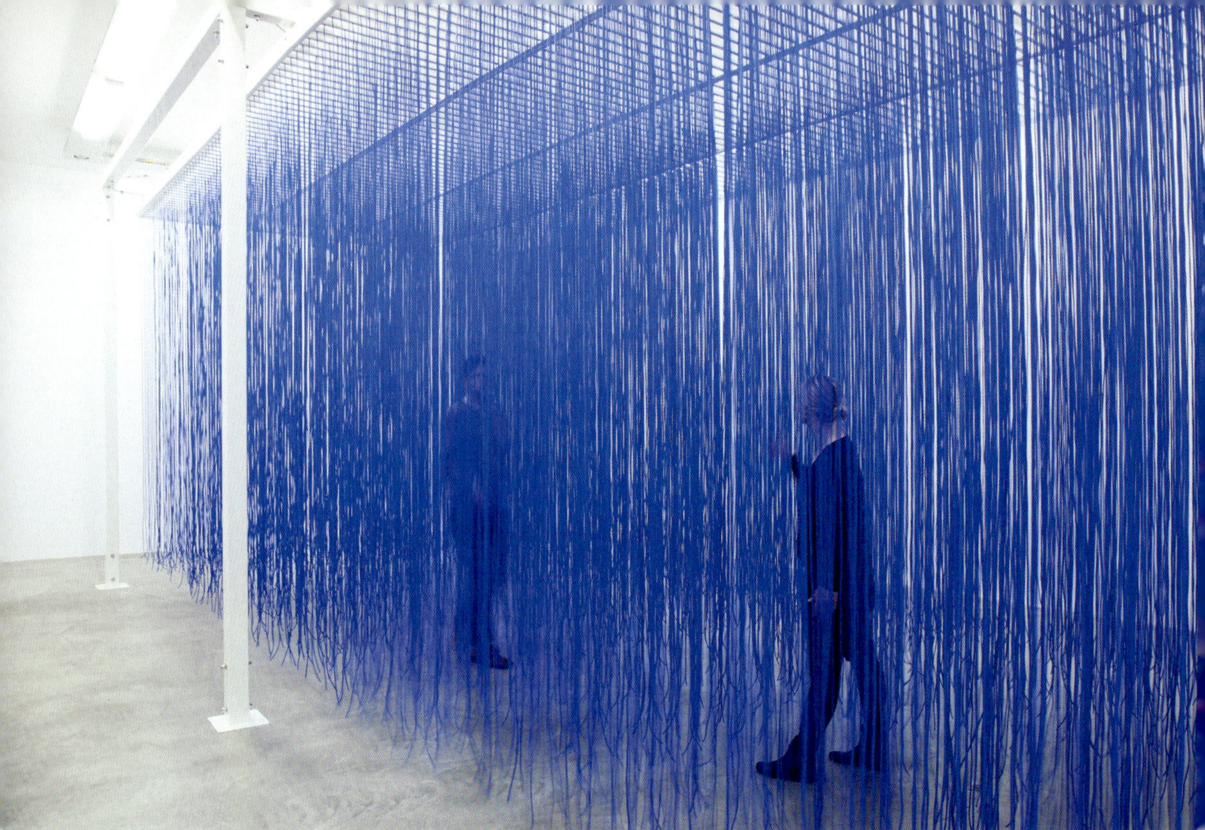

61. Jesús Raphael Soto (Venezuelan, 1923–2005). View of the exhibition "Chronochrome" at Perrotin, Paris, 2015

can get a good sense of what the full-size works would be like from their miniature mates.

Soto, on the other hand, is an artist best known for his kinetic sculptures: large-scale immersive works that he calls *Penetrables*. Made from hundreds of strands of fabric suspended from a ceiling or steel frame, they create a space that viewers enter and engage with physically (fig. 61). The works are activated by the bodies of their viewers. His work in miniature, a ring, essentially replicates that experience, with a lapis lazuli blue "ceiling" from which hang solid yellow- and white-gold strands (fig. 62). When worn on the finger, the entire ring can be animated in space. In the large *Penetrable*, the sculpture's frame is static and human viewers agitate it and provide the source of energy and movement.[6] With

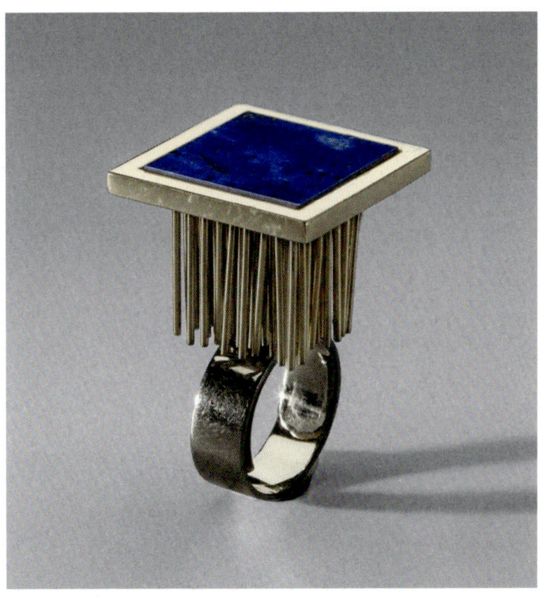

62. Designed by Jesús Raphael Soto (Venezuelan, 1923–2005), made by GEM Montebello (Italian, active 1967–78). Ring, 1968. 18 kt yellow and white gold; lapis lazuli, height: 4.3 cm (1¾ in.)

the ring, the human again provides the energy, as the sculpture moves around and with the wearer's hand. Enjoyable on its own as a ring with kinetic and musical elements (the gold filaments make a delightful clinking sound), this ring is more powerful and better understood when we know its parent object in Soto's body of work.

Wearable miniatures can communicate different things in different ways, sometimes by simply symbolizing a hobby, an interest, or some other affiliation. The beguiling sixteenth-century *Viol Player* print by the German engraver Albrecht Altdorfer is a miniature in and of itself, requiring extremely skilled engraving by the artist able to carve the small printing plate with such detail (fig. 63). Altdorfer is recognized as having a particular facility for making truly tiny prints.[7] Here, he has layered another miniature within the

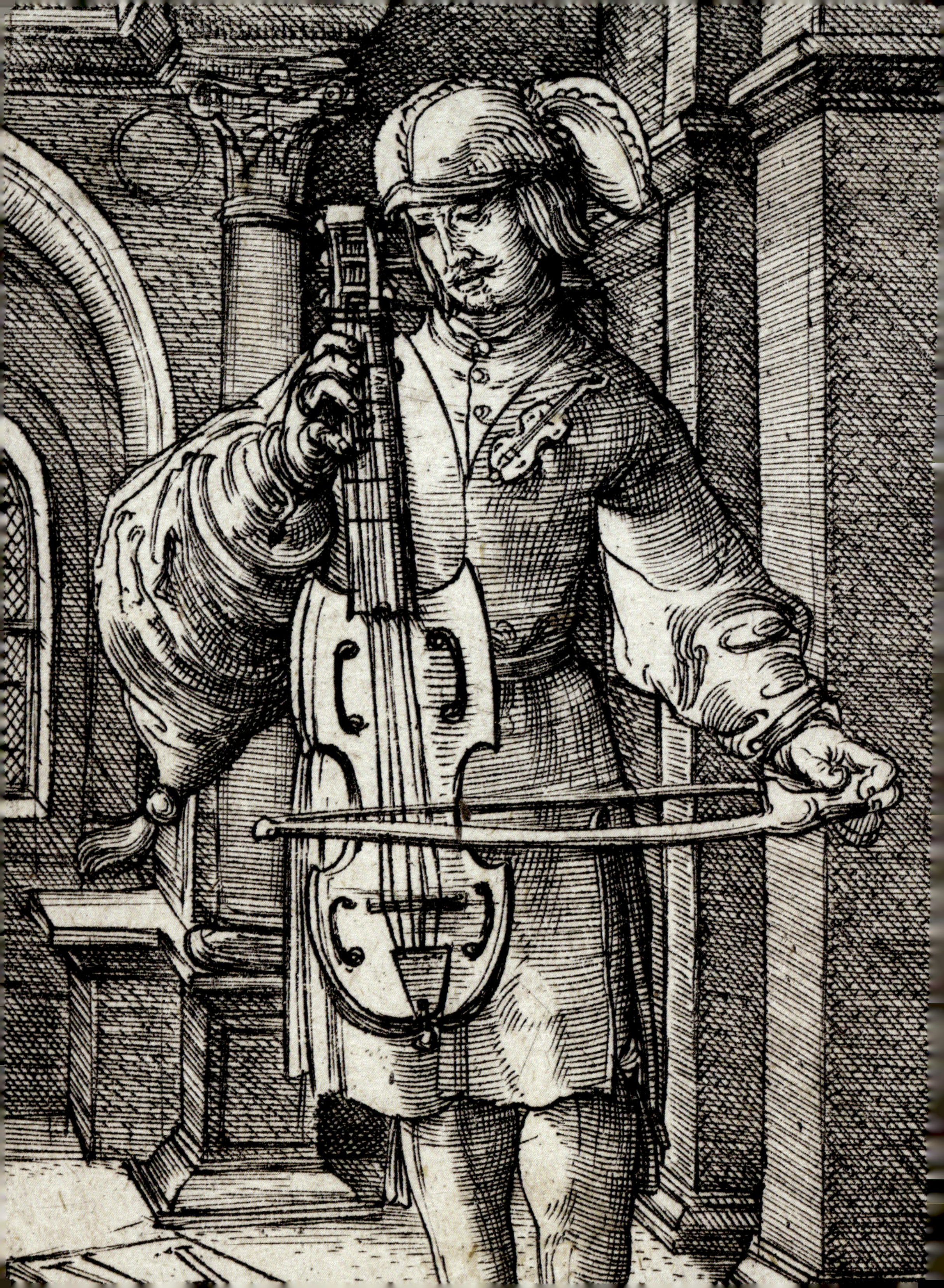

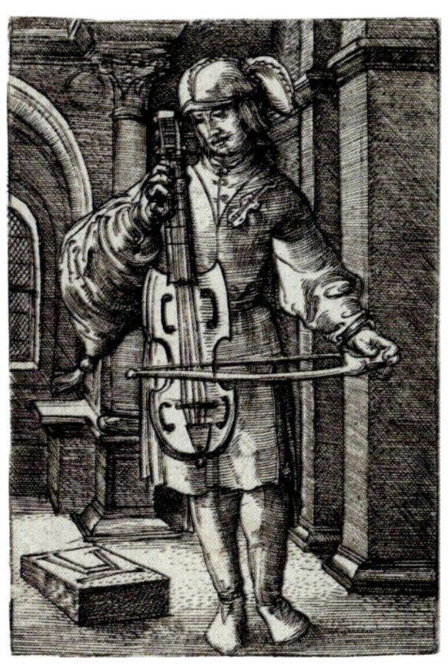

63. Albrecht Altdorfer
(German, about 1480–1538).
The Viol Player, 1519–25.
Engraving, 6.1 × 4.1 cm
(2⅜ × 1⅝ in.)

print: his viol player sports a small brooch of a viol, a miniature version of the instrument in his hands. Such a piece, like the watch pin in the shape of a lute, would have taken great skill to create and possibly would have incorporated gold, enameling, and jewels or pearls (fig. 64). Altdorfer demonstrated his facility for working small by showing off how he could engrave another even tinier viol on his miniature player's breast.

As we have seen, miniature objects can depend on and refer to other senses beyond seeing, including movement (Soto) and sound (Altdorfer). A small, gilded

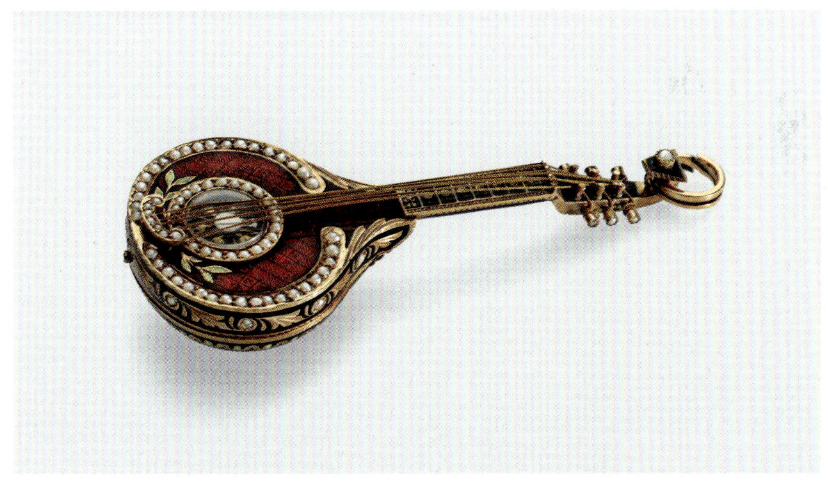

64. Watch in the shape of a lute, French, about 1800.
Gold, enamel, pearls, length: 7.3 cm (2⅞ in.)

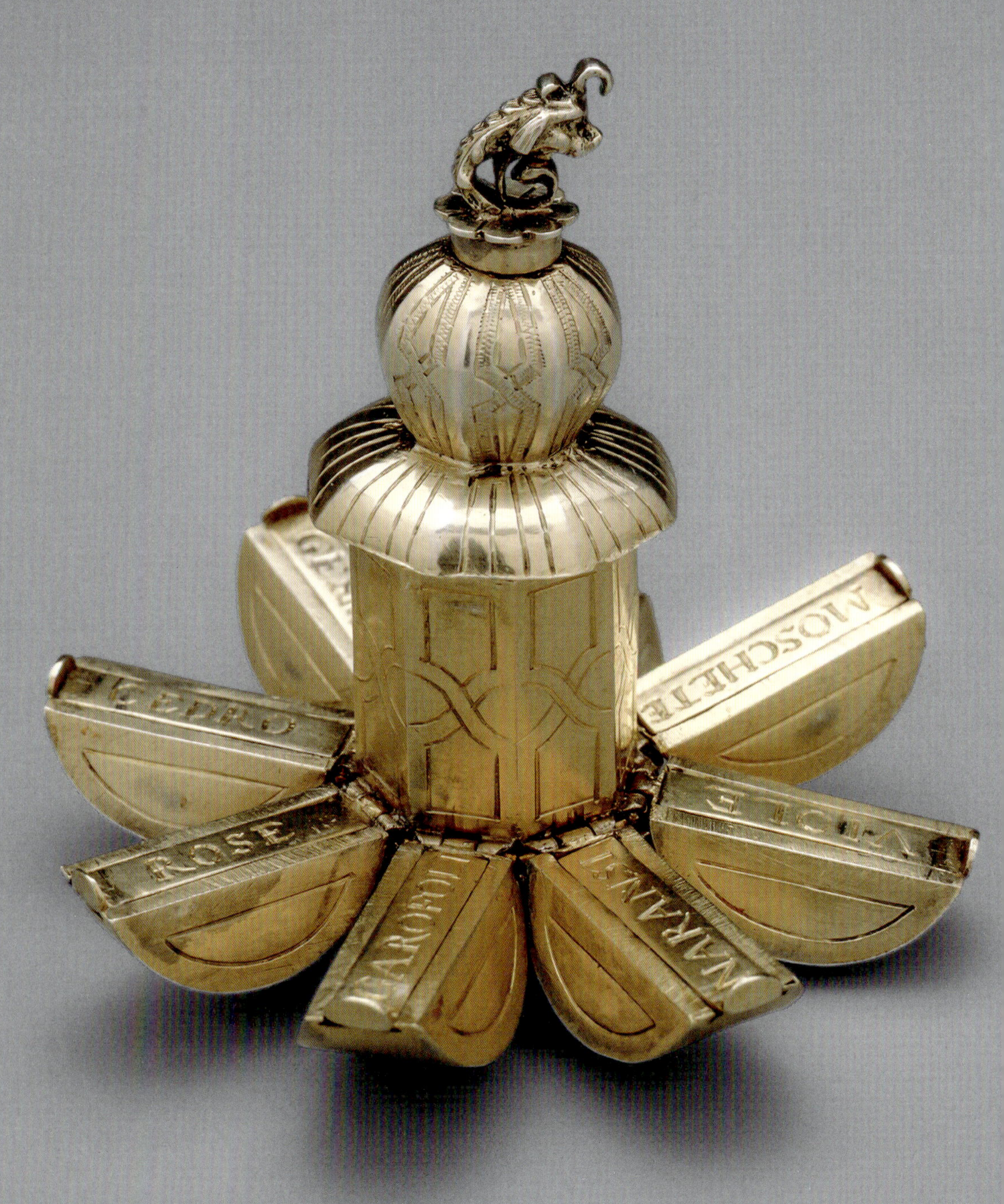

MOSCHITE
ROSE
TAROFOI
NARANA
VIOLE

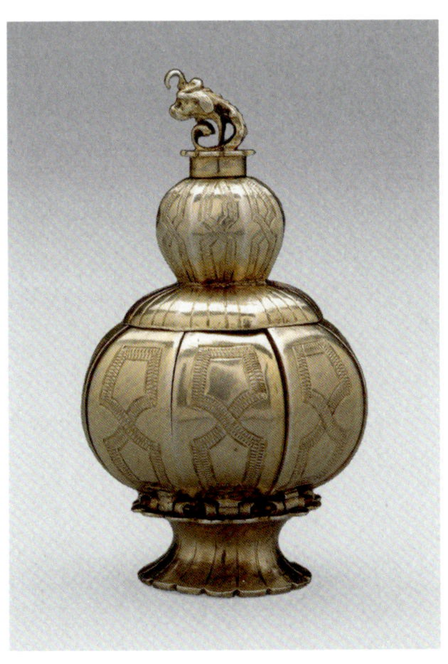

65. Pomander, English, about 1580. Gilded silver, height: 6.4 cm (2½ in.)

silver orb, called a pomander, adds scent to the equation (fig. 65). Taking the name from the French word for apple (*pomme*), pomanders were popular in the medieval period, before modern hygiene practices. This pomander, with its bulbous lower part, borrows its shape from its eponymous fruit. When the tapered finial is unscrewed, the body opens to reveal eight compartments that fold down like petals. Each one is labeled with the name of a substance or plant appreciated for its scent: rose, cedar, jasmine, ambergris, musk, violet, orange, and clove. When worn by a well-to-do woman or man, whether on a chain or leather strap around the neck or hanging from the waist by a girdle, the pomander could be lifted to the nose and sniffed whenever the surrounding atmosphere smelled unpleasant. Many of the spices and other elements it contained were believed to have medicinal purposes as well, and so the pomander brought together the kitchen garden and the apothecary in miniature form, to be carried on one's person when venturing out into the world.[8]

Two-dimensional works like prints and paintings are harder to categorize as miniatures per se, as they are often just smaller works than their creators typically make. Smallness in painting has often resulted in works called "cabinet" pictures, in reference to the fact that they were likely to be displayed and enjoyed in a small room of the home, rather than in a larger setting such as a church, an exhibition space like the annual French Salon, or some other grand interior. A description that often comes to mind when looking at a beautiful small painting is "jewel-like," and it is easy to assign such a term to the exquisite work titled *Les Plastrons*

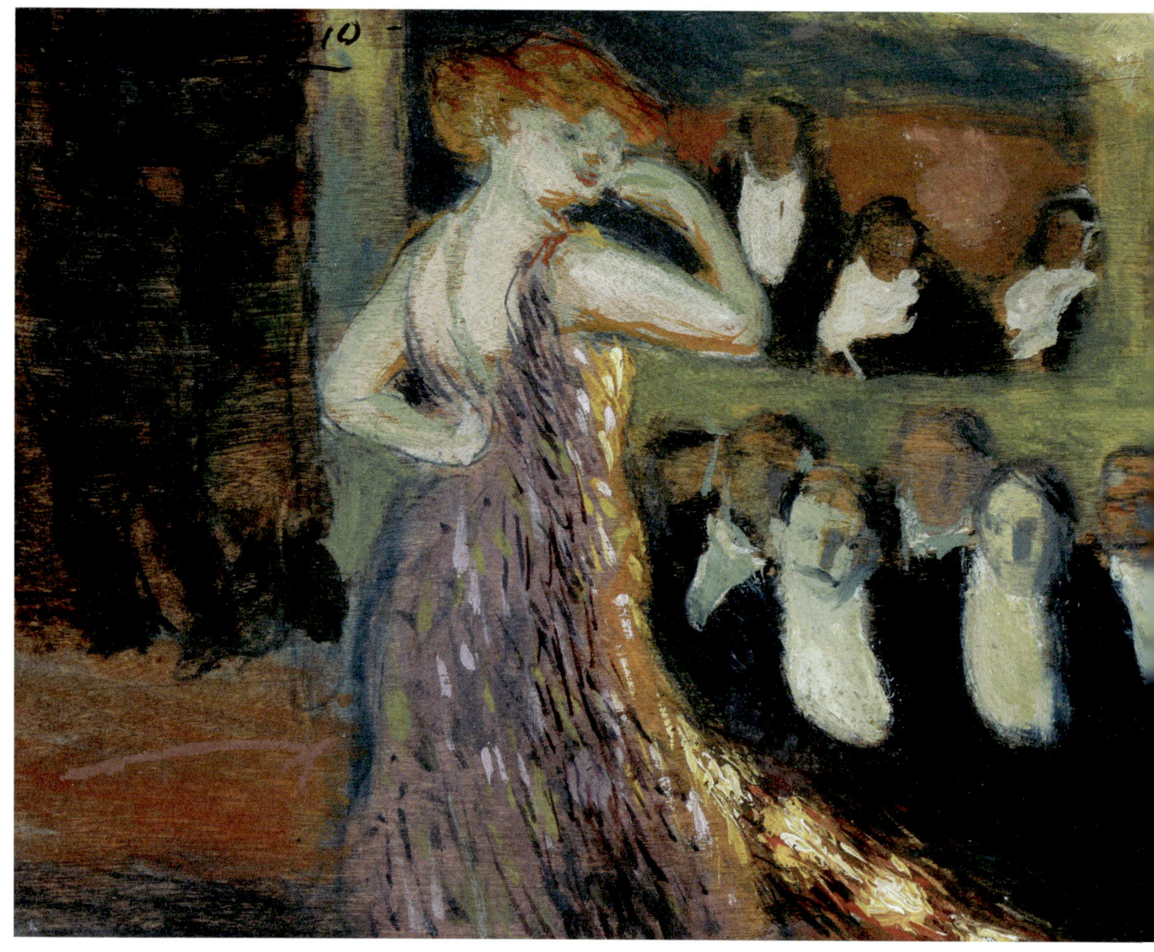

(*Stuffed Shirts*) by Pablo Picasso. Dating from 1900, right around the time of Picasso's move from his native Spain to Paris, the small painting shows a female performer standing onstage in a theater and a group of well-dressed men seated in the front of the audience, watching her (fig. 66). Miniature or small-scale paintings and prints also often require great technical mastery, whether in painting the tiny details with a very fine brush or engraving a plate with minute lines. Here, however, Picasso has eschewed detail in favor of a smudged and hazy vision of the scene at hand, creating a very different visual experience.

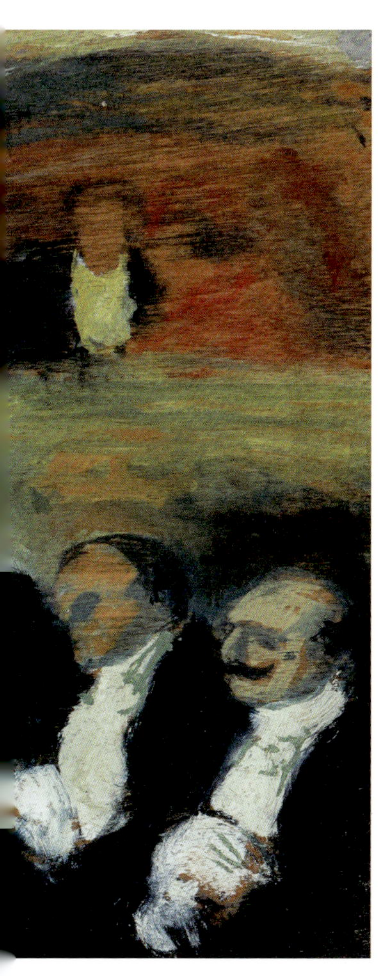

66. Pablo Picasso (Spanish, active in France, 1881–1973). *Les Plastrons (Stuffed Shirts)*, 1900. Oil on panel, 13.6 × 22.5 cm (5⅜ × 8⅞ in.)

This gets to the heart of the appeal of the miniature: it is often surprising. We can easily be caught off guard by something small, as our eye can pass over it more easily than a large work that fills our gaze. Do we miss it, or dismiss it? Perhaps. But when we do turn our attention to it, we often engage with a miniature more deeply, as we have to focus closely to see the details, the materials, even what it shows us or represents. Our eyes and brain must work harder with miniatures: not just to *see* them but to make the mental calculations about relative scale necessary to compare the miniature with what we may know about its parent or a full-size example.

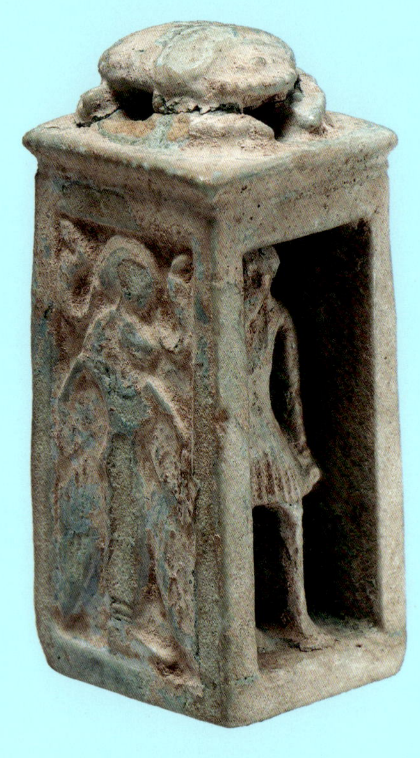

Why Miniatures Matter

The resistance of miniatures to falling neatly into categories is what makes them universal and of enduring interest. One source of their lasting meaning and impact, as we have seen, can be their connection to a full-size object believed to have special powers, or through their association with the relics or memory of someone deceased.

In that spirit, miniature shrines have been popular across many different religious traditions and cultures as a focus for private worship, or for burial or entombment with the deceased so that they may have the protection of the god or gods venerated in the shrine. By extension, miniatures can also call to mind an actual shrine where relatives may have paid for services or given donations in memory of their loved ones. A fifteenth-century Jain example from western India, just under 5 inches tall, is made of brass and silver, with doors that swing open to reveal its interior (fig. 67). While the Jain religion does not worship any gods, it has a tradition of lavish, architecturally impressive temples, of which this is a small-scale version.

Gods feature prominently in a different shrine dating from almost 2,000 years earlier, a Nubian miniature made of blue faience (fig. 68). This ancient piece depicts three different deities: it has a standing figure of Horus in its open inner chamber, a relief of a winged Hathor on one side, and a relief of a winged Bastet on the opposite side. Under 3 inches tall, it is even smaller than the Jain example. Both miniature shrines reconfigure the place of worship in the community—a shrine or temple—making it into something worshippers could hold in their hands and contemplate in private.

Beyond channeling power, miniatures also can serve one function while taking on the appearance of something else. Examples include decorative elements designed to look like much larger structures, placed in a different context. Medieval European craftsmen, in particular, gravitated to using architectural elements, usually drawn from cavernous Gothic cathedrals, and miniaturizing them in smaller decorative metalwork. A fragmentary finial, for example, from the mid-fourteenth to mid-fifteenth century, possibly German, likely sat atop something larger that is now lost (fig. 69). Crafted to resemble a cathedral tower, its maker gave it three

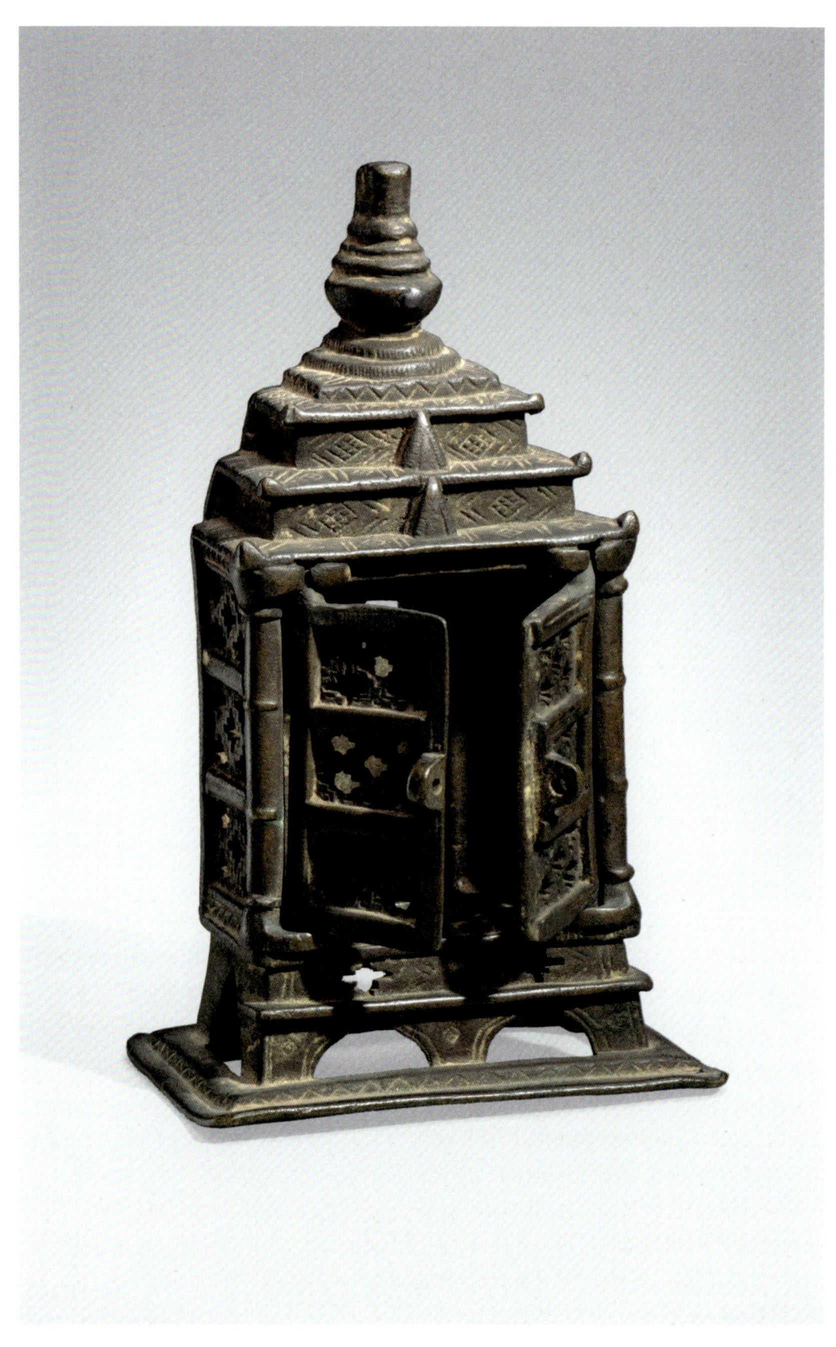

67. Miniature Jain shrine, Indian, 1487–88. Brass and silver,
height: 12.3 cm (4⅞ in.)

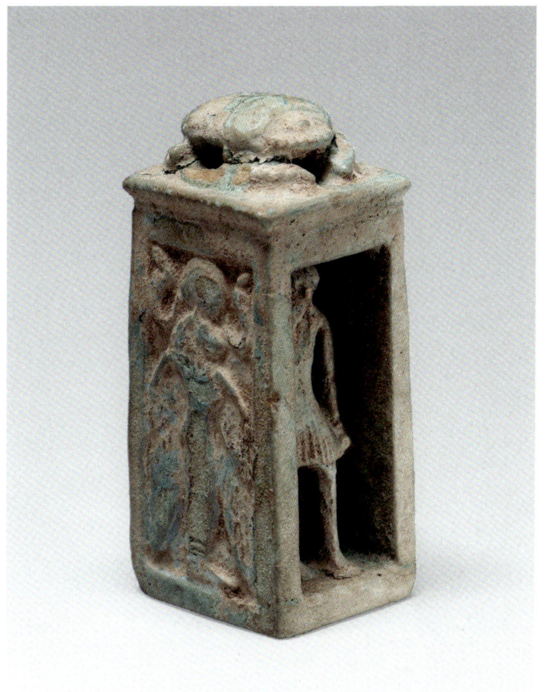

68. Miniature shrine, Nubian, 743–712 BCE. Faience, height: 7 cm (2¾ in.)

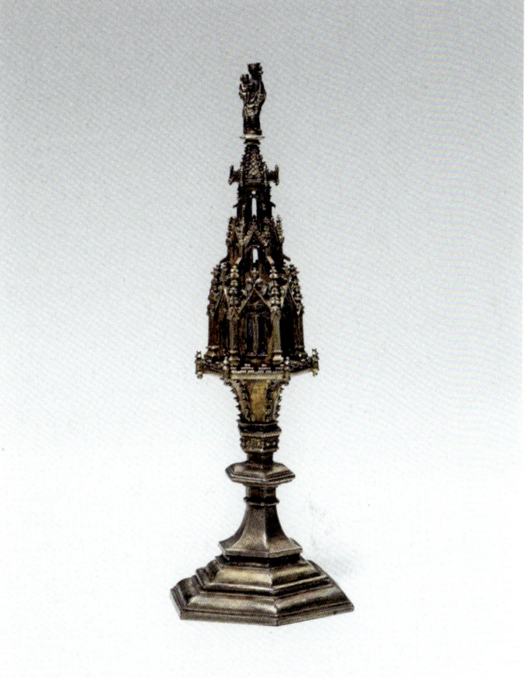

69. Finial, possibly German, mid-14th to mid-15th century. Silver with gilding and translucent enamel, height: 7.5 cm (3 in.)

stories of windows separated by buttresses, culminating in a pyramidal roof surmounted by a statue of the Virgin Mary and the Christ child. Each window is represented by an enameled panel, to replicate stained glass. With its fine details, it looks just like the spires of cathedrals of the same period. A similar example of architectural metalwork, though a bit later and likely French in origin, is a lock and lock plate, or hasp, made for a chest. Like the finial, this work is fragmentary, as we do not have the chest that it may have secured. However, we can clearly see that the metalsmith created this durable iron lock plate to look like the portal of a Gothic cathedral (fig. 70).[1] The keyhole stands in the place of the doorway, surrounded by tracery that resembles carved stone; at left, on a

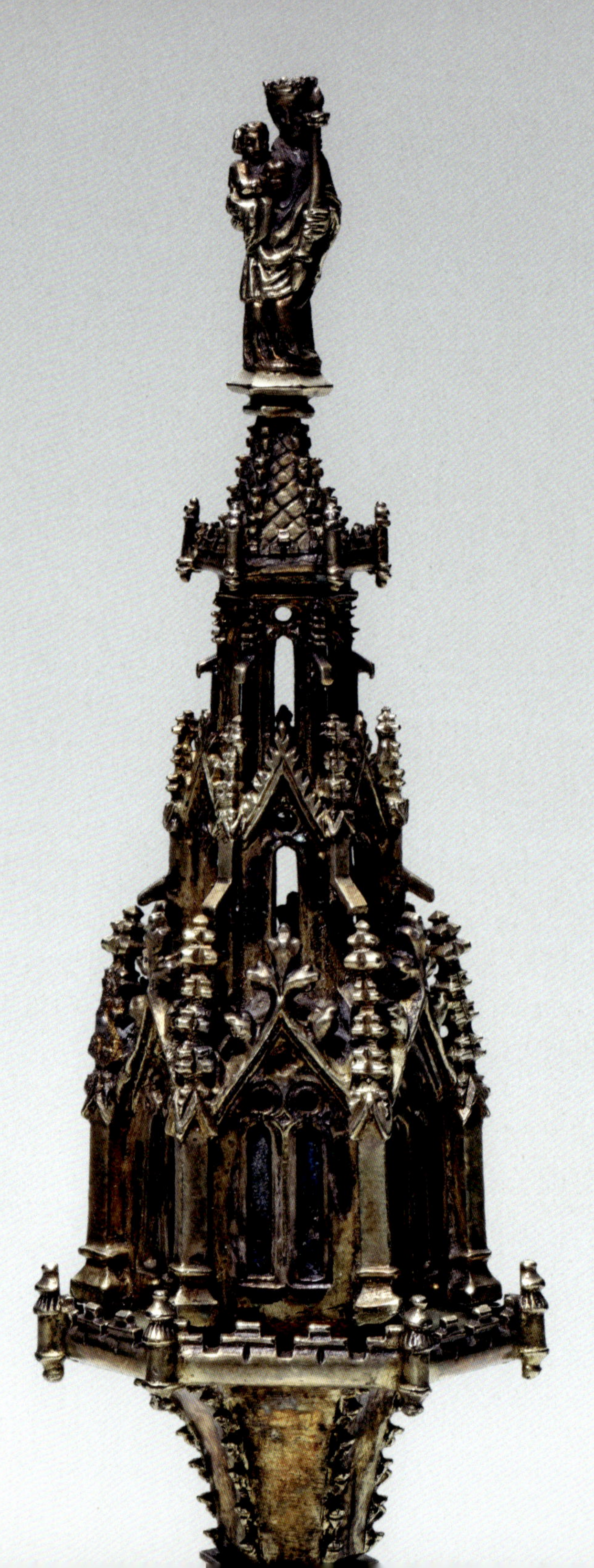

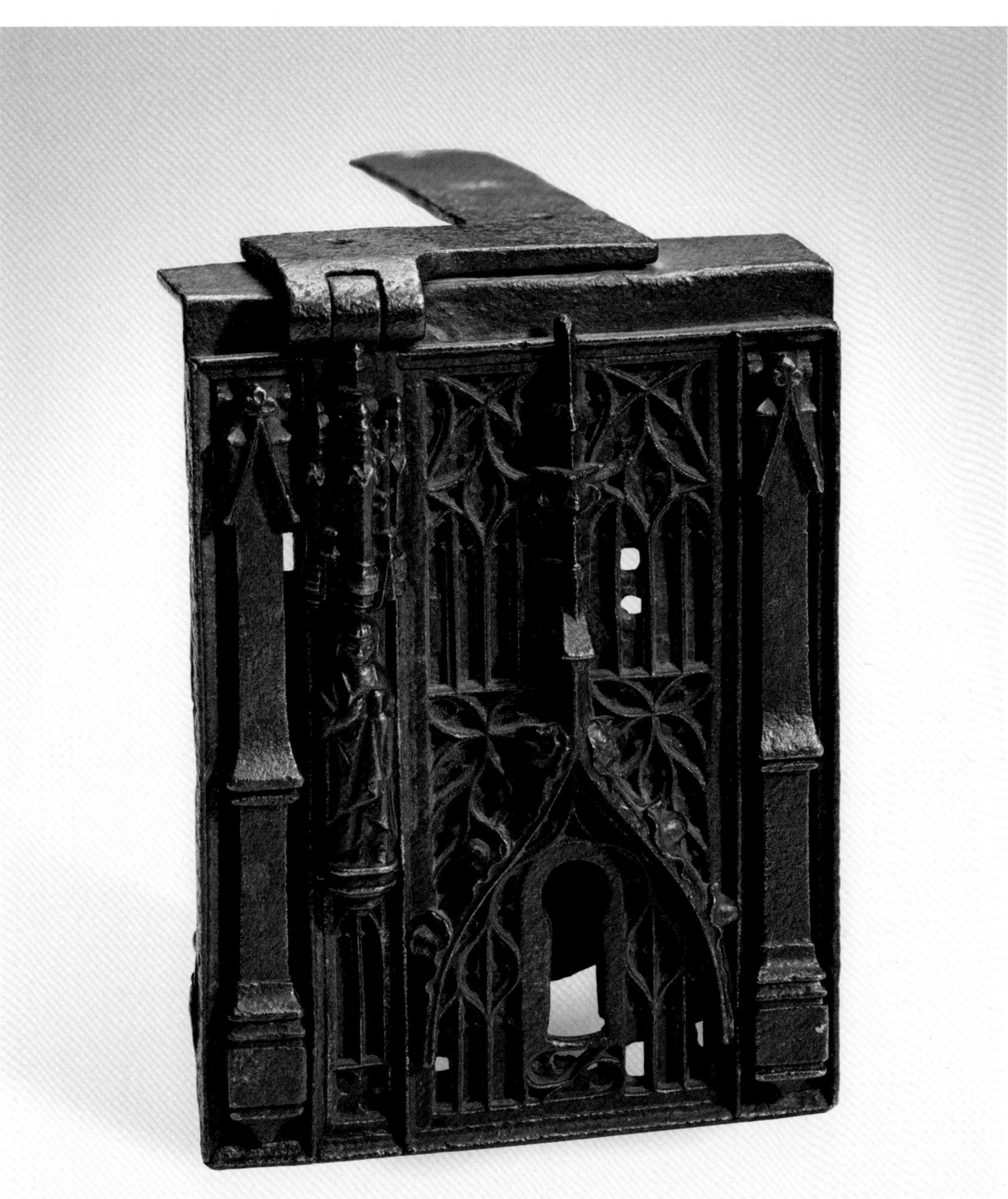

70. Lock and hasp for a chest, possibly French, late 15th to
early 16th century. Iron, height: 12.7 cm (5 in.)

Opposite: Detail of fig. 69

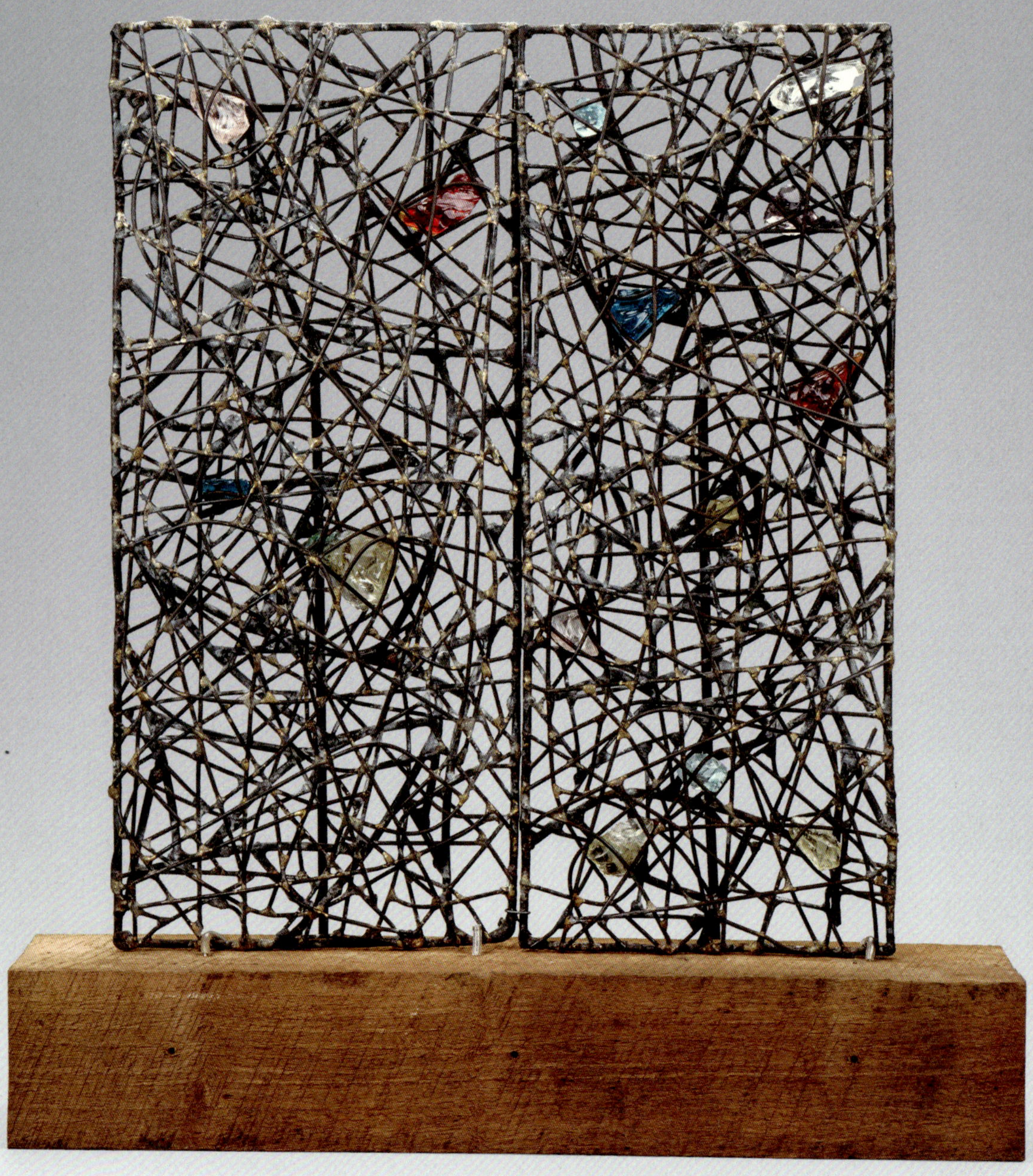

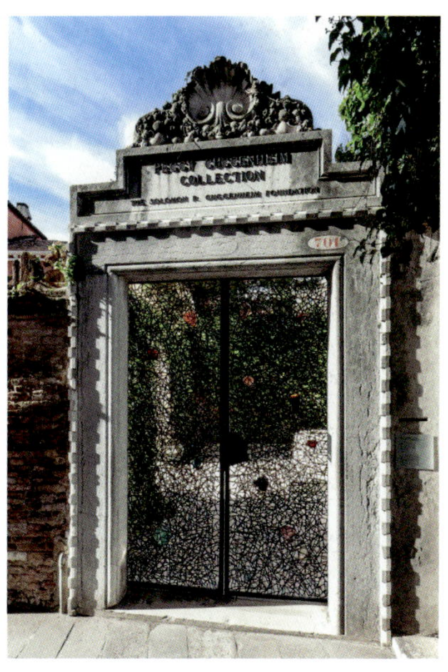

72. Claire Falkenstein (American, 1908–1997). Entrance gates to the Palazzo, 1961. Iron and colored glass, height: 277 cm (109 in.)

pedestal, stands a statue of a saint with a book and draped robes. A lock plate like this could have been used on multiple chests, since it would have been easy to move it from one to another. As with the finial, we can imagine the same doorway rendered in stone and on a monumental scale, part of an inspiring edifice that would have truly been the work of a lifetime.

Throughout history and across cultures, religion and faith have offered artisans ample opportunities to create miniature works. Objects that hearken back to a site of veneration like a shrine or a cathedral could transfer their spiritual meaning to something else or hold it within themselves. However, their specific meaning can be hard to pin down: faith and belief are intangible things, and the power of these miniatures likely did not lie in their material impact or role in the world. Other types of miniatures are, by contrast, fundamentally practical and play a specific part in the process of artistic creation, design, and construction.

In 1960 the American artist Claire Falkenstein received an important commission: to create entrance gates for the new Venetian palazzo of the art collector Peggy Guggenheim. As part of her design process, Falkenstein first crafted a scale model of her plan for the gates, using painted copper wire and glass (fig. 71).[2] The miniature version, only 17½ inches tall compared with the 109-inch height of the gates themselves, is a work of art in its own right. Falkenstein, who was also known for her work in jewelry, could bend and manipulate copper wire for the model

Opposite: 71. Claire Falkenstein (American, 1908–1997). Model for *New Gates of Paradise*, Guggenheim Foundation, 1961. Painted copper wire and glass, height: 44.5 cm (17½ in.)

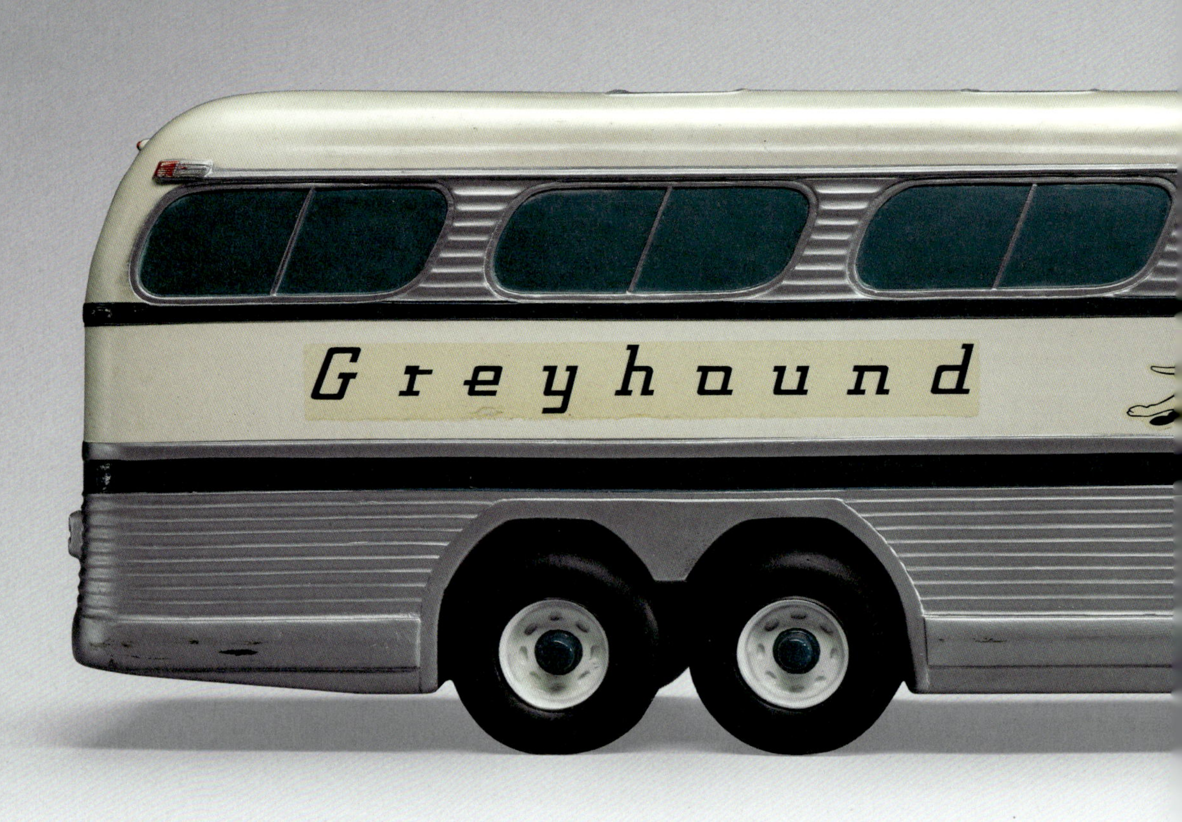

more easily than she could the iron rods in the final piece. She was also used to working in miniature and envisioning how her model might scale up to create a finished work. The full-size work of iron and colored glass was completed in 1961 and now stands in Venice (fig. 72).

Model airplanes, buses, and cars, while most often created as collectibles or toys for personal enjoyment, have also had practical

73. Designed by Raymond Loewy (American, born in France, 1893–1986). Greyhound Scenicruiser bus model, mid-1950s. Painted plaster, printed decals, wood, length: 101.6 cm (40 in.)

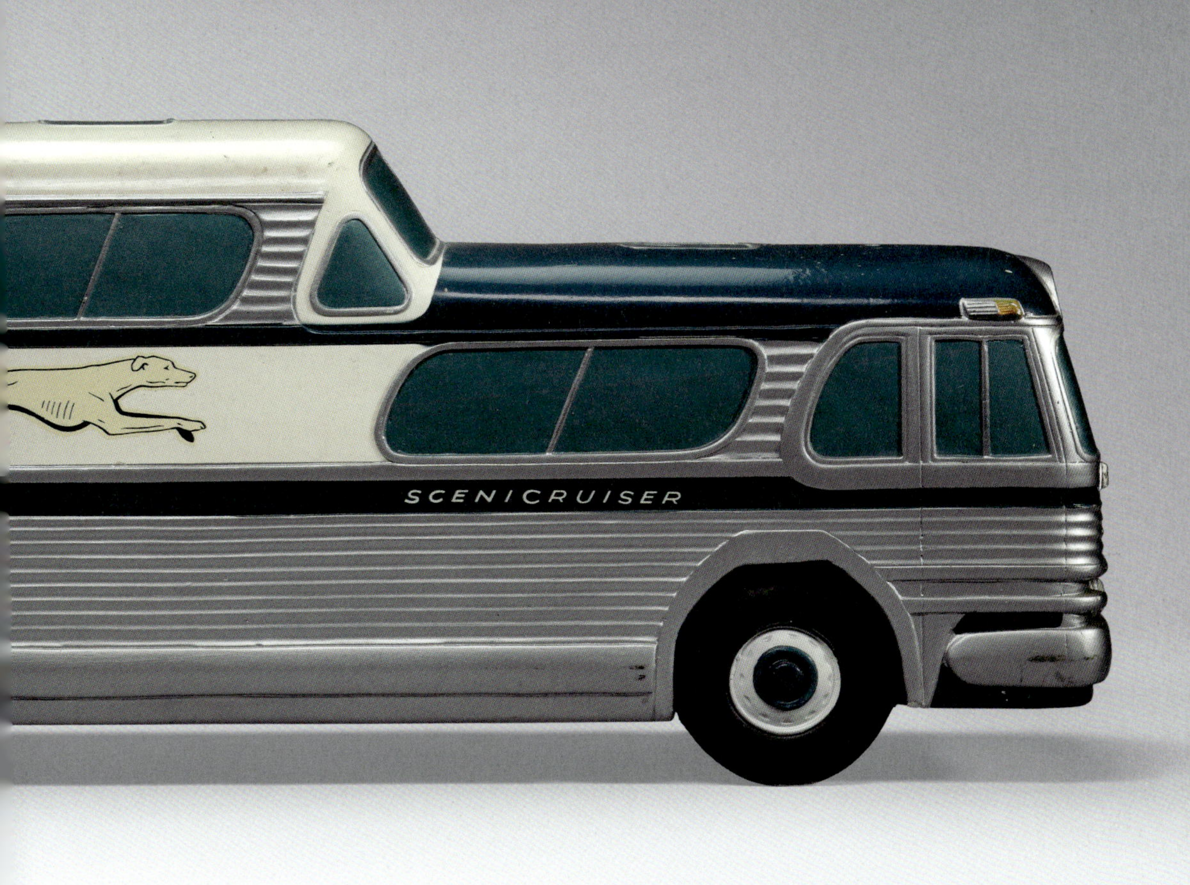

real-world purposes. Miniatures of the iconic Greyhound Scenicruiser bus, for example, were produced as sales and marketing
tools (fig. 73). Created for General Motors in the 1950s by the indus-
trial designer Raymond Loewy, the Scenicruiser featured a sleek,
modern design and upper-level seats that gave road travelers a
better view; the popular split-level buses began operating in 1954
and remained in use into the 1970s.[3] As promotional pieces, miniature Scenicruiser buses like this were sent out to Greyhound sales
offices throughout the United States, so that prospective customers could see for themselves the style in which they would be
traveling on their long-distance bus journey. It was far easier to
use a 40-inch-long model than a full-size bus!

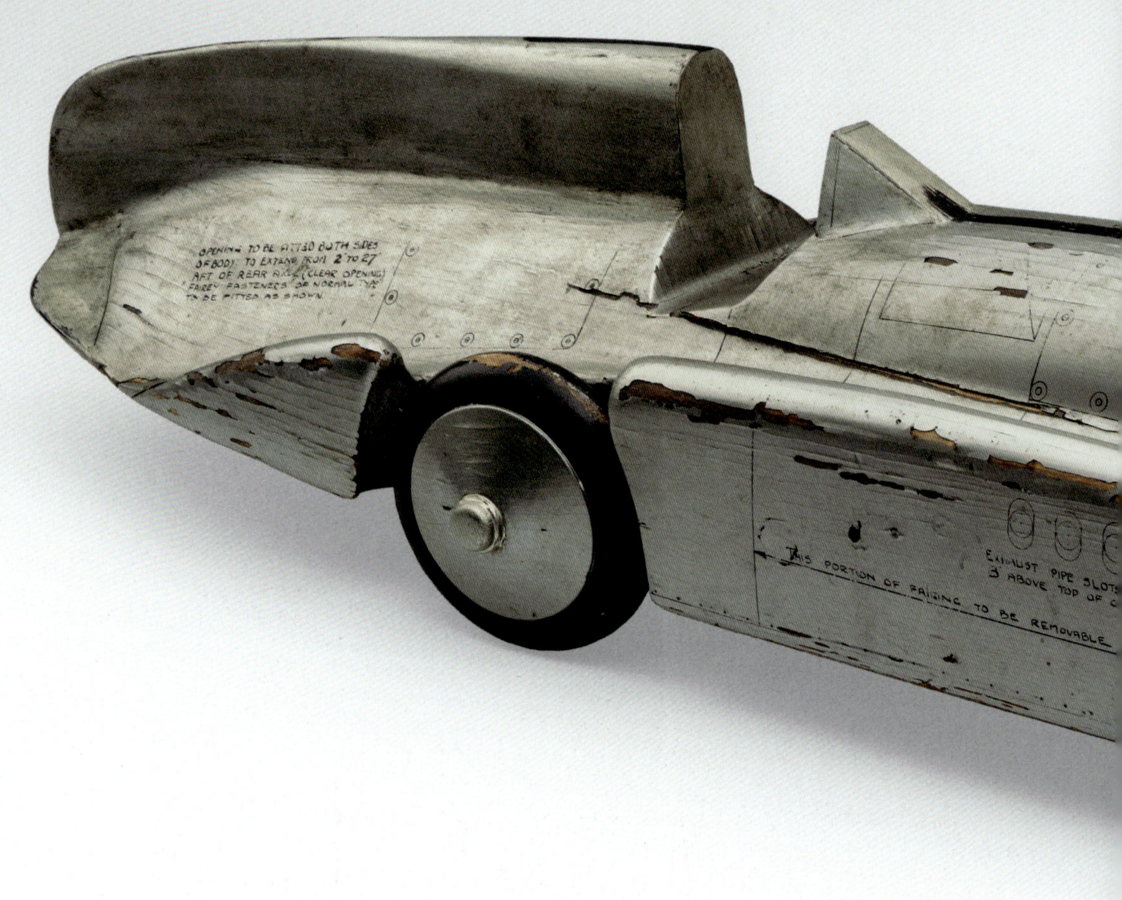

A vehicle model of a different sort is a miniature of the Speed of the Wind, a test car built for British inventor and racing driver Captain George Eyston, who broke long-duration speed records with it in 1935 and 1936. This wooden model, made of painted pine with metal and pine wheels, shows the lines of the car's body, marked with stripes and designs related to its aerodynamics (fig. 74). In its

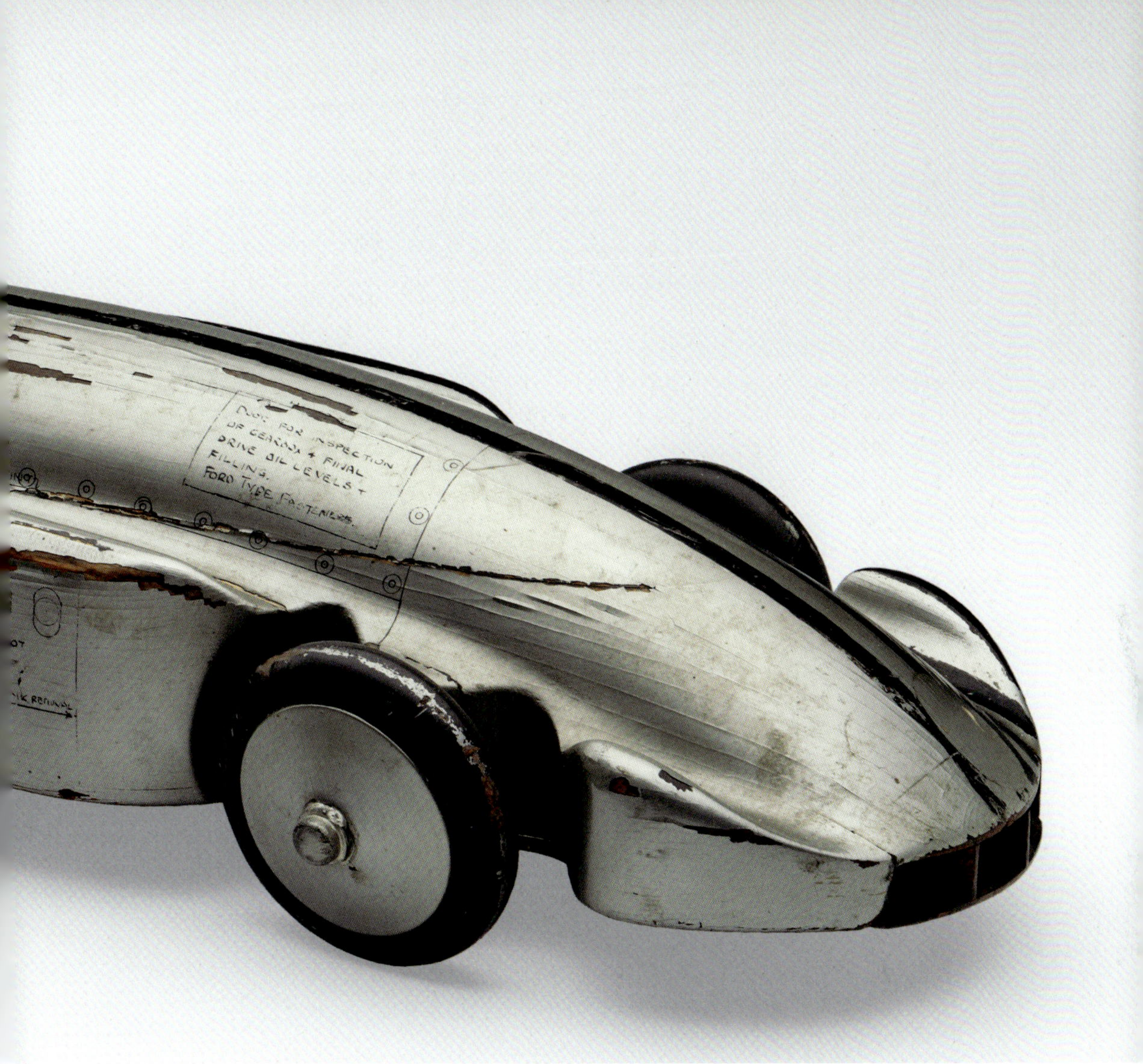

74. Speed of the Wind wind-tunnel model, American, about 1935.
Painted pine, length: 88.9 cm (35 in.)

construction, the actual Speed of the Wind was designed for maximum endurance, and it broke records on the Utah salt flats. Made of humble materials, the miniature version is a purely functional object that models the shape of the car: a miniature simplified out of practicality.

In contrast, an intricate Edo-period print by an unknown artist in Japan, *One Hundred Poems by One Hundred Poets*, is the essence of impracticality and smallness for smallness' sake (fig. 75). After Japanese artists in the early nineteenth century found ways to imitate copperplate etchings by European artists, they discovered that the technique allowed them to preserve an immense level of detail. Artists began to demonstrate their

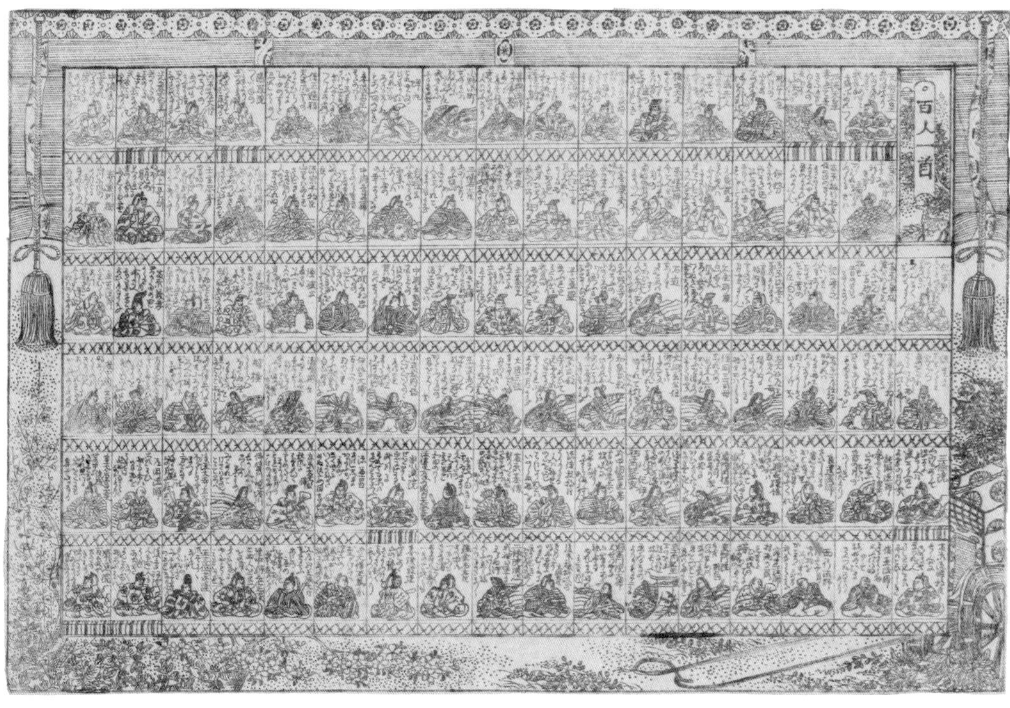

75. *One Hundred Poems by One Hundred Poets*, Japanese, early 19th century. Copperplate etching on paper, 9.9 × 14.6 cm (3⅞ × 5¾ in.)

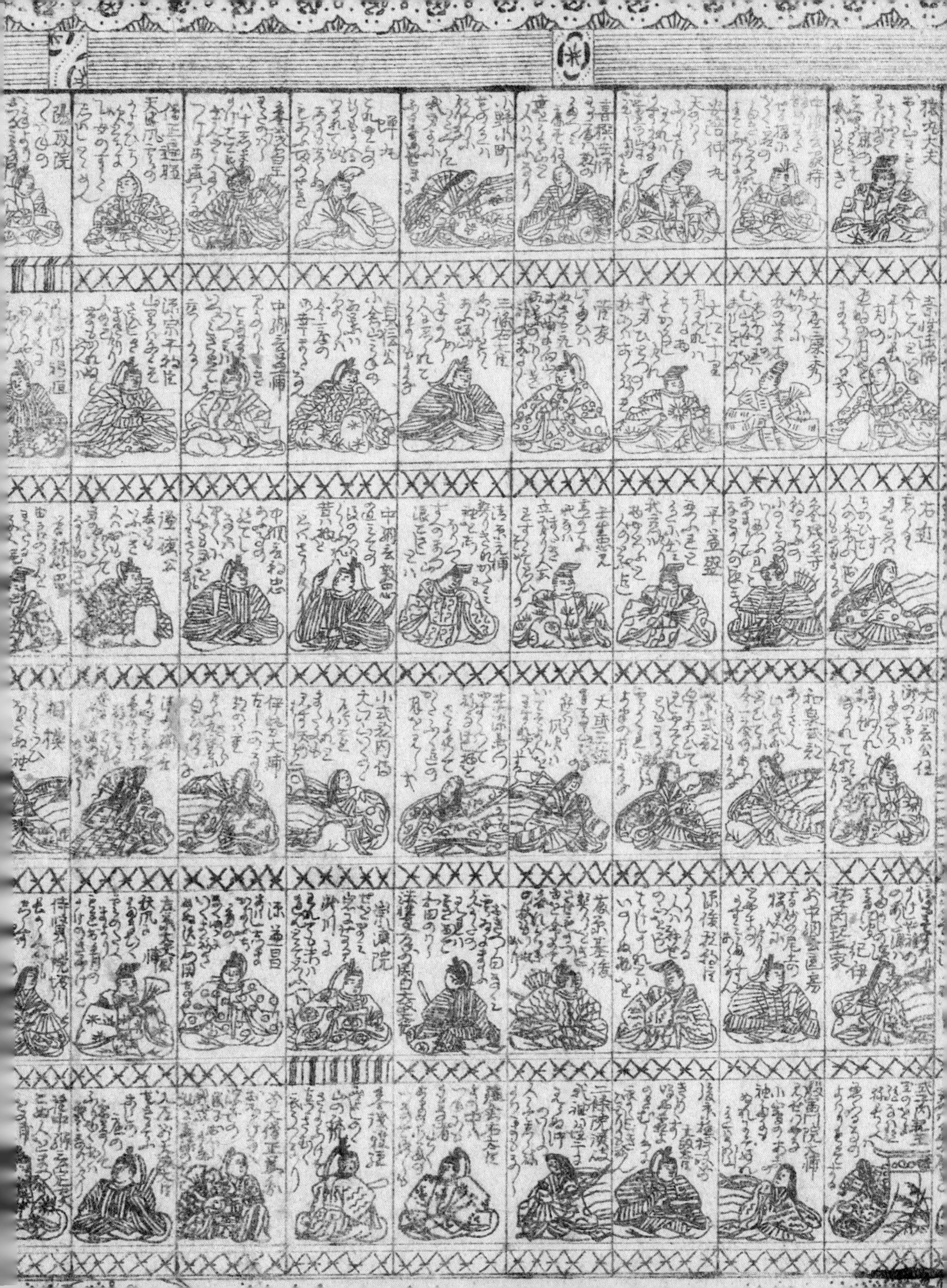

virtuosity by producing the tiniest prints they could, shrinking down both text and images to an extremely small scale. This example, produced by an artist of great skill, combines 100 poems and portraits of their authors in a print less than 4 inches high. Nearly illegible without magnification, this is a miniature that is small just because it can be.

Miniature ceramic vases by the French art potter Auguste Delaherche have both a practical and an impractical, purely aesthetic function. Delaherche is recognized as one of a group of artists in France who were producing art pottery around the turn of the twentieth century. The French art potters were interested in crafting simple works; they rejected the emphasis on ornament and decoration in earlier artistic traditions. Like artisans in the Art Nouveau and British Arts and Crafts movements, the French potters valued artistic uniqueness and craftsmanship above all.[4] Delaherche embodied these beliefs in his work, and he was particularly interested in experimentation, as he tried out new techniques for making his stoneware. His group of fifty miniature vases, all marked on the bottom with the artist's initials, "A D L H," and individual model numbers, speak to Delaherche's obsession with testing new shapes for his vases and new colored slips and glazes. Like Falkenstein, who produced a small version of *New Gates of Paradise* before the full-size gates, Delaherche chose to experiment with techniques first in his miniatures: they required less clay, less glaze, less time, and less space in the kiln. By signing them and giving them identifying numbers, he also claimed the miniature vases as an integral part of his artistic process and unique works of art on their own, something very much in keeping with the tenets of art pottery and the importance of the craft. An example of Delaherche's full-size functional works, a stoneware vase from around 1889 demonstrates the usefulness of his experimentation. Here, he combined multiple glaze colors to create a floral design delineated by carefully incised marks in the clay. The larger vase is more beautiful to us when we know the care and time that he put into working in miniature to discover and test new glazes (fig. 76).

As we have seen throughout this book, miniatures are more than just cute, childish objects. To relegate them to the world of toys and dollhouses is to miss their point entirely: miniatures contain worlds within them. We will be rewarded for stopping to look closely and think deeply about them.

Following pages: 76. Auguste Delaherche (French, 1857–1940). Vase, about 1889. Stoneware, slip and incised decoration, height: 25.4 cm (10 in.). Miniature vases, 1930s. Stoneware with slip decoration, each, height: about 4.5 cm (1¾ in.)

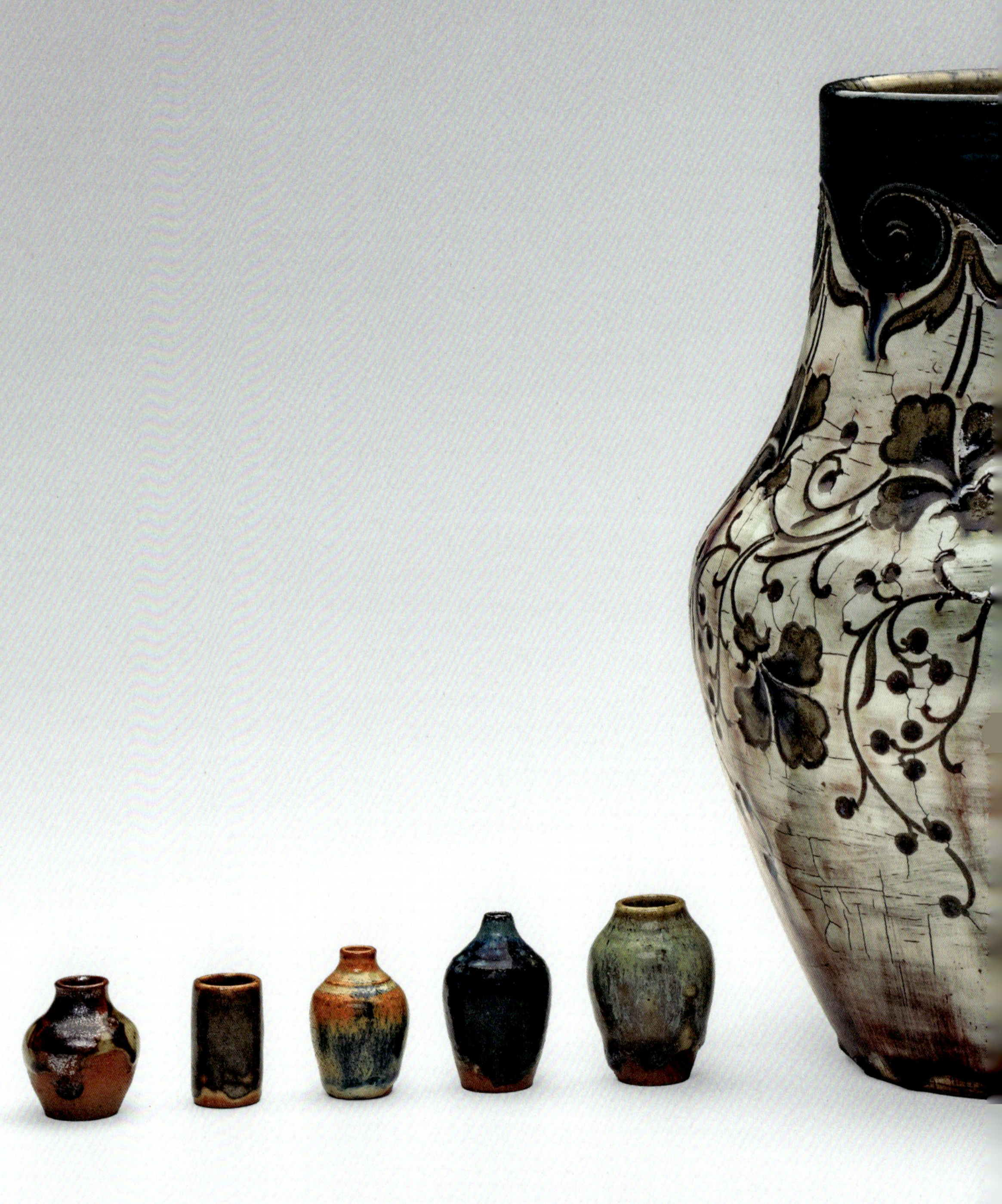

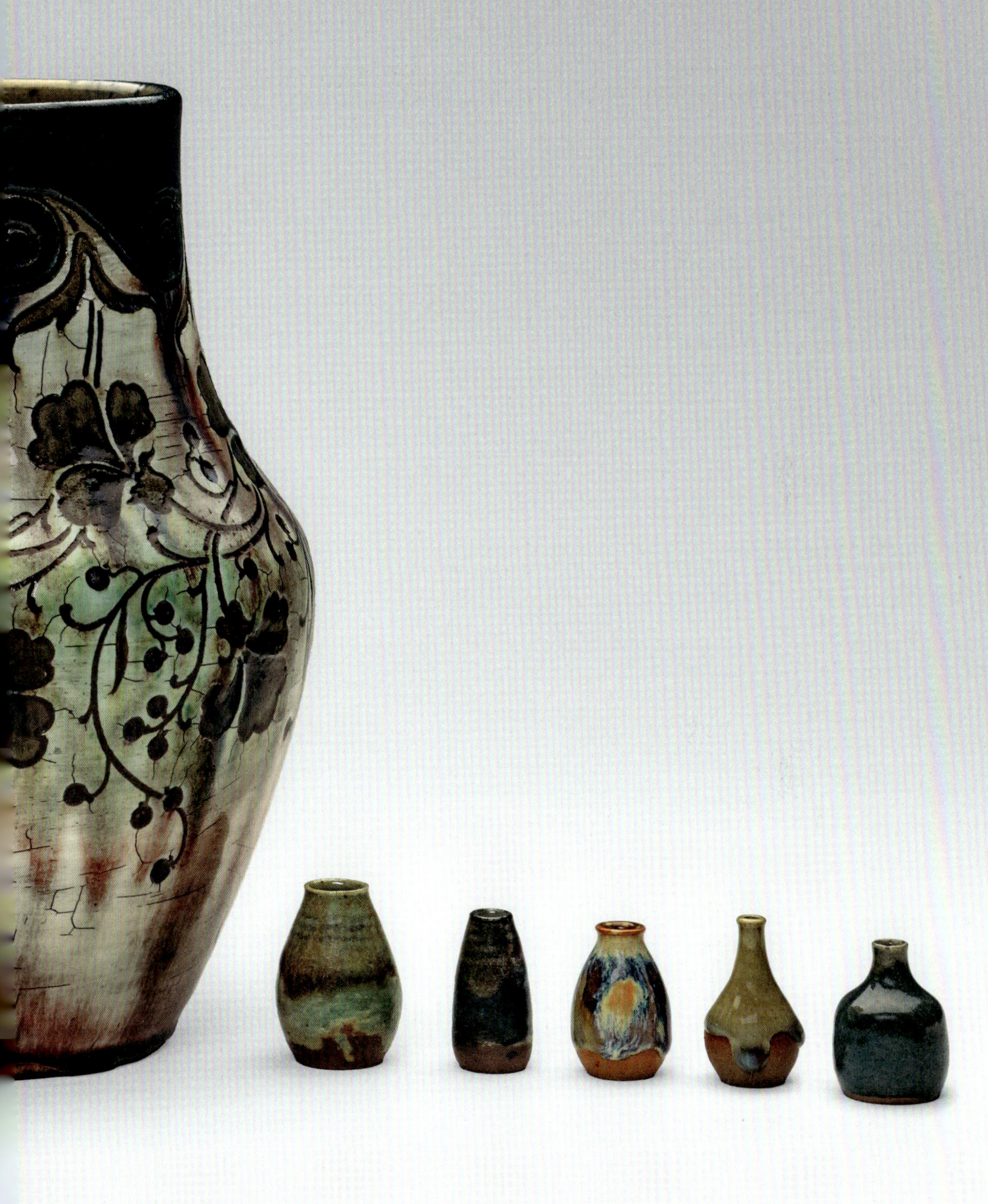

Notes

What Makes a Miniature?

1. Susan Stewart, *On Longing: Narratives of the Miniature, the Gigantic, the Souvenir, the Collection* (Durham, NC: Duke University Press, 1993), 55–56.

2. John Mack, *The Art of Small Things* (Cambridge, MA: Harvard University Press, 2007), 20–21.

3. Catharine MacLeod with Rab MacGibbon et al., *Elizabethan Treasures: Miniatures by Hilliard and Oliver* (London: National Portrait Gallery, 2019).

4. Mack, *Art of Small Things*, 27–31. See also Sheila R. Canby, *Persian Painting*, Eastern Art (London: Trustees of the British Museum, 1993).

5. Julius von Schlosser, *Art and Curiosity Cabinets of the Late Renaissance: A Contribution to the History of Collecting* (Los Angeles: J. Paul Getty Trust, 2021).

6. Clara Sue Ball, "The Early History of the Compound Microscope," *BIOS* 37, no. 2 (May 1966): 51–60.

7. Indeed, the phenomenon of miniatures in English literature and culture is a field of study unto itself. For a full discussion, see Melinda Alliker Rabb, *Miniature and the English Imagination: Literature, Cognition, and Small-Scale Culture, 1650–1765* (Cambridge: Cambridge University Press, 2019).

8. Laura Forsberg, "Nature's Invisibilia: The Victorian Microscope and the Miniature Fairy," *Victorian Studies* 57, no. 4 (2015).

9. Eben Haines, Michelle Millar Fisher, and Courtney Harris, "Shelter in Place "Gallery," in *Interiors in the Era of Covid-19: Interior Design between the Public and Private Realms*, ed. Penny Sparke et al. (London: Bloomsbury Publishing, 2023). See also @shelterinplacegallery on Instagram and the website www.shelterinplacegallery.com.

10. Stewart, *On Longing*, 171–72.

11. For recent scholarship, see Chloe Wigston Smith and Beth Fowkes Tobin, *Small Things in the Eighteenth Century: The Political and Personal Value of the Miniature* (Cambridge: Cambridge University Press, 2022), which records papers given at a symposium in June 2019 at the University of York.

When Small Is Powerful

1. Barbara Drake Boehm and Alexandra Suda, "The Material," in *Small Wonders: Gothic Boxwood Miniatures*, ed. Lisa Ellis and Alexandra Suda (Toronto: Art Gallery of Ontario, 2016), 17.

2. Barbara Drake Boehm and Alexandra Suda, "Devotion, Private Prayer," in *Small Wonders*, 77–83.

3. Adrian R. Bell and Richard S. Dale, "The Medieval Pilgrimage Business," *Enterprise & Society* 12, no. 3 (September 2011): 606.

4. Thomas S. Michie, *MFA Highlights: European Decorative Arts* (Boston: MFA Publications, 2014), 29.

5. Nancy Netzer, ed., *Secular Sacred: 11th–16th Century Works from the Boston Public Library and the Museum of Fine Arts, Boston* (Chestnut Hill, MA: McMullen Museum of Art, Boston College, 2006), cat. no. 62.

6. Diana Webb, *Pilgrimage in Medieval England* (London: Bloomsbury Publishing, 2007), 63–92.

7. Bell and Dale, "Medieval Pilgrimage Business," 623.

8. Yvonne J. Markowitz, "Triptych Pendant Depicting Martyrdom of Saint Barbara, Mary Magdalen, and Saint Gereon," in *Artful Adornments: Jewelry from the Museum of Fine Arts, Boston* (Boston: MFA Publications, 2011), 40.

9. Isabel Stünkel, "Ancient Egyptian Amulets," in *Heilbrunn Timeline of Art History* (New York: Metropolitan Museum of Art, 2000–).

10. Deborah Lutz, "The Dead Still among Us: Victorian Secular Relics, Hair Jewelry, and Death Culture," *Victorian Literature and Culture* 39, no. 1 (2011): 128.

11. Lutz, "The Dead Still among Us," 129–30.

12. Yvonne J. Markowitz, "Mourning Pendant Brooch," in *Artful Adornments*, 113. The inscription bears the names and ages of the two boys, "In Memory of / T. M. McC. / Aged six years & three months / and / W. H. McC. / Aged 2 years & 10 months" as well as the manufacturer and date: Parry & Musgrave, Philadelphia, Sept. 13, 1792. With this information, it was possible to identify the mother of the two deceased boys as Ruth McConnell of Philadelphia.

The Miniature at Home

1. Michelle Moseley-Christian, "Seventeenth-Century *Pronk Poppenhuisen*: Domestic Space and the Ritual Function of Dutch Dollhouses for Women," *Home Cultures* 7, no. 3 (November 2010): 344.

2. *Miniature Rooms: The Thorne Rooms at the Art Institute of Chicago* (New York: Abbeville Press, 1983).

3. *Silver of the Americas, 1600–2000: American Silver in the Museum of Fine Arts, Boston*, ed. Jeannine Falino and Gerald W. R. Ward (Boston: MFA Publications, 2008).

4. See the excellent extant example of a large, intact tile stove in the collection of the Victoria and Albert Museum, made in 1577 by Hans Kraut for the Convent of St. Wolfgang at Engen, Baden, and later relocated to a home in Engen im Hegan near Switzerland. V&A accession number 498:1 to 6-1868, collections.vam.ac.uk.

5. John David Farmer, *The Virtuoso Craftsman: Northern European Design in the Sixteenth Century* (Worcester, MA: Worcester Art Museum, 1969), 189, cat. no. 101.

6. Clive Edwards, "Reclining Chairs Surveyed: Health, Comfort, and Fashion in Evolving Markets," *Studies in the Decorative Arts* 6, no. 1 (1998): 66.

7. Kelly Hays, "Boston Furnituremakers and the New Social Media, 1830–1860," in *Boston Furniture 1700–1900*, ed. Brock Jobe and Gerald W. R. Ward (Charlottesville: University of Virginia Press, 2016), 335–339.

8. Augustus Eliaers to United States Patent Office, Library Step-Chair, Specification of Letters Patent no. 10,151, dated October 25, 1853.

9. For an exploration of artists working in the field of miniatures in the last quarter of the twentieth century and first decade of the twenty-first, particularly those focused on model making and "world creating," see David Revere McFadden, *Otherworldly: Optical Delusions and Small Realities* (New York: Museum of Art and Design, 2011).

Miniature Worlds Observed

1. David Brewster, *The Stereoscope: Its History, Theory, and Construction, with Its Application to the Fine and Useful Arts and to Education* (Chapel Hill, NC: FB&C Limited, 2015); first published in 1856 by John Murray (London).
2. See Inge Reist and Malcolm Baker, *Sculpture Collections in Europe and the United States 1500–1930: Variety and Ambiguity* (Leiden: Brill, 2021), 147–149, on Permoser's work in gardens.
3. Yvonne J. Markowitz, "The Balletta Bulldog," in *Artful Adornments: Jewelry from the Museum of Fine Arts, Boston* (Boston: MFA Publications, 2011), 93.
4. Joe Earle, *Netsuke: Fantasy and Reality in Japanese Miniature Sculpture* (Boston: MFA Publications, 2004).
5. For further discussion of this episode in Komachi's life, see Earle, *Netsuke*, cat. 33.
6. In 2022, for example, Anthony Hillman published his fourth instructional book on the subject: *Carving Miniature Duck Decoys: Easy-to-Use Templates and Complete Instructions for Making 16 Decorative Carvings* (Brattleboro, VT: Echo Point).

Small Size, Big Style

1. Laura Cerwinske, *Russian Imperial Style* (New York: Prentice Hall, 1990), 54.
2. T. J. Burleigh, J. R. Schoenherr, and G. L. Lacroix, "Does the Uncanny Valley Exist? An Empirical Test of the Relationship between Eeriness and the Human Likeness of Digitally Created Faces," *Computers in Human Behavior*, 29, no. 3 (2013): 759–771.
3. Yvonne J. Markowitz, "Bicycle Brooch," in *Artful Adornments: Jewelry from the Museum of Fine Arts, Boston* (Boston: MFA Publications, 2011), 89.

4. Jeanette Hanisee Gabriel et al., *Micromosaics: The Gilbert Collection* (Wappingers Falls, NY: distributed in the US and Canada by Antique Collectors' Club Limited, 2000).
5. Samuel Wittwer, Richard Baron Cohen, and Sarah Louise Galbraith, *Refinement & Elegance: Early Nineteenth-Century Royal Porcelain from the Twinight Collection, New York* (Munich: Hirmer Verlag: 2007), cat. no. 35, 208 and 451.
6. Justo Pastor Mellado et al., *Inverted Utopias: Avant-garde Art in Latin America* (New Haven, CT: Yale University Press, 2004), 253.
7. For more information on Altdorfer and the Dresden school, see Giulia Bartrum, *German Renaissance Prints 1490–1550* (London: Trustees of the British Museum, 1995), 183–185.
8. Luisa Coscarelli, "The *Balsambüchse*: A Portable Seventeenth-Century Medicine Cabinet," in *The Routledge Handbook of Material Culture in Early Modern Europe*, ed. Catherine Richardson, Tara Hamling, and David Gaimster (London: Routledge, 2016), 236–237.

Why Miniatures Matter

1. François Bucher, "Micro-Architecture as the 'Idea' of Gothic Theory and Style," *Gesta* 15, no. 1/2 (1976): 71–89.
2. Susan M. Anderson, Michael Duncan, and Maren Henderson, *Claire Falkenstein* (Los Angeles: Falkenstein Foundation, 2012).
3. Fred Rayman and Tom McNally, *Greyhound Scenicruiser* (Xenia, OH: Ertel Publishing, 2013).
4. Elizabeth J. Fowler, "Paris 1900: Art Nouveau Ceramics," in *Paris 1900* (Oklahoma City: Oklahoma City Museum of Art, 2007), 130–49.

List of Illustrations

All artworks are from the collections of the Museum of Fine Arts, Boston, unless stated otherwise. Dimensions are given as height × width × depth.

1
Nicholas Hilliard (English, 1547–1619)
Queen Elizabeth I, 1572
Watercolor on vellum
5.1 × 4.8 cm (2 × 1⅞ in.)
National Portrait Gallery, Purchased, 1860, Primary Collection, NPG 108
Photograph © National Portrait Gallery, London

2
Terrestrial globe compass, France (Dieppe), around 1675–85
Ivory with ink decoration, brass compass
Diameter: 5.7 cm (2¼ in.)
Gift of the heirs of Bettina Looram de Rothschild, 2015.109a-b

3
Robert Hooke (English, 1635–1703)
Engraving of a flea, from *Micrographia* (1665)
33 × 43 cm (13 × 16⅞ in.)
Wellcome Collection, Attribution 4.0 International (CC BY 4.0)

4
Miniature magnifying glass, possibly English, 18th century
Brass and glass lens with ivory handle
Length: 5.2 cm (2 in.)
Gift of Mrs. F. O. North in memory of Thomas L. Sprague, RES.29.43a-c

5
Yagi Akira (Japanese, born in 1955)
Nesting covered boxes, 1994
Porcelain with pale blue glaze
Largest box, height: 17.1 cm (6¾ in.)
Gift of Halsey and Alice North, 2006.829.1–11
Reproduced with permission

6
Rooster, Chinese (for export), mid-18th century
Hard-paste porcelain
Height: 15.9 cm (6¼ in.)
Gift of Miss Aimée and Miss Rosamond Lamb, 58.1337

Chris Templeman (American, born in 1979)
"Make and Take" Rooster, 2017
3-D-printed polyactide (PLA) plastic
8 × 5 × 4 cm (3⅛ × 2 × 1⅝ in.)
Collection of the artist
Reproduced with permission

7
Eben Haines (American, born in 1990)
Shelter in Place Gallery, 2020
Foamcore, matboard, acrylic and latex paint, balsa wood, redwood, plexiglass, adhesive backed vinyl, adhesive backed polyvinyl, and aluminum
53.3 × 61 × 80.6 cm (21 × 24 × 31¾ in.)
The Wornick Fund for Contemporary Craft, 2020.502
© Eben Haines Studio

8
Katarina Burin (Slovakian, active in Canada and the United States)
Hotel Nord-Sud model, 1932–34, 2010–17

Chipboard and paint
61.5 × 19 × 11.5 cm (24¼ × 7½ × 4½ in.)
Charles Amos Cummings Fund, 2021.116
© Katarina Burin

9
Prayer bead with depictions of Saint James
and Saint George, Netherlandish, about
1500–1530
Boxwood
4 × 3.5 × 4.3 cm (1⅝ × 1⅜ × 1¾ in.)
Art Gallery of Ontario
Purchase, with funds from the sale of deaccessioned European art work and the Thomson
European Collection Acquisition Fund, 2017,
2017/18
Photograph © Art Gallery of Ontario

10
Reliquary casket "Emly Shrine," Irish, late
7th–early 8th century
Champlevé enamel on bronze over yew wood;
gilt bronze moldings, inlay of lead-tin alloy
9.2 × 4.1 × 10.5 cm (3⅝ × 1⅝ × 4⅛ in.)
Theodora Wilbour Fund in memory of
Charlotte Beebe Wilbour, 52.1396

11
Box, Northern European, mid-14th century
Silver
4.8 × 4.4 × 1.9 cm (1⅞ × 1¾ × ¾ in.)
Arthur Mason Knapp Fund, 46.1249

12
Pilgrim's badge of the shrine of Saint Thomas
Becket at Canterbury, English (Canterbury),
1350–1400
Cast tin-lead alloy
7.9 × 6.4 × .3 cm (3⅛ × 2½ × ⅛ in.)
Metropolitan Museum of Art, Gift of Dr. and
Mrs. W. Conte, 2001, 2001.310
Image copyright © The Metropolitan Museum
of Art
Image source: Art Resource, NY

13
Triptych Pendant depicting Martyrdom of Saint
Barbara, Mary Magdalen, and Saint Gereon,
German (Cologne), 1504
Basse-taille enamel and gilding on silver
Open: 7.2 × 6.3 × .7 cm (2⅞ × 2½ × ¼ in.)
1941 Purchase Fund, 47.1450a-b

14
Bastet amulet inscribed for Pamay, Egyptian,
724–712 BCE
Gold
4.7 × .8 × 1 cm (1⅞ × ⁵⁄₁₆ × ⅜ in.)
Harvard University—Boston Museum of
Fine Arts Expedition, 23.335

15
Bracelet, American or European, 1864
Gold, glass, and hair
2.1 × 7.5 × 9.5 cm (⅞ × 3 × 3¾ in.)
Gift of Mrs. Joseph A. Cushman, 64.735

16
Brooch, American, 19th century
Enamel, gold, crystal, braided hair
1.8 × 1.4 cm (¾ × ½ in.)
Bequest of Dr. Samuel A. Green, 19.3706

17
Memorial ring, Central European, late
18th century
Gold, pearls, paint, enamel, and glass
2.8 × 1.7 cm (1⅛ × ⅝ in.)
Bequest of Mrs. Arthur Croft—The Gardner
Brewer Collection, 01.6608

18
Rowland Parry (American, active about 1790–96)
Mourning pendant brooch, 1792
Gold, watercolor on ivory, hair, glass
5.7 × 4.8 × 1.3 cm (2¼ × 1⅞ × ½ in.)
The Daphne Farago Collection, 2006.418

19
Miniature Hanukkah lamp, possibly Italian,
20th century
Silver
Height: 6.8 cm (2½ in.)
Charles and Lynn Schusterman Collection,
2013.936

20
Made at Bezalel School of Arts and Crafts,
Jerusalem (British Mandate Palestine)
Sabbath candlesticks, probably 1920s
Silver
Each: 6.5 × 5.5 cm (2½ × 2⅛ in.)
Charles and Lynn Schusterman Collection,
2013.939.1-2

21
Robert W. Ebendorf (American, born in 1938)
Traveling communion service, 1967
Silver vessel with rosewood and silver box
Vessel: 11.8 × 4.1 cm (4⅝ × 1⅝ in.)
Box: 12.7 × 15.2 × 7.6 cm (5 × 6 × 3 in.)
Anonymous gift, 1992.265.1a-d, .2a-b
Reproduced with permission

22
Dollhouse, Dutch, 17th–18th century
Wood, silver miniatures, porcelain, glass,
oil on copper, mother of pearl, and pen and
ink drawings
196 × 150 × 57 cm (77⅛ × 59 × 22½ in.)
Rose-Marie and Eijk van Otterloo Collection

23
Arnoldus van Geffen (Dutch, 1728–1769)
Dining room with silver miniatures, second
half of the 18th century
Mixed media
37 × 48 × 30 cm (14⅝ × 18⅞ × 11¾ in.)
Rose-Marie and Eijk van Otterloo Collection

24
Miniature teapot and stand, English (London),
about 1730
Silver
9.7 × 7 × 4.8 cm (3⅞ × 2¾ × 1⅞ in.)
Theodora Wilbour Fund in memory of
Charlotte Beebe Wilbour, 55.978a-c

25
Miniature plate, English (Staffordshire),
19th century
Lead-glazed earthenware
Diameter: 7.6 cm (3 in.)
Gift of Mrs. Ralph Lowell in memory of
Mrs. Thacher Loring (Margaret Fuller
Channing) from her granddaughter
Mrs. Ralph Lowell, 54.1604

26
Arthur Stone (American, born in England,
1847–1938)
Miniature two-handled covered cup, 1895–97
Silver
5.5 × 4.6 × 2.3 cm (2⅛ × 1¾ × ⅞ in.)
Gift of Miss Alma Bent, 1979.190a-b

27
Miniature stove, Southern German, late
16th century
Lead-glazed earthenware
80.5 × 43.4 × 12.7 cm (31¾ × 17⅛ × 5 in.)
Gift of Dr. Lloyd E. Hawes, 60.1304

28
Wrought Iron Range Co., St. Louis, Missouri,
1864–1960
"Home Comfort" salesman sample range and
travel box, about 1940
Iron and enamel
Stove: 40.6 × 40.6 × 17.8 cm (16 × 16 × 7 in.)
Collection of Frederic and Jean Sharf

29
Augustus Eliaers (American, active 1849–65)
Patent model for library step-chair, 1853
Mahogany
17.8 × 11.4 × 11.4 cm (7 × 4½ × 4½ in.)
H. E. Bolles Fund, 1977.336

30
Augustus Eliaers (American, active 1849–65)
Library step-chair patent drawing (as
"Step-Ladder Chair")
U.S. Patent 10,151, issued October 25, 1853
United States Patent and Trademark Office,
Washington, DC

31
Augustus Eliaers (American, active 1849–65)
Library step-chair, about 1854–60
Oak, brass, original oilcloth upholstery
101.6 × 64.8 × 86.4 cm (40 × 25½ × 34 in.)
H. E. Bolles Fund, 1976.762

32
Emerita Membache (Wounaan, active late
20th–early 21st century)
Pictorial basket, 2003
Nahuala and chunga plant fibers, natural
and artificial dyes
10.3 × 5 × 7.4 cm (4 × 2 × 2⅞ in.)
Gift of Charles and Patricia McLure, 2022.118
Reproduced with permission

33
Francis Williams (Nuu-chah-nulth, 1919–1996)
Miniature basket, about 1990
Woven reeds or grass, dyed
5.7 × 5.1 cm (2¼ × 2 in.)
Gift of Dale and Doug Anderson, 2012.386a-b
Reproduced with permission

34
Designed by Philippe Starck (French, born
in 1949)
Manufactured by Vitra International AG (Swiss)
Miniature of "Louis 20" chair and crate,
designed 1992, manufactured 1996
Blown polypropylene body; aluminum rear legs
Chair: 14 × 8 × 9.4 cm (5½ × 3⅛ × 3¾ in.)
Crate: 16 × 10.1 × 11.1 cm (6¼ × 4 × 4⅜ in.)
Gift of Vitra Design Museum, 1996.130a-b
© Starck Network

35
Isamu Noguchi (American, 1904–1988)
Miniature coffee table, second half of the
20th century
Glass and wood
6.4 × 20.3 × 15.2 cm (2½ × 8 × 6 in.)
Collection of Brett Angell
© 2023 The Isamu Noguchi Foundation and
Garden Museum, New York/Artists Rights
Society (ARS), New York

36
Ron Ho (American, 1936–2017)
TV Guide, 1992
Silver, patinated copper, polymer clay; silk cord
10.8 × 10.8 × 2.5 cm (4¼ × 4¼ × 1 in.)
The Daphne Farago Collection, 2006.251
Reproduced with permission

37
Liliana Porter (Argentine, active in the United
States, born in 1941)
Untitled with Fallen Chairs, 2009
Acrylic and assemblage on canvas
111.8 × 152.4 × 10.2 cm (44 × 60 × 4 in.)
Leigh and Stephen Braude Fund for Latin
American Art, and funds donated by the
Pinta Museum Acquisitions Program, and
Leigh Bonilla Braude, 2010.1
© Liliana Porter

38
London Stereoscopic Company (English,
active 1854–early 20th century)
Rievaulx Abbey from the South, 1850s
Stereocard, albumen prints mounted to
card stock
8.4 × 17.4 cm (3¼ × 6⅞ in.)
Edward Jackson Holmes Collection—Bequest
of Mrs. Edward Jackson Holmes, 65.3436

39
Katsushika Hokusai (Japanese, 1760–1849)
Bonsai Grower, from the series *Three Festival
Days*, 1803
Woodblock print (*surimono*); ink and color
on paper
19.2 × 12.7 cm (7½ × 5 in.)
Gift of Mrs. Jared K. Morse in memory of
Charles J. Morse, 53.2676

40
In the style of Balthasar Permoser (German,
1651–1732)
Model for a garden pavilion, early 18th century
Painted pine
73.7 × 34.9 × 28.6 cm (29 × 13¾ × 11¼ in.)
Charles Amos Cummings Fund, 1970.75

41
Jean-François Millet (French, 1814–1875)
Trees along a Rocky Stream Bed, 1866–67
Watercolor with pen and brown ink over
graphite on paper
5.4 × 10.4 cm (2⅛ × 4⅛ in.)
Gift of Martin Brimmer, 76.423

42
Léon Victor Dupré (French, 1816–1879)
Water Meadows and Cattle, mid-18th century
Oil on panel
8.9 × 15.8 cm (3½ × 6¼ in.)
Bequest of Ernest Wadsworth Longfellow,
23.493

43
Workshop of Peter Carl Fabergé (Russian,
1846–1920)
Spray of lilies of the valley, late 19th or early
20th century
Enamel, nephrite, gold in a rock crystal vase
Height: 9.5 cm (3¾ in.)
Bequest of Lila Stevenson, 1970.227

44
Workshop of Peter Carl Fabergé (Russian,
1846–1920)
The Balletta Bulldog, about 1905
Gold, silver, agate, diamond, and ruby
8.9 × 2.7 × 11.6 cm (3½ × 1⅛ × 4⅝ in.)
Gift of Sidney A. Levine, 1980.649

45
Scaraboid of a hedgehog, Egyptian,
760–332 BCE
Faience
1.3 × 1 cm (½ × ⅜ in.)
Gift of Mrs. H. W. Toulmin, 19.3

46
Okatomo of Kyoto (Japanese, about 1750–1800)
Hare and Mushroom, late 18th–early
19th century
Stained ivory and horn
3.3 × 4.5 × 2.2 cm (1¼ × 1¾ × ⅞ in.)
Gift of Dr. Ernest G. Stillman, 47.925

47
Shūōsai Hidemasa (Japanese, active early
19th century)
*Clamshell with the Vindication of Ono No
Komachi*, early 19th century
Stained ivory
3.1 × 4.4 × 3 cm (1¼ × 1¾ × 1⅛ in.)
William Sturgis Bigelow Collection, 11.23212

48
Duck decoy, possibly a male wood duck,
American, 19th century
Painted wood
6.3 × 10.8 × 5.1 cm (2½ × 4¼ × 2 in.)
Gift of Maxim Karolik, 59.946

49
Girdle book calendar, northeastern Spain or
southwestern France, about 1300–1350
Ink on parchment, silver handle with six
carnelian beads
Open: 6 × 4.5 cm (2⅜ × 1¾ in.)
Helen and Alice Colburn Fund, 46.458

50
Jean Louis Ernest Meissonier (French,
1815–1891)
Officer, mid-19th century
Oil on panel
10.5 × 8.3 cm (4⅛ × 3¼ in.)
Abbott Lawrence Fund, 03.623

51
Édouard Brandon (French, 1831–1897)
Juif Lisant (Jewish Man Reading), 1870
Oil on panel
13 × 7 cm (5⅛ × 2¾ in.)
Charles and Lynn Schusterman Collection,
2013.973

52
David Teniers the Younger (Flemish, 1610–1690)
After Titian (Tiziano Vecellio) (Italian, about
1488–1576)
Parma the Physician, 17th century
Oil on panel
17.1 × 12.1 cm (6¾ × 4¾ in.)
Gift of the Estate of Gardiner Howland Shaw,
66.266

53
Workshop of Peter Carl Fabergé (Russian,
1846–1920)
Miniature commode, late 19th century
Gold with nephrite
7.6 × 10.4 × 5.7 cm (3 × 4⅛ × 2¼ in.)
Gift of Mrs. Albert J. Beveridge in memory of
Delia Spencer Field, 49.1785

54
Possibly by Streeter & Co. (English)
Bicycle brooch, mid-1890s
Gold, enamel, diamond, and ruby
4 × 6.5 × 1 cm (1⅝ × 2½ × ⅜ in.)
Museum purchase with funds donated
anonymously, 2009.2419

55
Brooch, Italian, about 1870
Gold, onyx, and glass
4.6 × 5.7 × 1 cm (1¾ × 2¼ × ⅜ in.)
Gift of Miss Alice Williams Pearse, 46.884

56
Attributed to Giacomo Raffaelli (Italian,
1753–1836)
Box, about 1825
Micromosaic, gold, green porphyry
6 × 8.2 × 2.7 cm (2⅜ × 3¼ × 1⅛ in.)
Private collection

57
Königliche Porzellanmanufaktur, German
(Berlin)
Cup and saucer with micromosaic decoration,
about 1817
Hard-paste porcelain with gilding
Cup: 11.4 × 10.2 × 7.6 cm (4½ × 4 × 3 in.)
Saucer: 2.2 × 13.3 cm (⅞ × 5¼ in.)
Helen and Alice Colburn Fund, 2022.1857a-b

58
Miniature eyeglass case with eyeglasses,
French, late 18th century
Beadwork with glass beads (*sablé*)
Case: 7 × 1.5 cm (2¾ × ⅝ in.)
The Elizabeth Day McCormick Collection,
43.2287a-c

59
Shepherdess, France (Nevers), 18th century
Glass
Height: 14.6 cm (5¾ in.)
The Elizabeth Day McCormick Collection,
45.380

60
John La Farge, American, 1835–1910
Study for Skylight, about 1875–1900
Watercolor over graphite on paper
9.3 × 11 cm (3⅝ × 4⅜ in.)
Gift of Major Henry Lee Higginson, 11.2834

61
Jesús Raphael Soto (Venezuelan, 1923–2005)
View of the exhibition "Chronochrome" at
Perrotin, Paris, 2015
© Jesús Rafael Soto/ADAGP, Paris & ARS, NY
2023, courtesy Atelier Soto-Paris and Perrotin

62
Designed by Jesús Raphael Soto (Venezuelan,
1923–2005)
Made by GEM Montebello (Italian, active
1967–78)
Ring, 1968
18 kt yellow and white gold; lapis lazuli
4.3 × 2.5 × 2.5 cm (1¾ × 1 × 1 in.)
The Daphne Farago Collection, 2006.552
© 2023 Artists Rights Society (ARS), New York/
ADAGP, Paris

63
Albrecht Altdorfer (German, about 1480–1538)
The Viol Player, 1519–25
Engraving
6.1 × 4.1 cm (2⅜ × 1⅝ in.)
Gift of W. G. Russell Allen, 53.27

64
Watch in the shape of a lute, French,
about 1800
Gold, enamel, pearls
2.8 × 7.3 cm (1⅛ × 2⅞ in.)
Bequest of Mrs. Arthur Croft—The Gardner
Brewer Collection, 01.6649

65
Pomander, English, about 1580
Gilded silver
6.4 × 3.4 cm (2½ × 1⅜ in.)
Bequest of Frank Brewer Bemis, 35.1547

66
Pablo Picasso (Spanish, active in France,
1881–1973)
Les Plastrons (Stuffed Shirts), 1900
Oil on panel
13.6 × 22.5 cm (5⅜ × 8⅞ in.)
Gift of Mrs. Charles Sumner Bird (Julia
Appleton Bird), 1970.475
© 2023 Estate of Pablo Picasso/Artists Rights
Society (ARS), New York

67
Miniature Jain shrine, Indian, 1487–88
Brass and silver
Height: 12.3 cm (4⅞ in.)
Ross-Coomaraswamy Collection, 17.2353

68
Miniature shrine, Nubian, 743–712 BCE
Faience
Height: 7 cm (2¾ in.)
Harvard University—Boston Museum of
Fine Arts Expedition, 24.618

69
Finial, possibly German, mid-14th to
mid-15th century
Silver with gilding and translucent enamel
7.5 × 2.5 cm (3 × 1 in.)
Harriet Otis Cruft Fund, 55.467

70
Lock and hasp for a chest, possibly French,
late 15th to early 16th century
Iron
12.7 × 9.2 cm (5 × 3⅝ in.)
Gift of William Emerson, 42.530

71
Claire Falkenstein (American, 1908–1997)
Model for *New Gates of Paradise*, Guggenheim
Foundation, 1961
Painted copper wire and glass
44.5 × 36.8 × 2.5 cm (17½ × 14½ × 1 in.)
Gift of Mrs. Peggy Guggenheim, 64.317
© The Falkenstein Foundation, courtesy of
Michael Rosenfeld Gallery LLC, New York, NY

72
Claire Falkenstein (American, 1908–1997)
Entrance gates to the Palazzo, 1961
Iron and colored glass
277 × 90 cm (109 × 35⅜) and 277 × 91.2 cm
(109 × 35⅞ in.)
Peggy Guggenheim Collection, Venice, 76.2553
PG 203 (Solomon R. Guggenheim Foundation,
New York)
© The Falkenstein Foundation, courtesy of
Michael Rosenfeld Gallery LLC, New York, NY

73
Designed by Raymond Loewy (American,
born in France, 1893–1986)
Made by General Motors Corporation
(American, founded in 1908) or Greyhound
Lines (American, founded in 1914)
Greyhound Scenicruiser bus model, mid-1950s
Painted plaster, printed decals, wood
29.2 × 101.6 × 14 cm (11½ × 40 × 5½ in.)
Gift of Jean S. and Frederic A. Sharf, 2014.1251
Reproduced with permission

74
Speed of the Wind wind-tunnel model,
American, about 1935
Painted pine
19.1 × 88.9 × 27.9 cm (7½ × 35 × 11 in.)
Gift of Jean S. and Frederic A. Sharf, 2014.1244

75
One Hundred Poems by One Hundred Poets,
Japanese, early 19th century
Copperplate etching on paper
9.9 × 14.6 cm (3⅞ × 5¾ in.)
William Sturgis Bigelow Collection, 11.45842.18

76
Auguste Delaherche (French, 1857–1940)
Vase, about 1889
Stoneware, slip and incised decoration
Height: 25.4 cm (10 in.)
Museum purchase with funds by exchange
from The John Axelrod Collection, 2017.4441

Auguste Delaherche (French, 1857–1940)
Miniature vases, 1930s
Stoneware with slip decoration
Each: about 4.5 × 3.2 cm (1¾ × 1¼ in.)
Gift in the name of Robert Hatton Monks,
RES.27.19.1, 4, 11, 13, 14, 18, 30, 32, 33, 34

Acknowledgments

This book and the accompanying exhibition have come together very quickly, and many people helped make it possible on an incredibly short timeline.

It was a true pleasure to work with my editor, Julie Hagen, who provided helpful insights and refinement of the text throughout the editing process. In MFA Publications, Jennifer Snodgrass and Hope Stockton were guiding lights for keeping me on track throughout the writing process.

Early collaborators on this project were Sarah Schwetterman and Seth Riskin, co-leaders of the course "Vision in Art and Neuroscience" at MIT in fall 2019, who helped with providing the neuroscientific background behind what we see and how our brains process visual input.

I am grateful to my curatorial colleagues across departments who have generously supported this project with their expertise and their objects: Ai Fukunaga; Angie Simonds; Emily Stoehrer, Rita J. Kaplan and Susan B. Kaplan Curator of Jewelry; Patrick Murphy, Lia and William Poorvu Associate Curator of Prints and Drawings; Ben Weiss, Leonard A. Lauder Senior Curator of Visual Culture, Department of Prints and Drawings; Karen Haas, Lane Senior Curator of Photographs; Simona di Nepi, Charles and Lynn Schusterman Curator of Judaica; Antien Knaap; Katie Hanson; Nonie Gadsden, Katharine Lane Weems Senior Curator of American Decorative Arts and Sculpture; and Michelle Millar Fisher, Ronald C. and Anita L. Wornick Curator of Contemporary Decorative Arts. Cara Wolahan was by my side through the many object moves and photography studio trips, and provided invaluable assistance with paperwork and logistics for which I am truly grateful. Marietta Cambareri, Senior Curator of European Sculpture and Jetskalina H. Phillips Curator of Judaica, has been a great colleague, offering insights, support, time, and guidance at every step of the process. Frederick Ilchman, Chair and Mrs. Russell W. Baker Curator of Paintings, Art of Europe, has helped with refining the checklist and this book text, and with pursuing loans.

Nearly every conservation laboratory has had their hands upon works for this project, in particular Gerri Strickler; Rhona MacBeth, Director of Conservation and Scientific Research, Eijk and Rose-Marie van Otterloo Conservator of Paintings and Head of Paintings Conservation; Gregg Porter, Christine Storti, and Annette Manick.

Christina YuYu, Matsutaro Shoriki Chair, Art of Asia and Chief of Curatorial Affairs and Conservation, and Kat Bossi and Angie Morrow in the exhibitions department made the scheduling and logistics of this exhibition possible. Maggie Loh and Diana Sibbald coordinated new photography, and Michael Gould in particular took many of the new photographs for the book. It has been a joy to work with Luisa Respondek on the exhibition design, Jadzia Genece on the graphics, and Catherine Johnson-Roehr and Jordan Cromwell on the interpretation.

While the exhibition, and this book, are rooted firmly in the MFA's collection, a few local lenders and good friends of the museum have generously supported this project with loans. At the Art Gallery of Ontario, I am grateful to Caroline Shields, Lisa Ellis, and Adam Levine, for going above and beyond to be helpful.

I am grateful to my parents, who have always encouraged me to seek knowledge, pursue excellence, and be myself. And finally, I am grateful to my husband for his support through the process of preparing this book, as well as to the wonderful staff of my daughter's school, who provide excellent care for her so we can both work. Thank you, Lucy, for bringing levity and joy to both this project and all of life.

Courtney Leigh Harris
Assistant Curator, Decorative Arts and Sculpture, Art of Europe
Museum of Fine Arts, Boston

Index

MFA∕Boston

MFA Publications
Museum of Fine Arts, Boston
465 Huntington Avenue
Boston, Massachusetts 02115
www.mfa.org/publications

Published in conjunction with the exhibition *Tiny Treasures: The Magic of Miniatures*, organized by the Museum of Fine Arts, Boston, from July 1, 2023, to February 18, 2024

Generous support for this publication provided by the Andrew W. Mellon Publications Fund

ISBN: 978-0-87846-893-5
Library of Congress Control Number: 2023931592

While the objects in this publication necessarily represent only a small portion of the MFA's holdings, the Museum is proud to be a leader within the American museum community in sharing the objects in its collection via its website. Currently, information about approximately 400,000 objects is available to the public worldwide. To learn more about the MFA's collections, including provenance, publication, and exhibition history, kindly visit www.mfa.org.

For a complete listing of MFA publications, please contact the publisher at the above address, or call 617 369 4233.

Cover: Detail, fig. 76

Illustrations in this book were photographed by the Imaging Studios, Museum of Fine Arts, Boston, except where otherwise noted.

Edited by Julie Ericksen Hagen and
    Jennifer Snodgrass
Proofread by Kathryn Blatt
Design and production by Rita Jules,
    Miko McGinty, Inc.
Principal photography by Michael Gould
Image research and permissions by Diana Sibbald
Typeset in Fakt and Utile by Tina Henderson
Printed on Gardamatt Ultra 150 gsm
Printed and bound at Trifolio S.r.l., Verona, Italy

Distributed by
ARTBOOK | D.A.P.
75 Broad Street, Suite 630
New York, New York 10004
www.artbook.com

FIRST EDITION
Printed and bound in Italy
This book was printed on acid-free paper.

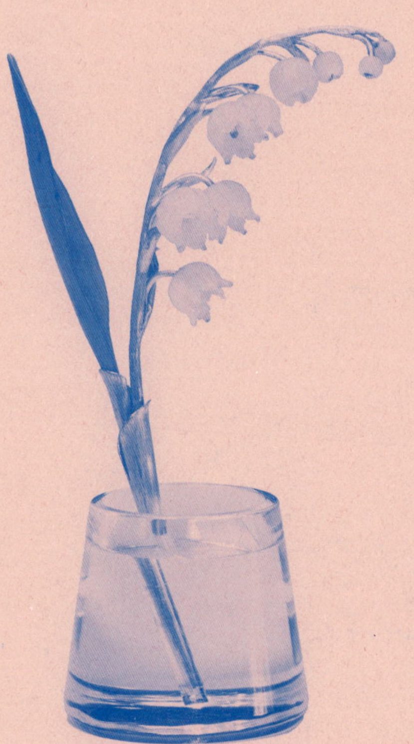
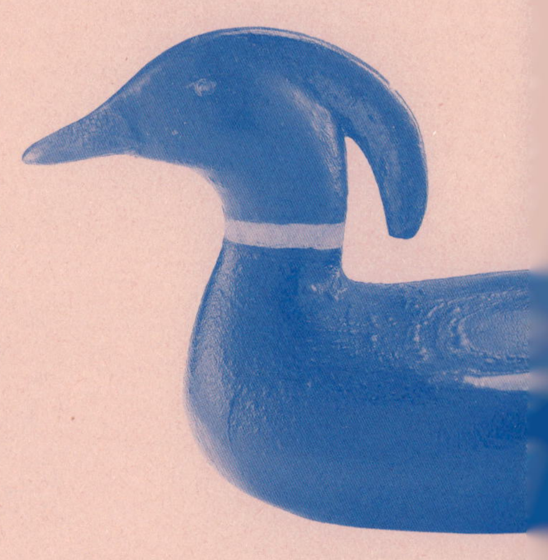

15
14
13
12
11
10
9
8
7
6
5
4
3
2
1 cm